THE LAWYER'S GUIDE TO

Adobe®

Acrobat®

THIRD EDITION

COVERS ADOBE ACROBAT 8.0 !

David L. Masters

 LawPracticeManagementSection

MARKETING • MANAGEMENT • TECHNOLOGY • FINANCE

Screen shots reprinted with permission from Adobe Systems Incorporated. © 2008 Adobe Systems Incorporated. All rights reserved. Adobe and Adobe Acrobat is/are either (a) registered trademark(s) of Adobe Systems Incorporated in the United States and/or other countries.

Cover design by Jim Colao.

Nothing contained in this book is to be considered as the rendering of legal advice for specific cases, and readers are responsible for obtaining such advice from their own legal counsel. This book and any forms and agreements herein are intended for educational and informational purposes only.

The products and services mentioned in this publication are under or may be under trademark or service mark protection. Product and service names and terms are used throughout only in an editorial fashion, to the benefit of the product manufacturer or service provider, with no intention of infringement. Use of a product or service name or term in this publication should not be regarded as affecting the validity of any trademark or service mark.

The Law Practice Management Section of the American Bar Association offers an educational program for lawyers in practice. Books and other materials are published in furtherance of that program. Authors and editors of publications may express their own legal interpretations and opinions, which are not necessarily those of either the American Bar Association or the Law Practice Management Section unless adopted pursuant to the bylaws of the Association. The opinions expressed do not reflect in any way a position of the Section or the American Bar Association.

© 2008 American Bar Association. All rights reserved.
Printed in the United States of America.

Library of Congress Cataloging-in-Publication Data
The Lawyer's Guide to Adobe® Acrobat®, Third Edition. David L. Masters:
Library of Congress Cataloging-in-Publication Data is on file.

10-digit: ISBN 1-59031-978-8
13-digit: ISBN 978-1-59031-978-9

12 11 10   5 4 3 2

Discounts are available for books ordered in bulk. Special consideration is given to state bars, CLE programs, and other bar-related organizations. Inquire at Book Publishing, American Bar Association, 321 N. Clark Street, Chicago, Illinois 60610.

Contents

About the Author   xi
Acknowledgments   xii
Introduction   xiii

CHAPTER 1
Why PDF?   **1**

CHAPTER 2
PDF File Types   **5**

2.1   Image-Only Files   5
2.2   Image-on-Text Files   5

CHAPTER 3
Getting Started   **7**

3.1   Menus   8
3.2   Toolbars   10
3.3   The Navigation Icons and Panes   14
3.4   Basic Navigation   16
3.5   Bookmarks   18
3.6   Links   18
3.7   Controlling How Pages Are Displayed   18
3.7.1   Page Display   19
3.7.2   Page Size   20
3.7.3   Zoom Tools (Toolbar buttons)   23
3.7.4   Full Screen Mode   25

3.8	Preferences	25
3.8.1	Preferences—Commenting	26
3.8.2	Preferences—Documents	26
3.8.3	Preferences—General	26
3.8.4	Preferences—Page Display	27
3.8.5	Preferences—Identity	27

CHAPTER 4
Creating PDF Files   **29**

4.1	Creating PDFs Using the Print Command	30
4.2	Creating PDF Files Using a Scanner	31
4.3	Creating PDF Files Using Drag and Drop	33
4.4	Converting an Existing File to PDF	33
4.5	Combining Multiple Files	35
4.5.1	Creating a Single PDF from Multiple Files	35
4.5.2	Creating a PDF Package	40
4.6	Creating PDF Files from Web Pages	42
4.7	Creating PDF Files from Clipboard Images	43
4.8	Creating PDF Files from Blank Pages	44

CHAPTER 5
Working with PDF Files   **47**

5.1	Add Pages	48
5.2	Replace Pages	49
5.3	Extract Pages	49
5.4	Delete Pages	51
5.5	Crop Pages	52
5.6	Rotate Pages	53
5.7	Rearranging Page Order Using Pages Panel	54
5.8	Document Open Options	55
5.9	Document Properties	57
5.10	Chapter 5 Wrap-up	59

CHAPTER 6
Adding Document Navigation Aids   **61**

6.1	Bookmarks	62
6.1.1	Using Bookmarks with Litigation Documents	62
6.1.2	Creating Bookmarks	63
6.1.3	Bookmarking Selected Text or Image	64
6.1.4	Changing Bookmark Appearance	65

6.1.5	Editing the Bookmark Destination	65
6.1.6	Deleting Bookmarks	66
6.1.7	Wrapping Long Bookmarks	67
6.1.8	Bookmark Hierarchy	68
6.1.8.1	Nesting a Bookmark Under Another Bookmark	68
6.1.8.2	Moving a Bookmark Out of a Nested Position	68
6.1.9	Bookmark Security	68
6.2	Links	69
6.2.1	The Link Tool	70
6.2.2	Creating Links	70
6.2.3	Setting the Appearance of Links	73
6.2.4	Link Properties	73
6.2.5	Moving and Resizing Links	73
6.2.6	Deleting Links	74
6.2.7	Link Destinations	74
6.2.8	Link Security	75
6.3	Page Numbering	76

CHAPTER 7
Commenting Tools
79

7.1	Commenting Toolbars	80
7.2	Sticky Notes	81
7.2.1	Adding Sticky Notes	82
7.2.2	Sticky Note Properties	82
7.2.3	Editing Sticky Notes	83
7.3	Text Boxes	84
7.4	Callout Text Boxes	85
7.5	Text Markup	86
7.6	Measuring Tools	87
7.6.1	Distance Measuring Tool	87
7.6.2	Perimeter and Area Measuring Tools	87
7.7	Comment Summaries	89
7.8	Lines and Shapes	90
7.9	Deleting Comments	93
7.10	Comment Properties	93
7.10.1	Viewing Comments	94
7.10.2	Pop-Up Open Behavior	95
7.10.3	Making Comments	95
7.11	Stamps	96
7.11.1	Ready-Made Stamps	96
7.11.2	Custom-Made Stamps	96

7.11.3   Creating a Stamp of Your Signature   98
7.11.4   Transparent Signature Stamps   98
7.11.5   Signature Stamp Security   99
7.12   Final Comment on Comments   101

CHAPTER 8
Digital Signatures   **103**

8.1   Using Acrobat Digital Signatures   104
8.1.1   Creating a Secure Digital Signature   105
8.1.2   Signing a Document with a Digital Signature   107
8.2   Validating Someone Else's Signature   109
8.2.1   Storing Someone Else's Certificate   111
8.2.2   Validating the Signature   112

CHAPTER 9
Extracting Content from PDF Files   **113**

9.1   Using Copy to Extract Text   113
9.2   Extracting Text Using Save As   114
9.3   Extracting Text with WordPerfect X3   116
9.4   Extracting Graphic Images   116
9.4.1   Using Copy to Extract Images   117
9.4.2   Using Save As to Extract Images   118
9.4.3   Using Export to Extract Images   119

CHAPTER 10
Search, Find, and Indexing   **121**

10.1   Creating Image-on-Text Files   122
10.2   OCR Quality Experiment   123
10.3   Searching Image-on-Text PDF Files   124
10.4   Refining Searches   126
10.5   Find   127
10.6   Indexing Using Catalog   129

CHAPTER 11
PDF File Security   **133**

11.1   Applying Document Open Security Through
          Document Properties   135
11.2   Applying Permissions Security Through
          Document Properties   138

11.3   Creating a Security Policy (Document Open)   141
11.4   Creating a Security Policy (Permissions)   145
11.5   Advanced PDF Security (Certificate)   149

CHAPTER 12
Saving Web Pages to PDF   **151**

12.1   Printing Web Pages to PDF   152
12.2   Creating a PDF File from a Web Site   153
12.3   Web Page Capture Settings   155
12.3.1   General Settings   155
12.3.2   Page Layout Settings   156
12.3.3   Additional HTML Capture Settings   157

CHAPTER 13
Plug-ins   **161**

13.1   Bates Numbering   162
13.2   StampPDF (Bates Numbering Plug-in)   163
13.2.1   Setting the Beginning Bates Number   163
13.2.2   Adding Prefixes to Bates Numbers   164
13.3   IntelliPDF BATES (Bates Numbering Plug-in)   165
13.3.1   Using IntelliPDF BATES   165
13.3.2   Position, Background, and Pages (Bates Section)   165
13.3.3   Properties and Font (Elements Section)   166
13.3.4   Preview (Bates Preview Section)   166
13.3.5   Advanced Options Section   166
13.3.6   Full Preview Section and Action Buttons   166
13.4   Redacting Information (Redax Redaction Plug-in)   167

CHAPTER 14
Display Mode   **169**

14.1   Using Full Screen View   171
14.2   PDF Exhibit Notebook   174
14.3   Full Screen View Preferences   176

CHAPTER 15
Electronic Briefs   **179**

15.1   Why Acrobat for Electronic Briefs?   179
15.2   Printing a Markup Copy   180
15.3   Printing to PDF   180

15.4	Scanning to PDF	180
15.5	Creating and Organizing the Source Materials	182
15.6	Planning and Organization	182
15.6.1	Organization of Complex Electronic Briefs	183
15.6.2	Organization of Simple Electronic Briefs	184
15.7	Creating the Links	185
15.7.1	Using Right-Click to Create Links	185
15.7.2	Using the Link Tool	186
15.7.3	Stylistic Considerations	187
15.8	Copying the Finished Product to CD	187
15.8.1	Creating and Including a Contents Page	188
15.8.2	Creating and Including an "About this CD" File	188
15.8.3	Indexing the CD Contents	188
15.8.4	Adding an Auto-run Feature	190
15.9	Service and Filing	190
15.9.1	Alternative 1	190
15.9.2	Alternative 2	191
	Sample Contents Page	191
	Sample "About this CD" File	192

CHAPTER 16
Acrobat in the Paper-Free Office
193

16.1	Why Go Paper Free with Acrobat?	193
16.2	Law Office Information Systems	194
16.3	Basic Document Management	196
16.4	The Digital Filing System	198
16.4.1	The Logical Folder System	199
16.4.2	The Dual-Folder System	201
16.4.3	File-Naming Conventions	202
16.4.4	The System in Action	203
16.4.5	Document Management Alternatives	204
16.5	Digital Document Storage Requirements	205

CHAPTER 17
Bates Numbering
207

CHAPTER 18
Redaction
213

18.1	Manual Mark for Redaction	215
18.2	Search and Mark for Redaction	215

18.3   Redaction Properties   219
18.4   Applying Redaction   220

CHAPTER 19
Acrobat PDF Forms   **223**

19.1   Creating Forms   223
19.2   Creating a Form from an Existing File   224

CHAPTER 20
Batch Processing   **229**

20.1   Creating a Batch Sequence   230
20.2   Running a Batch Sequence   234
20.3   Batch Process Summary   237

CHAPTER 21
Examine Document (Remove Metadata)   **239**

CHAPTER 22
Printing PDF Files   **243**

22.1   What to Print (Comments and Forms)   243
22.2   What to Print (Print Range)   245
22.3   Page Handling   246
22.4   Print PDF to PDF   247

CHAPTER 23
Reduce—Reuse—Recycle   **249**

CHAPTER 24
Keyboard Shortcuts and Resources   **253**

        Keyboard Shortcuts   253
        Web Sites   254

Index   **255**

About the Author

David Masters is a small firm general practitioner in Montrose, Colorado. His practice focuses on real estate and business matters, transactions and litigation, including personal injury, construction, and employment matters, for both plaintiffs and defendants. He writes and speaks frequently on the use of information technology in the practice of law. Outside the practice of law he loves to climb mountains.

David wrote "Electronic Briefs" (Chapter 23), *Colorado Appellate Practice Guide 5d*, Continuing Legal Education in Colorado, Inc. (2005); "Adobe Acrobat for E-Filing and More" (Chapter 34), *Flying Solo: A Survival Guide for Solo Lawyers*, Fourth Edition, American Bar Association, Law Practice Management Section (2005); "Securing Your Documents: Encryption, Digital Signatures and PDF" (Chapter 14), *Information Security for Lawyers and Law Firms*, American Bar Association, Law Practice Management Section and Science & Technology Section (2006); and, numerous articles and presentations on the use of information technology in the practice of law.

David attended the University of Montana School of Law, Missoula, Montana, and obtained his Juris Doctorate in 1986. David is a member of the American Bar Association (1986–present), the Law Practice Management Section (member of the ABA TECHSHOW® Planning Board, 2004–2007), and the General Practice Solo and Small Firm Section. He is also a member of the Colorado Bar Association (Vice President, District Six, 2003–2005); the Seventh Judicial District Bar Association (1986–present; President 1990—1992, 1999–2000); the West Publishing CD-ROM Advisory Board 1995; *The Colorado Lawyer* Board of Editors (1999–2004); and he is a member of the faculty at the National Institute for Trial Advocacy, Rocky Mountain Regional (2001–present).

Acknowledgments

The first edition of this book would not have been written without the help of my associate, Mindi Conerly, my legal assistant, Jennifer LeBlanc, and our administrative assistant, Barbara Forbes. Jeff Flax deserves credit as the Law Practice Management publications board member who persuaded the Section to pursue this project. Thanks to my family for allowing me the additional time to work on this project.

While the author is grateful to Adobe® for creating Acrobat®, there is no sponsorship, affiliation, or endorsement of this book by Adobe Systems Incorporated. The author has, since publication of the first edition, been compensated by Adobe Systems for writing two white papers and presenting two seminars. The Adobe Acrobat screen shots are reprinted with permission from Adobe Systems Incorporated.

David L. Masters

Introduction

READ ME FIRST

First, I hope this book both inspires and instructs. I hope it inspires you to appreciate the extent to which lawyers, for the most part, manage and process information, and instructs you on how Acrobat can help you make the transition from managing and processing paper-based information to information in digital form. Second, I hope you enjoy reading this book. Let's face it, in the end it's a reference work for a piece of software—boring. To combat the boring factor I have tried to make the discussion as entertaining a possible.

The transition from paper-based information to digital information has begun. If you are not completely comfortable with conducting legal research electronically, if you are not using a practice-management application, or performing a significant portion of your client communication electronically, you are not meeting the current standard of care and are on the road to extinction (with a call to your carrier along the way). As surely as the age of the scrivener has passed, so has the time for lawyers who rely on paper-based systems to manage and process information.

Lawyers throughout history have adapted to changes in information management: from the scrivener's pen to the clerk's typewriter; from carbon paper to photocopies; from stenographers and shorthand to Dictaphones and transcriptionists; from couriers to guaranteed 9:00 a.m. overnight delivery; from fax machines to electronic mail. In the change currently underway, the sources of information that lawyers work with are moving from paper-based systems to electronic or digital systems.

The transition from paper-based information to digital information has begun, and even if you don't see yourself on the path towards a paper-free office, chances are you've already taken the first steps. If you use a time and billing program you have already committed a significant portion of your practice (the income tracking portion) to the digital realm. Surely you use a computer and word processing software to generate documents. If you use a computer to manage your contact and calendar information, then another step has been taken. The step to storing and working with client files, discovery documents, and other large collections of paper in a digital format should be next. We are not looking at the future, we are practicing in the present; it is, after all, early in the twenty-first century.

The days of using paper as the substrate for storage and communication of information are waning. As the prominence of paper-based information systems fades, digital systems are on the rise. Working with digital information—storing, organizing, analyzing, retrieving and delivering it—may sound like a radical departure from your current situation, but it can be done using familiar concepts from paper-based systems. The idea here is to take the vast quantities of paper found in most every law office, convert it to digital form—specifically the ubiquitous Adobe Portable Document Format™ (PDF)—and use Adobe Acrobat™ to work with the newly digitized information in ways familiar to most lawyers.

This book was written to help lawyers use Acrobat to work with digital documents. You should not try to avoid working with digital documents by delegating this task to your staff. Working with digital documents does not require you to become a geek, an IT (information technology) professional or anything else. You need only understand and accept that the information on printed pages can be easily captured and displayed on your computer. When you move the information from paper to digital form few of the ideas and concepts that you currently use to work with the information are lost in the process. Most of your existing ideas and concepts for working with paper-based information will be brought to bear on the information in digital form. This is not rocket science.

The ideas and concepts expressed here are not necessarily unique; for example, the bookmark function was created by Adobe for an obvious purpose and there are only so many ways that bookmarks can be added to PDF files. That said, the "how and why" of bookmarks in the legal realm merits discussion. For example, take fifty different documents, put them together in a single file and bookmark each. Now, if those fifty documents happen to be fifty trial exhibits you have just created an electronic exhibit notebook with a hyperlinked (those "click and go there" things common to web pages) table of contents. The contents of the exhibit notebook can be replicated across multiple computer systems, transferred by electronic means, even displayed in the courtroom using a digital projector. But in the end, it's just an exhibit notebook.

There may be limits to the utility of Acrobat and therefore this book. This book was written based on one small law firm's experience using Acrobat to develop a virtually paper-free office. Over the course of several years the utility of Acrobat became more and more apparent, to the point that a book was called for. *The Lawyer's Guide to Adobe Acrobat* is aimed at newcomers to Acrobat and experienced users alike. The book should be helpful in putting Acrobat to use in any law practice, whether transactional or litigation oriented. The limit on the utility of Acrobat and this book may exist in scaling the information presented for use in large firms. As a lawyer who has never practiced in a firm with more than six attorneys, I'll leave it to you to imagine what I mean by "large firms."

For the most part, the chapters of the book stand independent of one another. That said, Chapters 1 and 2 cover some background information about the what and why of PDF. Also, Chapter 3, "Getting Started," covers the basic use of Acrobat, from a description of the work area to how to navigate within PDF files. New users may need to spend some time familiarizing themselves with Acrobat or at least refer back to initial chapters from time to time. The book should serve as a reference for Acrobat functions useful in the law office. If the user wants information about digital signatures, then only Chapter 8 need be consulted. The book does not attempt to catalog and describe every feature and function of Acrobat. That task has been done by Adobe in the Acrobat *User's Guide*.

Finally, I have no personal or financial interest in Adobe or Acrobat. Indeed, Adobe expressed no interest in publishing this book (they did approve the screen shots as required by the Acrobat EULA). As you will see, I think Acrobat is a great product that will be the next big thing in realm of legal technology. That said, even great products have weak points. Some "improvements" from one version to the next are (in my opinion) a step backwards. Unless we (you and I) can convince the software company to return prior functions that are dropped or crippled in the move to "advance" software, complaining about these changes will amount to no more than crying over spilt milk; we might as well accept the changes and get on with our work, or we might hope the big company hears our small voices, takes note and makes changes.

Why PDF?

1

Information is the lawyer's stock in trade. Lawyers process information. Historically, much of the information processed by lawyers has existed in paper form. As times have changed, so has the format of information. Today, much information exists in digital form, while much remains in paper. Digital information can be stored, manipulated, analyzed, and managed much more effectively and efficiently than information maintained in paper format. Someday, the vast majority of information will be created and maintained in digital format. In the meantime, the information that comes to lawyers on paper can be converted to digital format.

To convert paper-based information to digital information, you much first choose a digital format. Formats vary in what tools are available for working with the files, and how easily and universally the files can be shared with other people. With Acrobat, you can easily convert paper documents to digital files and then work with them in many different ways. You can also convert other digital file types, such as word processing files or spreadsheets. Virtually any file that can be printed on paper can be converted to Portable Document Format (PDF). Acrobat does more than just allow you to work with digital documents in the same ways you work with paper documents. It does not, however, replace your word processing application (such as Microsoft Word, Corel WordPerfect, and so on).

Digital information can exist in many formats. Just as paper-based information may be bound in books or jotted on the backs of cocktail napkins, and be written in many different languages, digital information can exist in a variety of media and formats (although the choice of format is more important than the choice of medium). Converting existing stocks of paper-based information into digital information also requires a choice of image format. Today, common image formats include JPEG, TIFF, and PDF. The choice of format appears to have been made: courts and government institutions have chosen PDF.

Portable Document Format was invented by Adobe Systems, Inc. Refined and perfected over 15 years, Adobe PDF lets legal professionals capture and view information—from any application, on any computer system—and share it with anyone around the world. PDF files can be viewed and printed on any computer system—Macintosh, Microsoft® Windows®, UNIX®, and many mobile platforms. Adobe PDF files look just like original documents, regardless of the application used to create them. Paper documents scanned to PDF look just like their hard-copy counterparts and can be quickly turned into computer-searchable files. Unlike PDF files, documents scanned to Tagged Image File Format (TIFF) lose their original appearance when converted to searchable files. When it comes to long-term file retention, the PDF/Archive standard (PDF/A) enables organizations to archive documents electronically in a way that ensures preservation of content for later retrieval and reuse with a consistent and predictable result over an extended period of time in the future. The International Organization for Standardization (ISO) has approved PDF/A as an archive standard. PDF is an open specification and has been implemented by more than 1,800 hardware and software vendors. A PDF is a PDF no matter what software was used to create it. As a result, PDF has become the de facto standard for the secure and reliable distribution and exchange of electronic documents, and has a proven track record. PDF is a universal file format that preserves the fonts, images, graphics, and layout of any source document, regardless of the application and platform used to create it. PDF files are compact and complete, and can be shared, viewed, and printed by anyone with the free Adobe Reader program. To date, more than 500 million copies of Reader have been distributed.

You can use Acrobat to convert, create, distribute, and exchange secure and reliable PDF files (you cannot create PDF files using Reader). There are alternatives to Acrobat for the creation of PDF files, such as 1-Step RoboPDF, absolutePDF Creator Easy, activePDF Composer, and Pdf995, to name a few (**www.planetpdf.com** lists almost three hundred tools under the category "Creation & Conversion").

Governments and enterprises around the world have adopted PDF to streamline document management, increase productivity, and reduce reliance on paper. For example, PDF is the standard format for the electronic submission of drug approvals to the U.S. Food and Drug Administration. The federal judiciary's Case Management and Electronic Case Files (CM/ECF) system has been implemented in almost all district and bankruptcy courts. CM/ECF allows the courts to have case file documents in electronic format and to accept filings via the Internet. CM/ECF systems are now in use in 89% of the federal courts: 89 district courts, 93 bankruptcy courts, the Court of International Trade, and the Court of Federal Claims. Most of those courts accept electronic filings. More than 27 million cases are on CM/ECF systems, and more than 200,000 attorneys and others have filed documents via the Internet.

The CM/ECF system stores case and related information as PDF files. Most legal professionals find the system easy to use—filers prepare a document using their word processor of choice, then save it to PDF for electronic filing with the court. Attorneys practicing in courts offering the electronic filing capability can file documents directly with the court via the Internet. When documents are filed electronically, the system automatically generates and sends a verifying receipt by electronic mail—no more waiting or paying for conformed copies. Other parties in the case automatically receive notification of the filing. There are no added fees for electronic filing in federal court (existing document filing fees apply). Litigants receive one free PDF copy of every document electronically filed in their cases, which they can save or print for their files.

CM/ECF also provides courts the ability to make their documents available to the public over the Internet via the Public Access to Court Electronic Records (PACER) program. PACER offers users a fast and inexpensive way to obtain comprehensive case and docket information as PDF files from federal appellate, district, and bankruptcy courts via the Internet. Electronic access requires registration with the PACER Service Center, the judiciary's centralized registration, billing, and technical support center.

The volume of documents produced as PDF files through disclosure and discovery in litigation continues to grow. Recognizing the power and efficiency of electronic documents, attorneys employing best practices—be they co-counsel, opposing counsel, or in-house counsel—expect that documents will be exchanged as PDF files. Likewise, clients have come to expect legal professionals to provide documents as PDF files. Given the widespread adoption of PDF as the standard for electronic files, lawyers need to work with those files using Acrobat.

Acrobat provides good image-acquisition capabilities, including the ability to perform optical character recognition (OCR) while retaining an exact image of the scanned pages. Recent versions of Word and WordPerfect contain drivers to publish word processing files to PDF. Because PDF is an open standard, companies like Corel and Microsoft can develop and include PDF tools in their software applications.

Besides acquiring images, Acrobat makes PDF files truly useful. For example, bookmarks and sticky notes can be added to image-only files. If the files have a text background, the text can be formatted with highlighting, strikethroughs, or underlining. PDF files with background text can be searched; image-only files cannot be searched but information contained in the Document Summary or in attached notes is included in indexes of document collections. PDF files can be reviewed and annotated; the annotation can be summarized and published to PDF with just a few keystrokes or mouse clicks.

Acrobat allows lawyers to work with digital documents in much the same way they work with paper documents. That does not mean that Acrobat replaces your word processor. Just as you cannot effectively edit a paper document, you cannot effectively edit documents using Acrobat. You can mark them up, like you would a paper document, but the real work of editing remains the domain of word processing applications. While Acrobat adheres to many of the familiar techniques we employ to work with paper-based documents, it allows lawyers to work with digital documents more efficiently, more effectively, and with greater mobility. With a scanner and Acrobat, any law office can become a paper-free office. The person who does the paper filing becomes the person who scans incoming documents. When documents are scanned and saved they are "filed." For more information on how Acrobat can provide the foundation for a paper free-office, see Chapter 16, "Acrobat in the Paper-Free Office."

PDF File Types

2

Not all PDF files are created equally. PDF files can be divided into two broad categories: image-only and image-on-text. Understanding the fundamental difference between image-only and image-on-text files is absolutely critical; a short explanation of the difference appears more than once throughout this book. Regardless of whether you work with image-only or image-on-text files, the image produced by scanning paper to PDF remains an exact duplicate of the original (one of the key advantages of PDF).

§ 2.1 Image-Only Files

Image-only PDFs are just that—images only, just digital photocopies of paper documents. Think of image-only PDF files as pages in a notebook; you can look at the pages but you cannot search the notebook without reading each page. Even though image-only files cannot be searched, they are still more useful than a notebook full of paper pages. Using Acrobat, image-only files can be annotated with comments and graphics. Comments can be searched and summarized (see Chapter 7, "Commenting Tools") with Acrobat. PDF image-only files that contain comments content can be searched for with Windows Explorer and other computer-based search programs.

§ 2.2 Image-on-Text Files

Image-on-text files are created by printing an existing computer file to PDF (word processing and spreadsheet files are good examples), or by running a PDF image-only file through an Optical Character Recognition (OCR) application. When using OCR applications other than the functionality built into Acrobat, care must be taken to select a final file type that produces an exact image on text; otherwise, the visible text in the PDF image may be changed to comport with the interpretation of the OCR application. Acrobat has the built-in ability to create OCR PDF files; Acrobat calls this function OCR Text Recognition. For more information on creating and working with image-on-text files, see Chapter 10, "Search, Find, and Indexing."

Image-on-text files contain an exact image of the paper copy, with a text layer behind the image. Engage your imagination for a moment here and picture two PDF image-only files created by scanning two different pieces of paper. On one piece of paper is a photograph of the Statute of Liberty and on the other is double-spaced black text against a white background. When you look at these two PDF files on your computer, you are looking at image-only files. The image-only file that shows the Statute of Liberty contains no text for an OCR application to work with. The image-only file that shows double-spaced black text against a white background, while just a picture of the text, does contain information in the form of small black shapes that an OCR application can work with. The OCR application looks at each discrete mark on the page, compares the image to its catalog of characters, and makes its best guess at what character the mark on the page corresponds to. After the OCR application has examined each mark and assigned a corresponding character that information is saved as a layer of text behind the image. In PDF image-on-text files, the recognized characters in the text layer are mapped to the corresponding mark in the image file. The mapping between the two layers allows you to select areas of the image that correspond with the text characters. This allows you to search, copy and highlight the marks on the image portion of the file as though they were text characters. Pretty cool!

Many lawyers think image-on-text PDF files are the holy grail of legal document management. When paper documents are scanned to other image formats such as TIFF or JPEG, only a digital image of the paper exists. If characters that comprise that image are converted to text, the conversion process inevitably changes the appearance of the text in the image file. Not so with PDF files; the image remains an exact duplicate of the original while the interpreted text exists independently behind, or a layer below, the image. The text file behind or below the image can be searched. Depending on the quality of the paper documents scanned, thousands of pages can be captured as exact copies and made searchable through the use of OCR applications. There are limits and caveats with OCR technology that are discussed in more detail in chapter 10. (See Section 10.2, "OCR Quality Experiment.")

Getting Started

3

Before looking at specific features of Acrobat, and how those features might be used in the practice of law, we need to take some time to become familiar with the application that makes working with digital documents as comfortable and familiar as working with paper-based documents. To start with, Acrobat 8 comes in four varieties:

Acrobat 8 Professional—Acrobat 8 Professional provides essential tools for the legal community to create and combine electronic documents, manage reviews, build forms, compare PDF files, create and use batch processes, and secure information. Acrobat 8 Professional also contains features specifically created for the legal community, including redaction and Bates numbering. With Acrobat 8 Professional, PDF files can be enabled to allow users who have only free Adobe Reader® 8 software to review, add comments, fill in PDF forms, and digitally sign PDF files.

Acrobat 8 Standard—Acrobat 8 Standard offers reliable ways to create, combine, protect, and share Adobe PDF files. Acrobat Standard generates PDF files that accurately represent the original document, whether paper or electronic.

Acrobat 8 Elements—Acrobat 8 Elements, available through volume licensing (100 seats per order), enables legal professionals to easily and reliably create secure Adobe PDF files.

Adobe Reader—The freely available Adobe Reader allows users to view, print, and search PDF files, and it also makes

PDF files freely shareable across multiple operating systems. More than 500 million copies of the free Adobe Reader have been distributed, making the ability to view a PDF file ubiquitous

Acrobat Standard and Professional are the "full" versions of the program and are the applications for working with PDF files. The primary differences between the Standard and Professional versions are tools for Bates numbering, redaction, creating PDF forms and enabling features (such as commenting) in PDF files so that users of the free Reader program can do more with the PDF files you send them. Having the ability to create forms can virtually eliminate the need for a typewriter in the law office. You can scan any document to PDF, then create form fields that can be filled in and printed. With Acrobat 8 Professional you can enable forms to allow Reader users to fill in the form, save it and return it to you. Without the "enabling" enhancement, Reader users can only fill in and print the completed form.

Acrobat looks much like any other software application (such as a word processor, spreadsheet, or database manager). If you make Acrobat fill the entire display on your computer you are looking at the user interface.

With Acrobat 8, Adobe revamped significant portions of the user interface to make it more useable and to maximize the space available for the work area. The user interface includes a number of components such as menus, toolbars, the navigation pane, and icons. The large area in the middle (the work area) displays PDF files and is where most of the action takes place (Figure 3.1). Before moving on to describing the action, take a look at the various components of the user interface and how tasks are described in this book.

§ 3.1 Menus

Many Acrobat tasks can be performed through menu selections. Menus are the second row of information displayed in the user interface (the top row displays the name of the currently open PDF file). In Acrobat 8 Professional, there are ten menus, from left to right: File, Edit, View, Document, Comments, Forms, Tools, Advanced, Window, and Help. Figure 3.2 shows the Tools menu pulled down and extended to select the Hand Tool.

Throughout this book as tasks are described, the menu commands are listed and in some cases illustrated. Menu commands list the sequence of items to be selected and appear as follows:

Menu (Edit Preferences): **Edit > Preferences**

The menu description states, in parentheses, the task to be accomplished (shown above as **Edit Preferences**), followed by the menu to select

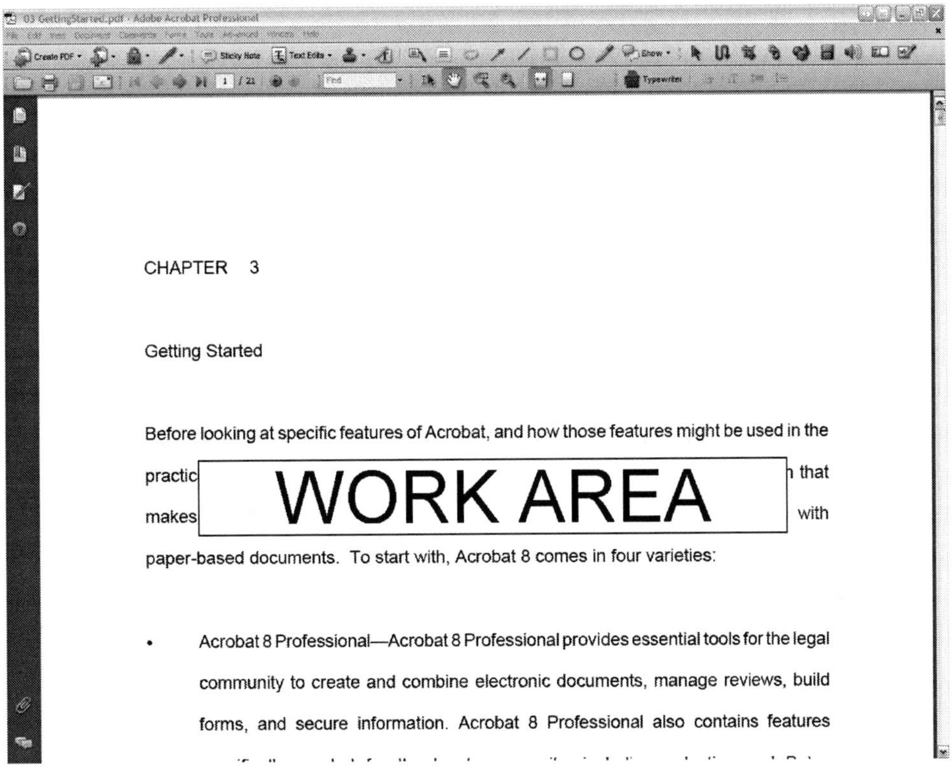

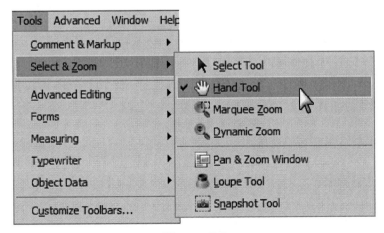

Figure 3.1

(shown above as **Edit**), followed by the item or items to be selected in sequence from the menu (shown above as **Preferences**). The first menu item is followed by ">," then the next item to be selected is listed. Some menus are several levels deep. In those cases, the menu items are separated by ">" in the order that they are to be selected.

Figure 3.2

When it is possible to execute menu commands by a series of keystrokes, those shortcuts follow the menu description and are shown as follows:

Keystroke (Edit Preferences): **Alt+E or Ctrl+K**

The keystroke descriptions throughout this book use the following conventions:

- ◆ **Alt** refers to the Alt key
- ◆ **Ctrl** refers to the Ctrl (or Control) key
- ◆ **Shift** refers to the Shift key
- ◆ When the plus symbol (+) appears between key references, the keys must be pressed simultaneously (for example, **Shift+Ctrl+N** means hold down the Shift, Control, and N keys all at the same time)
- ◆ When a hyphen (-) appears between key references, the keys are pressed in sequence

Keystroke combinations can offer a time-saving way to accomplish frequently repeated tasks in most computer applications, not just Acrobat. The trick to effectively using keystroke combinations is to not try to memorize more than you use on a regular basis. Chapter 24 provides a list of keystroke combinations that are particularly useful for legal professionals.

§ 3.2 Toolbars

In addition to menus and keystrokes, some Acrobat tasks can be performed by clicking an icon on one of the toolbars. Indeed, some tasks can be performed only by clicking on a toolbar icon. Acrobat opens with a set of default toolbars; more specialized and advanced toolbars can be displayed at your command. Acrobat 8 Professional groups tools into 16 toolbars (17 if you count the Properties Bar as a toolbar) (Figure 3.3). The list of available toolbars can be displayed using the following menu commands:

Menu (Display Toolbars): **View > Toolbars**
Keystroke (Display Toolbars): **Alt+V-T**

Acrobat 8 allows users to customize the toolbars by selecting which tools will be displayed. As you begin to work with PDF files on a regular basis you will find it worth the time spent to customize the toolbars to display regularly used tools and hide the ones that are rarely, if ever, used. To customize the toolbars, right-click anywhere in the toolbar area (you can right click on a

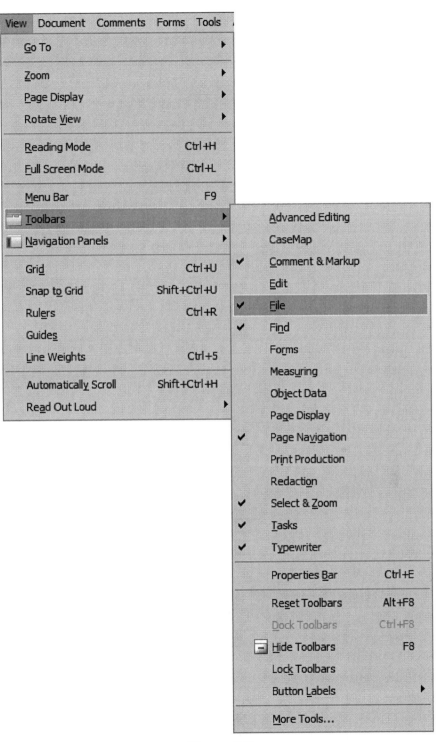

Figure 3.3

tool or in an unused area to the right of the active toolbars). Right-clicking in the toolbar area displays a menu; near the bottom of that menu select the **More Tools** item (Figure 3.4). After making this selection the **More Tools** dialog box opens.

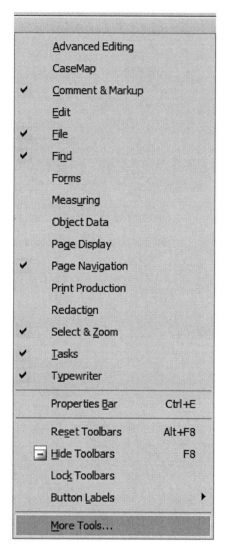

Figure 3.4

In the **More Tools** dialog box you can select which toolbars are displayed and which tools will be shown on the selected toolbars. In Figure 3.5 the Measuring, Object Data, Page Display, and Print Production toolbars have not been selected. The **Page Navigation** toolbar has been selected by clicking and placing a checkmark in the box next to its name. In addition, each of the tool

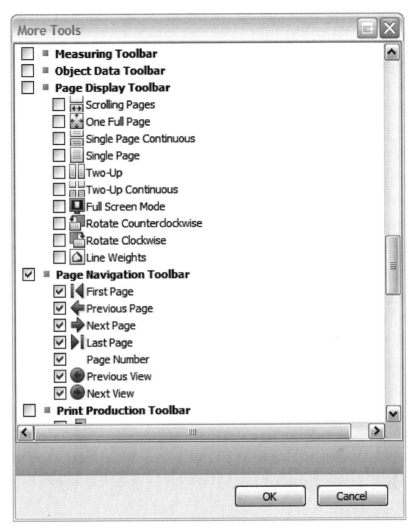

Figure 3.5

buttons on the **Page Navigation** toolbar have been selected (by default, when Acrobat 8 was installed, only the Previous Page and Next Page tool buttons were selected).

Toolbars can "float" in the work area, or be docked with the other toolbars. You may find it handy to display and float a seldom used toolbar in the work area. In Figure 3.6, the **Redaction Toolbar** floats in the work area.

You can display some or all toolbars. To quickly display all toolbars, right-click in the toolbar area and select **Dock All Toolbars**, or

> Menu (Show/dock all toolbars): **View > Toolbars > Dock All Toolbars**
> Keystroke (Show/dock all toolbars): **Alt+Ctrl+D**

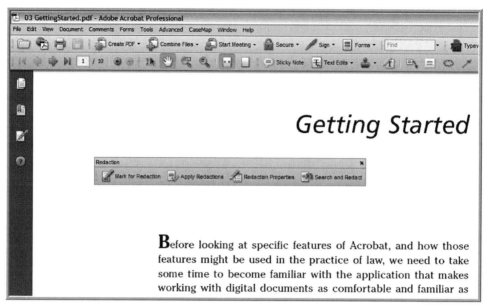

Figure 3.6

or

Keystroke (Show/dock all toolbars): **Alt+V-T-D**

To quickly hide all of the toolbars press the F8 key. This can be handy if you need maximum display real estate, such as when you have a word processing application and Acrobat open side by side on the screen. Why would you want to do that? It's just like looking at your draft answer (the word processing document) next to the complaint (PDF file). You can go through paragraph-by-paragraph and compare the answers to the allegations in the complaint. When you want to see the toolbars again, just press F8 and they will return. If you forget that F8 will hide and show the toolbars, the same result can be achieved through the View menu.

Menu (Hide/Show Toolbars): **View > Toolbars > Hide Toolbars/Show Toolbars**

§ 3.3 The Navigation Icons and Panes

A principal attribute that recommends Acrobat for use in the legal profession is the ability to navigate through PDF files in much the same way as you would browse through a file folder or notebook full of paper. But you can navigate through PDF files with Acrobat in more ways than you can with a paper file. One way is by using the navigation panes located on the left side of the document window. Specific navigation panes (e.g., Pages and Bookmarks) are activated by clicking on their respective icons. The Acrobat 8 Navigation Icons (Figure 3.7) are Pages, Bookmarks, Signatures, How To, Attachments, and Comments.

Clicking on one of the icons displays the navigation pane for that type of navigational aid. For example, clicking on the **Bookmarks** navigation icon (Figure 3.8) displays the **Bookmarks** pane. If the document contains bookmarks they are displayed in the navigation pane. The same goes for comments. Clicking on any one of the bookmarks (or comments if that icon was selected) takes you to the point in the document where the bookmark (or comment) was created. If the document does not contain bookmarks or comments, then the respective navigation panes will be empty. The **Pages** icon (Figure 3.9) always displays all the pages in the document (it's never "empty").

Figure 3.7

Figure 3.8

Figure 3.9

§ 3.4 Basic Navigation

Basic navigation of PDF files can be achieved by simply paging through the document. Another simple mode of navigation is going to a specific page number. More sophisticated navigation involves using Bookmarks, Links, Comments, or Thumbnail (page) views. Paging through a document calls to mind turning pages in a book or file; you can turn forward or backward one page at a time. To navigate through a document one page at a time, use the **Previous Page** and **Next Page** buttons on the button bar at the top of the document window (Figure 3.10).

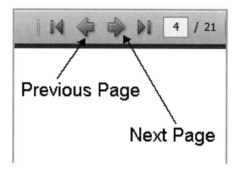

Figure 3.10

Or, use the **Page Up** and **Page Down** keys, or the **left-right** or **up-down** arrow keys on your keyboard. Note: this only works when the document is displayed in the Fit Page view; if it is displayed in Actual Size or Fit Width, pressing **Page Up** or **Page Down** first moves the document in the window up or down some distance before moving to the next or previous page; pressing the up-down arrow keys scrolls up or down the page until reaching the page break; but, pressing the left-right arrow keys moves to the previous or next page respectively. To jump to the beginning or end of a document, use the **First Page** and **Last Page** buttons (Figure 3.11) (Note: the First and Last Page buttons are not displayed by default in Acrobat 8); or use the keyboard command **Ctrl+Home** and **Ctrl+End**, respectively. To browse forward or backward in a document, one page at a time, use the following commands:

Menu (Go to next or previous page): **View > Go To > Next Page (or Previous Page)**

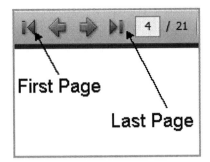

Figure 3.11

Keystroke (Go to next or previous page): **Page Up (or Page Down)** Note: this only works when with the document displayed in the Fit Page view; if displayed in Actual Size or Fit Width, pressing **Page Up** or **Page Down** first moves the document in the window up or down some distance before moving to the next or previous page.

Specific pages can be located by using the Go To function:

Menu (Go To Page *n*): **View > Go To > *n*** (insert page number *n*)
Keystroke (Go To Page *n*): **Alt+V-G-*n*** (insert page number *n*)
Keystroke (Go To Page *n*): **Shift+Ctrl+*n*** (insert page number *n*)

Your navigational course within a document or across multiple documents can be retraced by using the view buttons, **Next View**, and **Previous View**, which are adjacent to the Page buttons (Note: the View buttons are not displayed by default in Acrobat 8). As with most other tasks in Acrobat, the Next View and Previous View can also be achieved using menu commands or keyboard commands:

Menu (Go To Previous/Next View): **View > Go To > Previous View** (or **Next View**)
Keystroke (Go To Previous/Next View): **Alt+Left Arrow** (or **Alt+Right Arrow**)

When navigating through documents by paging through or using bookmarks, the view buttons may receive little use. But when navigating by way of links, the view buttons become indispensable. When you click on a link, the quickest way back to the point where you clicked is by clicking the **Previous View** button. Think of the view buttons as comparable to the Forward and Back buttons in browsers like Firefox and Internet Explorer.

§ 3.5 Bookmarks

Bookmarks are like a table of contents, except that clicking on a bookmark takes you to a predetermined page within a PDF file. Bookmarks may be one of the most powerful features of PDF files for lawyers. As you page through a document, bookmarks can be added with the keystroke **Ctrl+B**, followed by typing a short name for the bookmark. Bookmarks can be nested (arranged in a hierarchy) and differentiated by font style (plain, bold, italics, or bold and italic) or font color. The creation and use of bookmarks is discussed in more detail in Chapter 6, "Adding Document Navigation Aids."

Think of the basic four-part file folder: with the center section turned to the right, pages containing your notes may be on the left and correspondence on the right; flip the center section to the left and miscellaneous documents may be on the left and pleadings on the right. If the entire file contents were a single PDF file, then you could have four main bookmarks for notes, correspondence, miscellaneous, and pleadings. Under each of the main categories you could have bookmarks for each of the individual documents (such as a separate bookmark for each item of correspondence). Using a standard four-part file folder as an example of how bookmarks might be used provides a good illustration, but is probably not the best practice. It would be better to have a folder (directory) representing the paper file folder that contained subfolders (subdirectories) for each of the types of documents (notes, correspondence, miscellaneous, and pleadings). A discussion of digital filing systems appears in Chapter 16, "Acrobat in the Paper-Free Office."

§ 3.6 Links

Links in PDF files are like hyperlinks in Web pages. Clicking on a link takes you to a new location. Links can take you to a specific page in the current document, to the first page of another document, to a specific page in another document, or to a Web site; they can open another file type, play audio or video, and more. The creation and use of links is discussed in more detail in Chapter 6, "Adding Document Navigation Aids." Links are the essence of electronic briefs, discussed in Chapter 15, "Electronic Briefs."

§ 3.7 Controlling How Pages Are Displayed

Acrobat splits page displays according to two functions (three if you count full-page view as a separate function). You can set defaults for all three functions in Preferences (**Edit > Preferences** or **Ctrl+K**) (Figure 3.12).

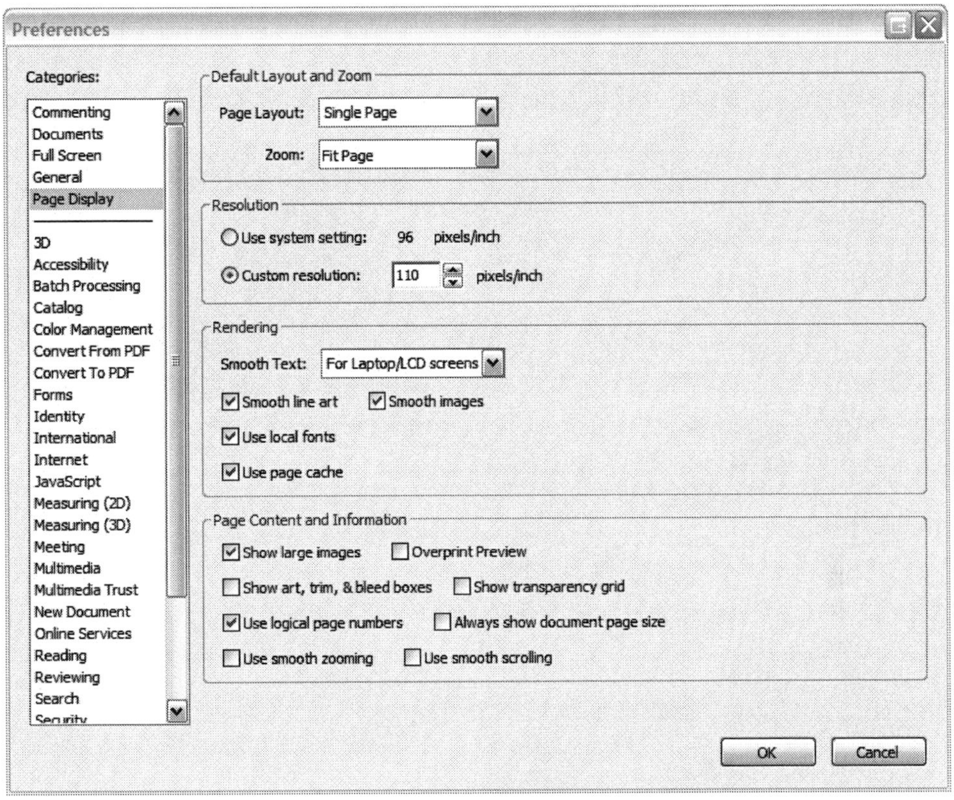

Preferences

Categories:

Commenting
Documents
Full Screen
General
Page Display

3D
Accessibility
Batch Processing
Catalog
Color Management
Convert From PDF
Convert To PDF
Forms
Identity
International
Internet
JavaScript
Measuring (2D)
Measuring (3D)
Meeting
Multimedia
Multimedia Trust
New Document
Online Services
Reading
Reviewing
Search
Security

Default Layout and Zoom

Page Layout: Single Page
Zoom: Fit Page

Resolution

○ Use system setting: 96   pixels/inch
● Custom resolution: 110   pixels/inch

Rendering

Smooth Text: For Laptop/LCD screens
☑ Smooth line art   ☑ Smooth images
☑ Use local fonts
☑ Use page cache

Page Content and Information

☑ Show large images   ☐ Overprint Preview
☐ Show art, trim, & bleed boxes   ☐ Show transparency grid
☑ Use logical page numbers   ☐ Always show document page size
☐ Use smooth zooming   ☐ Use smooth scrolling

OK   Cancel

Figure 3.12

§ 3.7.1 Page Display

"Page Display" refers to page layout and orientation. You can set a preferred default page display in Preferences (**Edit > Preferences > Page Display—Page Layout** or **Ctrl+K—Page Display—Page Layout**). You can change the page display mode for the currently open PDF file from the View Menu (Figure 3.13).

Menu (Page Display): **View > Page Display**
Keystroke (Page Display): **Alt+V-P**

- *Single Page* displays one page at a time, with no portion of other pages visible.
- *Single Page Continuous* displays pages in a continuous vertical column that is one page wide.
- *Two-Up* displays each two-page spread with no portion of other pages visible.
- *Two-Up Continuous* displays facing pages side by side in a continuous vertical column.

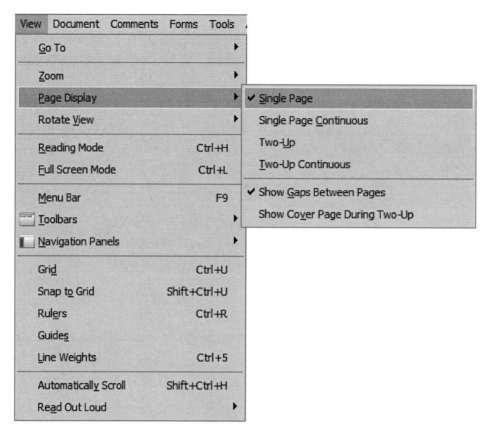

Figure 3.13

§ 3.7.2 Page Size

Acrobat displays document pages in a variety of views. The default view can be defined in Preferences (**Edit > Preferences—Page Display** or **Ctrl+K—Page Display**). When you look at a piece of paper in a file folder or notebook, you typically see the entire page. You might use a ruler or sheet of paper to cover portions of the page so that you can focus on specific areas. The three primary views in Acrobat are Actual Size, Fit Page, and Fit Width.

◆ *Actual Size view* displays the current page proportionally within the document window. The amount of the page that you see depends on the capabilities of the computer and your display settings. To display the current document in Actual Size, click on the **Actual Size** icon on the toolbar, or:

Menu (View Actual Size): **View > Actual Size**

Keystroke (View Actual Size): **Ctrl+1.** Figure 3.14 shows a page displayed with Actual Size selected (19" 4:3 flat panel display).

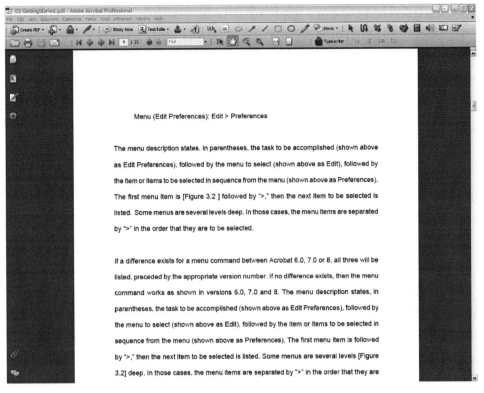

Figure 3.14

◆ *Fit Page view* displays the full current page from top to bottom. On smaller monitors it may be difficult to read the text on the page displayed, but this may be the preferred view for browsing through a document (you can always zoom in). To display the current document in Fit Page view, click on the **Fit Page** icon on the toolbar, or:

    Menu (Fit Page View): **View > Fit Page;**

    Keystroke (Fit Page View): **Ctrl+2**.

Figure 3.15 shows a page displayed with Fit Page selected (19" 4:3 flat panel display).

◆ *Fit Width view* displays the current page at maximum width. This view always chops off the bottom of the page, making it necessary to use the **Page Down** key, the scroll bar, or the scroll wheel on your pointing device to see the bottom of the page. If you need to read the text of a document this may be the best view because it provides the largest image that can be viewed with the least amount of scrolling (Fit Width does not require any side-to-side scrolling that may be necessary if the view is zoomed in closer than page width). To display the current document in Fit Width view, click on the **Fit View** icon on the toolbar, or:

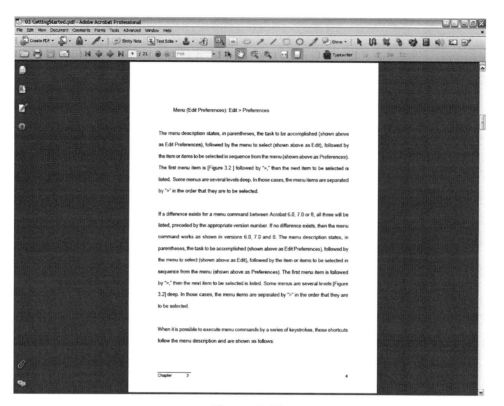

Figure 3.15

> Menu (Fit Width View): **View > Fit Width**;
> Keystroke (Fit Width View): **Ctrl+3**.

Figure 3.16 shows a page displayed with Fit Width selected (19" 4:3 flat panel display). TIP: Based on years of daily use of Acrobat to work with PDF files, here's my preferred view setup. First, uncheck the Page Display toolbar (see Section 3.2 for how to customize the toolbars). Then, check to display the Select & Zoom toolbar. On the Select & Zoom toolbar check the following: Select Tool; Hand Tool; Marquee Zoom; Dynamic Zoom; Fit Width; and, Fit Page. You won't need the Zoom In, Zoom Out, or Zoom Value buttons (Figure 3.17).

In addition to the three primary views, Acrobat includes the ability to zoom in (magnify) or zoom out (reduce). Zooming becomes important if you work with large-format documents such as survey maps or plats, or are concerned with the fine print or fine markings in a standard-size document. When a 24-inch by 36-inch survey map has been scanned or printed to PDF and displayed on your monitor, what you see is substantially smaller than the origi-

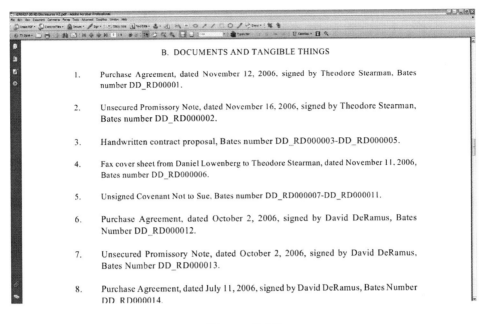

Figure 3.16

nal document (unless, of course, you have a 42-inch monitor). For example, a 24" x 36" survey plat displayed in Fit Page mode is reduced to 35 percent of its actual size. But not to worry—Acrobat can zoom in (magnify) to an incredible 6,400 percent. To zoom the view in or out from the current display:

Menu (Zoom In or Out): **View > Zoom To** [select the desired magnification or view]

Keystroke (Zoom In or Out): **Ctrl+M** [select the desired magnification or view]

Keystroke (Zoom In/Out respectively): **Ctrl++/Ctrl- -**

Okay, that last set of keystroke combinations needs an explanation. To Zoom In (make document appear larger) press the **Control** key and the "+" key at the same time; each time you press this key combination the display sizes increases. To Zoom Out (make the document appear smaller) press the **Control** key and the "-" key at the same time; each time you press this key combination the display size decreases.

§ 3.7.3 Zoom Tools (Toolbar buttons)

In addition to the zoom features available through the menus or keystrokes, Acrobat has a pair of zoom tools (Marquee and Dynamic) that are handy to

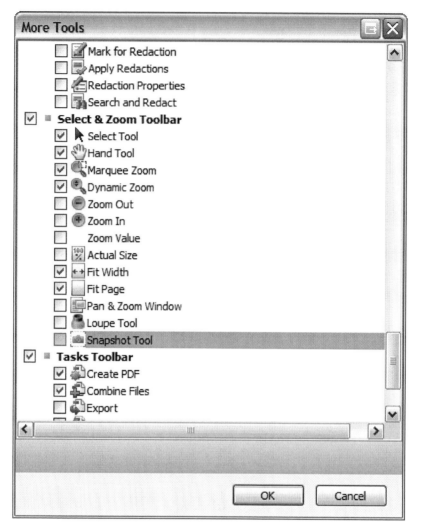

Figure 3.17

have displayed on the **Select & Zoom** Toolbar (Figure 3.18). The **Dynamic Zoom** tool lets the user zoom in or out simply by holding down the left mouse or pointer button and dragging the mouse or pointer up or down. The

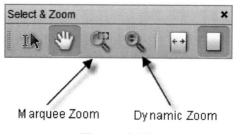

Figure 3.18

amount of zoom (magnification or reduction) is displayed in the Zoom tool-bar as a percentage (if you have included that feature on the Zoom & Select Toolbar). With the **Marquee Zoom** tool, you left click and "drag" a box around any area of the currently displayed file; when you release the left mouse button the area within the box fills the document window. The Marquee and Dynamic zoom tools are two of the things that you can use only by clicking the tool icon on the toolbar. When you are done examining the area of the document that you zoomed in on, simply click on the preferred view button in the toolbar (Actual Size, Fit Page, or Fit Width). These zoom tools are especially useful for examining documents using a digital projector in set-tlement conferences, depositions, or the courtroom. Note, however, that the Marquee and Dynamic zoom tools do not work in Full Screen view (this is dis-cussed below).

§ 3.7.4 Full Screen Mode

Acrobat also has a display feature called Full Screen Mode. This display op-tion presents each page in Fit Page mode and removes the work area from the display so that the page displayed is all that you see (except for a black or color border that fills the rest of the screen). Full Screen view works well for slide show type presentations, or even the presentation of evidence, but be-cause all of the tools are hidden you cannot zoom in or out or add comments to the displayed image. To activate the Full Screen view:

> Menu (Activate Full Screen View): **Window > Full Screen View**
> Keystroke (Activate Full Screen View): **Ctrl+L**

To exit Full Screen view, press the **Esc** key. For more information on using Full Screen view, see Chapter 14, "Display Mode."

§ 3.8 Preferences

Preferences, or default operating conditions, can be set from the **Edit** menu. For example, if you prefer to have documents open in the Fit Page view, this can be set as an operating default.

> Menu (Edit Preferences): **Edit > Preferences**
> Keystroke (Edit Preferences): **Ctrl+K**

The **Preferences** dialog box presents a bewildering list of options that can be set, more than can be described here, but we'll touch on a few. The **Preferences** dialog box has two primary parts. On the left is a list of "Cate-gories." On the right, the choices for the selected category are displayed (Figure 3.19).

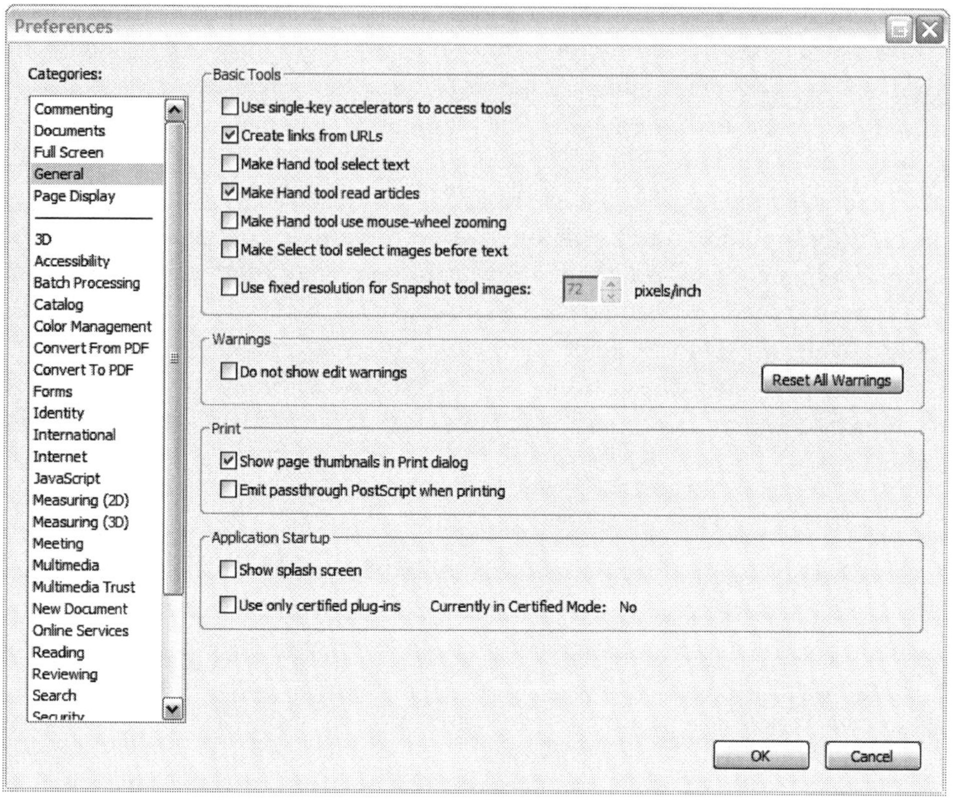

Figure 3.19

§ 3.8.1 Preferences—Commenting

In the **Viewing Comments** section select your preferred font and font size for comments (sticky notes, text boxes, call outs). In the **Making Comments** section check (or uncheck) the option to **Copy selected text into Highlight**. If you review image-on-text files, such as deposition transcripts in Acrobat, selecting text into highlights can be quite helpful. As you review a deposition you simply highlight important sections. As you highlight the text it is copied into a comment. The comments can be reviewed in the comments window.

§ 3.8.2 Preferences—Documents

In the Open Settings section you may want to increase the number of documents in the recently used list. That's the list you see at the bottom of the **File** menu (**Alt+F**). If you use the Organizer feature, you can select the "look back" period for which Organizer will remember opened files.

§ 3.8.3 Preferences—General

In the **Basic Tools** section, you can activate (check) the **Hand** tool to select text. If you use a mouse with a wheel, you can activate the wheel to zoom

(+/-) the view; this gives up using the mouse wheel to scroll through pages, but if you do a lot of zooming in and out, this might be worth trying. In the **Print** section, leave or place a check mark to show page thumbnails in the print dialog. This helps confirm what will, or will not, print.

§ 3.8.4 Preferences—Page Display

If you don't set any other preferences, take time to review and customize the settings here. First, pick a Page Layout that you prefer (single page works well). Next, choose a Zoom setting that you like (fit page works well). Keep in mind that you can quickly change the zoom depending on the tools you have selected to display on the **Select & Zoom** toolbar. If you work on a laptop computer or use an LCD (flat panel) display, select **For Laptop/LCD Screens** on the **Smooth Text** drop-down menu in the **Rendering** section.

§ 3.8.5 Preferences—Identity

The information on the Identity preferences page will be used with comments, review, and digital signatures. Take a minute to fill your name, firm name, and electronic mail address.

If you looked at the preferences discussed above, you saw that Acrobat allows you to make default settings for more things than you'll probably ever want to tinker with.

Creating PDF Files

4

PDF files can be created by using Acrobat to "print" to PDF, by scanning to PDF, by converting existing files, by combining files, and by capturing Web pages. Using Acrobat as a standard tool in the law office, on par with a word processing application, is no longer just beneficial—it is approaching the level of necessity. Just as law firms depend on word processing applications to create documents, lawyers are depending on Acrobat to create PDF files and work with them. With various state and federal courts implementing (and in some cases mandating) electronic filing, basic knowledge of creating and working with PDF files has become as necessary as proficiency in using a word processor or electronic legal research tools such as WestLaw and LexisNexis.

PDF is an excellent choice for the law office because it preserves the fonts, formatting, and graphics of the source file, regardless of the application and platform used to create it. A variety of file formats can be converted to PDF. As a general rule, if an electronic file can be printed on paper with a physical printer, it can be printed to PDF. For instance, a set of interrogatories can be created in WordPerfect or Word, printed to PDF, and then sent via electronic mail to opposing counsel or the client. Likewise, a spreadsheet prepared using Excel or QuattroPro can be printed to PDF and sent via electronic mail as an attachment to someone who does not have the source application software to open or read an Excel or QuattroPro file. PDF files are compact and can be exchanged, viewed, navigated, and printed by anyone with the free Adobe Reader software, while maintaining document integrity. In addition to creating PDF files from virtually any software application, you can also create PDF files by scanning paper documents and by downloading and converting Web pages.

As mentioned above, one of the main benefits to using Acrobat in the law office is the ease with which you can convert a word processing or other document simply by printing it to PDF. To create PDF files by printing to PDF you need a PDF printer (which is software, not hardware). Acrobat installs a single PDF printer, Adobe PDF. Adobe PDF is like any other printer driver, but it writes out PDF files instead of printer commands. The Adobe PDF printer appears in the Windows Printers folder and is available to all applications that use associated Windows printers (see Figure 4.1).

Figure 4.1

The default Acrobat installation adds Convert to Adobe PDF buttons to the toolbars in Microsoft Word, Excel, Internet Explorer and PowerPoint that allow you to create PDF files quickly and easily from within those applications. Adobe PDF is also added to the menu bar. By default, PDF files created using these commands and buttons preserve hyperlinks, styles, and bookmarks present in the source file. In Windows XP, if the Convert to Adobe PDF buttons are not visible in the Microsoft application, choose **View > Toolbars > PDF-Maker 6.0**.

Another incredible benefit of using PDF in the law office is the ability to scan all the information that comes into the law office in paper format and save it on your hard disk drive (or better still, on a drive shared over a local area network). Once you become comfortable with Acrobat, you are on your way to operating a paper-free office.

§ 4.1 Creating PDFs Using the Print Command

The most common way to create PDF files from existing files is to use the Print to PDF function. As mentioned earlier, Acrobat installs a Convert to PDF button on the toolbars of Microsoft Word, Excel, Internet Explorer, and PowerPoint. Adobe encourages use of the PDF Maker buttons when available because they create PDF files with bookmarks, tagging, hyperlinks, etc. A Publish to PDF button can be installed on the toolbar in WordPerfect (version 9.0 and later). This PDF functionality is written and provided by Corel, not Adobe. If you have a Print, Publish, or Convert to PDF button on the toolbar, you need only click it to start the process. Otherwise, to print a document to PDF:

1. Open the file that you want to convert to an Adobe PDF file in its authoring application, and choose **File > Print**.
2. Choose **Adobe PDF** from the list of printers.
3. From the **Print** dialog box, click **OK.**

By default, the PDF file is saved in the same folder (directory) as the source file, using the same filename, but with a .pdf extension. The conversion of files to PDF also uses the printer settings or page setup you have chosen for the application that created the file. For example, if you are using Microsoft PowerPoint and choose **Handouts** from the **Print Dialog** box, the resulting PDF file is based on the Handouts version of the presentation.

Corel WordPerfect includes a PDF writer that can be executed from the **File** menu (**File > Publish To PDF**). Using the Corel PDF writer will produce a PDF file with page breaks and pagination exactly as it appears on screen at the time of printing. Using the Adobe PDF printer may produce different pagination results. Accordingly, to ensure correct pagination when using the Adobe PDF printer with WordPerfect files, do the following:

1. In WordPerfect, select **Print** from the File menu, click the **Select Printer** button on the toolbar or press **F5.**
2. Select the **Adobe PDF** printer and click the **Close** button in the bottom right corner of the Print To dialog box.
3. Select View Page (**View > Page**, or **Alt + F5**).
4. Browse through the document and make appropriate adjustments to produce the desired page breaks and pagination results.
5. Print the file (**File > Print**; **Ctrl+P**; or **F5** and click **Print**.

§ 4.2 Creating PDF Files Using a Scanner

Perhaps the ultimate utility of Acrobat is the ability to convert paper documents into digital PDF files using a scanner. Discovery documents, incoming mail, and pleadings can all be converted to digital files using Acrobat and a scanner. To create a PDF file using a scanner:

1. Place the document to be scanned in the scanner, then click the **Create PDF** button (Figure 4.2) and select **From Scanner**; alternatively, use the menu or keyboard commands shown below.
    Menu (Create PDF from Scanner): **File > Create PDF > From Scanner**
    Keystroke (Create PDF from Scanner): **Alt+F-F-S**

Figure 4.2

2. The Acrobat Scan dialog box opens (Figure 4.3). Select your scanner device. Choose the format (single-sided or double-sided) and specify whether to create a new PDF file or append the converted scan to the currently open PDF file. Check the compatibility level. By default, pages are compressed for compactness and edge shadows are removed. The biggest determinant of the size of image-only PDF files is the type of compression used. If you adjust the file size slider all the way to the left, you'll get the smallest file size.

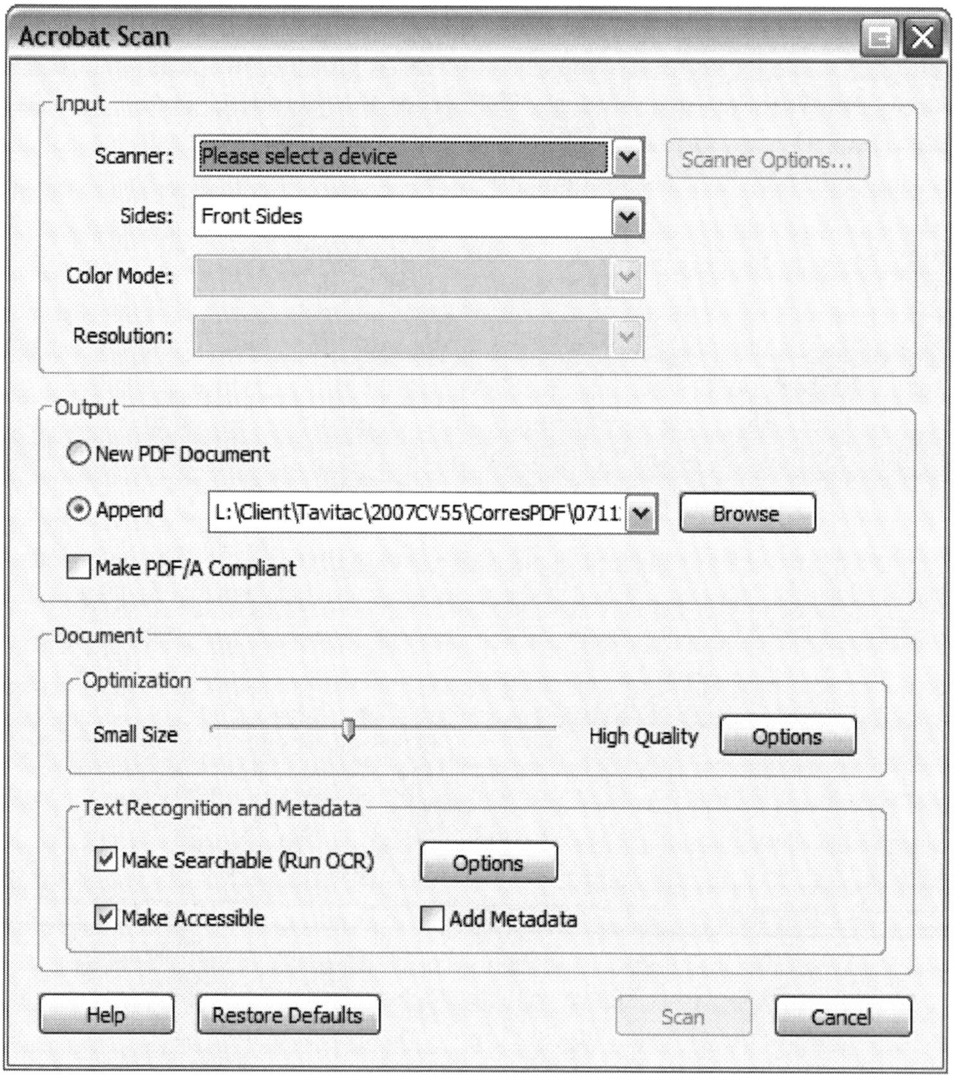

Figure 4.3

3. Click the Scan button, and the Saved Scanned Files As window appears. Navigate to the folder where you want to save the PDF file being created and supply an appropriate file name. Note: If you choose **Create > From Scanner** while a PDF file is open, you will have the option to append pages to it. Some lawyers like to build one large case file this way. If no document is open, Acrobat will ask you to first name the new document.

4. Click **Scan**. At this point a new dialog box appears that allows selection of additional scanning options such as paper size and the type of file to be created (color, gray scale, or black and white). This dialog box is a function of the software that came with the scanner (the scanner driver) and its contents vary depending on the make and model of scanner used. Accordingly, its precise contents cannot be described here. However, unless you need a color or gray-scale image of the paper document, always select **black-and-white** (sometimes listed as **text**). Documents scanned as black-and-white images produce substantially smaller PDF files sizes compared to documents scanned as color or gray-scale images. If you click on the **Scanner Options** button, you can choose to hide the scanner's native interface. This may make scanning faster, check it out.

5. Click **Next** if you are scanning multiple pages to the same file; click **Done** when finished scanning.

The document scanned to PDF is now visible in the work area of the Acrobat window.

§ 4.3 Creating PDF Files Using Drag and Drop

PDF files can be created by dragging image files (.jpg, .tif, etc.) and Microsoft files (Word, Excel, etc.) into the document pane of the Acrobat window or onto the Acrobat icon. This can be useful for people who use the functionality of the Windows desktop. To convert files to PDF by dragging and dropping, drag the file into the open Acrobat window or onto the Acrobat icon. Note: if you have a file open in the Acrobat window and you drag a file into the document pane, the converted file opens as a new PDF file. Once the conversion has taken place the new PDF file appears in the document window; save it to an appropriate location on the local computer or network.

§ 4.4 Converting an Existing File to PDF

A number of file types can be converted to PDF using this feature. Notably, WordPerfect files are not presently among the file types that can be converted. For the most part, only image files (.jpg, .tif, etc.) and files from Microsoft applications can be converted using this feature. To convert one existing file to PDF:

Click the **Create PDF button** and select **From File**; alternatively, use the menu or keyboard commands shown below:

Menu (Create PDF from File): **File > Create PDF > From File** (Figure 4.4)

Keystroke (Create PDF from File): **Ctrl+N**; or Keystroke (Create PDF from File): **Alt+F-F-F**

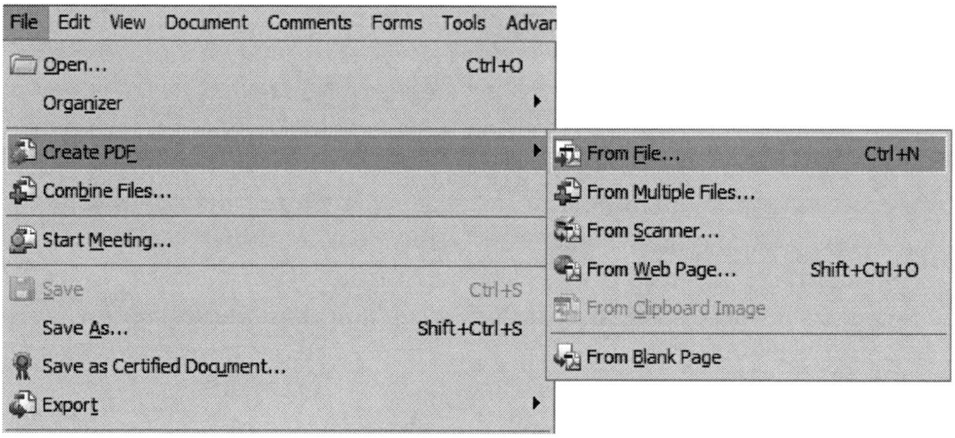

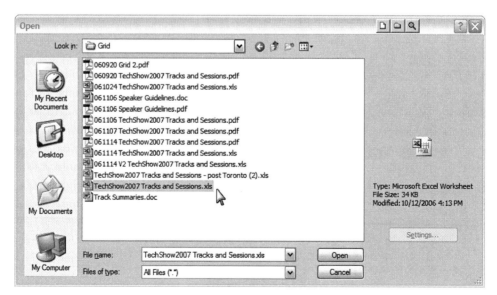

Figure 4.4

The **Open File** dialog box appears (Figure 4.5). Navigate to the folder that contains the file you want to convert to PDF. Select the file and click **Open**. The file will be converted and open in a new Acrobat window.

Figure 4.5

§ 4.5 Combining Multiple Files

There are many advantages to saving multiple files to a single PDF file or a PDF package. One example is the creation of electronic briefs or a real estate closing, or any other deliverable that would benefit from conversion to a single file, rather than multiple files. For instance, a lawyer can now combine all files to deliver to the client at the close of a matter. Rather than sending multiple emails with multiple attachments, printing out the documents and binding them, or burning individual documents to a CD or DVD, lawyers can now save all the files to a single PDF or in a PDF package. The resulting file provides all the features and functions of a PDF file—platform independence, the ability to search, links, bookmarks, comments, etc. Creating a single PDF from multiple files can involve *conversion* of other (convertible) file types (generally image and Microsoft Office file formats), *combining* multiple PDF files into a single file or *PDF Package*, or both *conversion* and *combining*. The starting point varies slightly, depending on whether the files to be combined are non-PDF or PDF, but after that, the process is the same.

§ 4.5.1 Creating a Single PDF from Multiple Files

To create a single PDF from multiple files, click the **Create PDF** button and select **From Multiple Files** to launch the Combine Files wizard, click the **Combine Files** button (Figure 4.6); alternatively, use the following menu or keyboard commands:

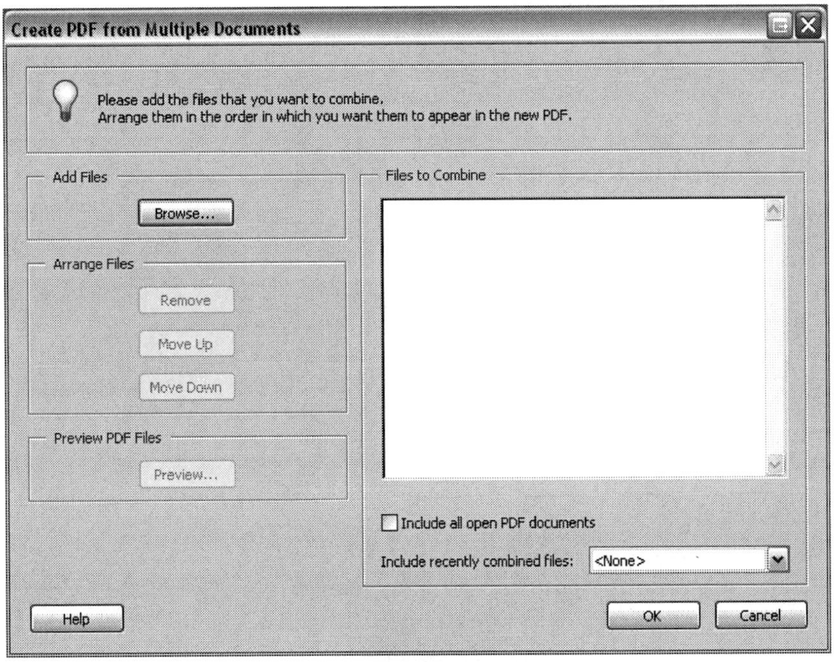

Figure 4.6

Menu (Create PDF From Multiple Files): **File > Create PDF > From Multiple Files**

Keyboard (Create PDF From Multiple Files): **Alt+F-F-M**

The **Combine Files** wizard appears on the screen (Figure 4.7).

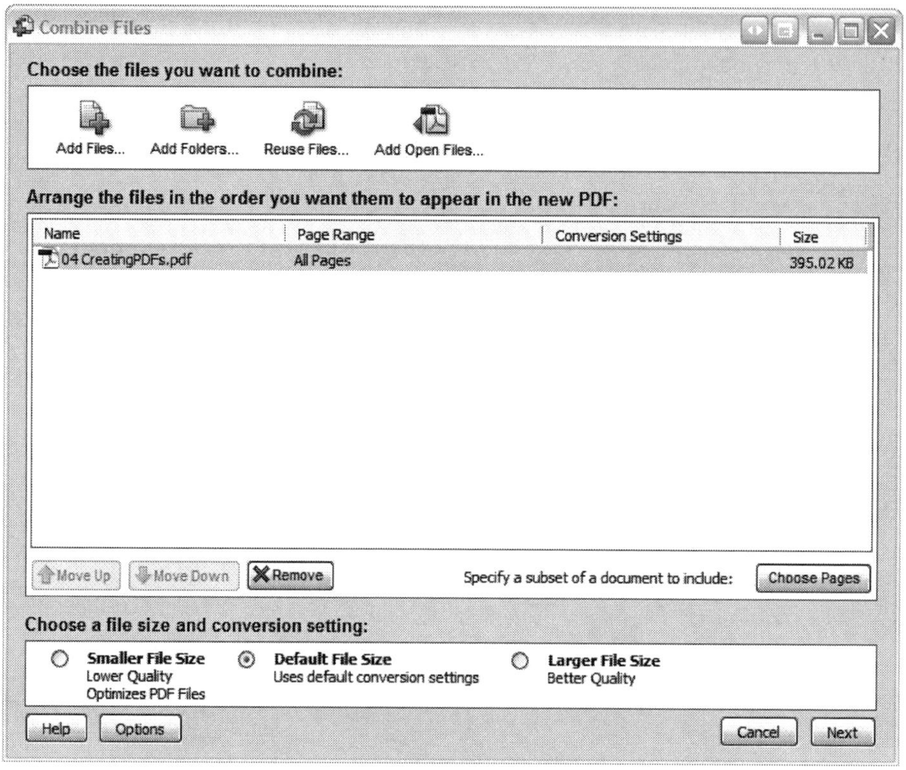

Figure 4.7

To create a single PDF file using Acrobat 8 launch the **Combine Files** wizard (described above) and select the files to be combined. The Combine File wizard allows you to add files, folders, open files or reuse files (Figure 4.8). The **Options** button in the first screen is important. Using this option, you can tell Acrobat to create bookmarks in the file. In Word, heading styles will automatically be converted to bookmarks. Clicking the **Add Files** button will bring

Figure 4.8

up an **Add Files** dialog box that permits browsing and selecting the files to be added (Figure 4.9).

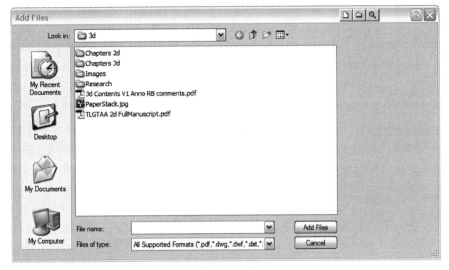

Figure 4.9

Clicking the **Add Folders** button brings up the **Browse for Folder** dialog box that permits browsing for entire folders to be selected for addition to the combine files list (Figure 4.10). Clicking the **Reuse Files** button produces the

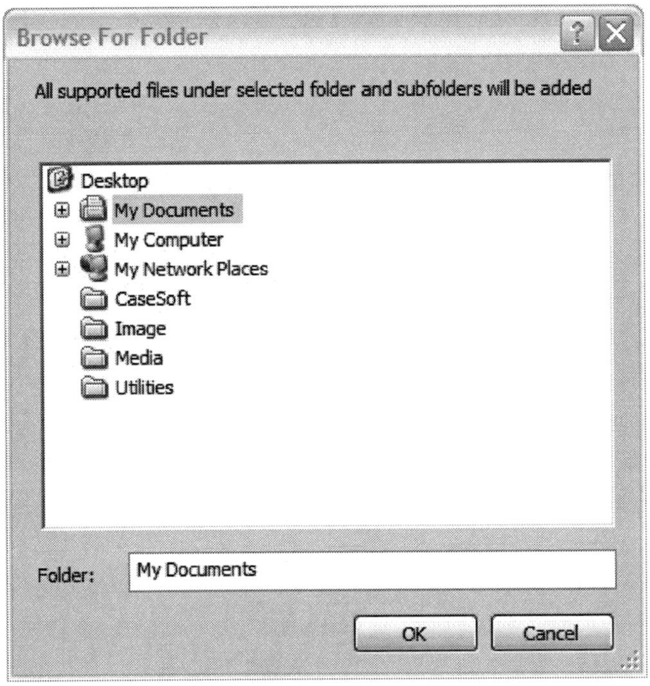

Figure 4.10

(you guessed it) **Reuse Files** dialog box (Figure 4.11). This window might be a bit bewildering at first glance, but the display is rather straightforward. On the left is a list of recently combined files and on the right a list of the recently

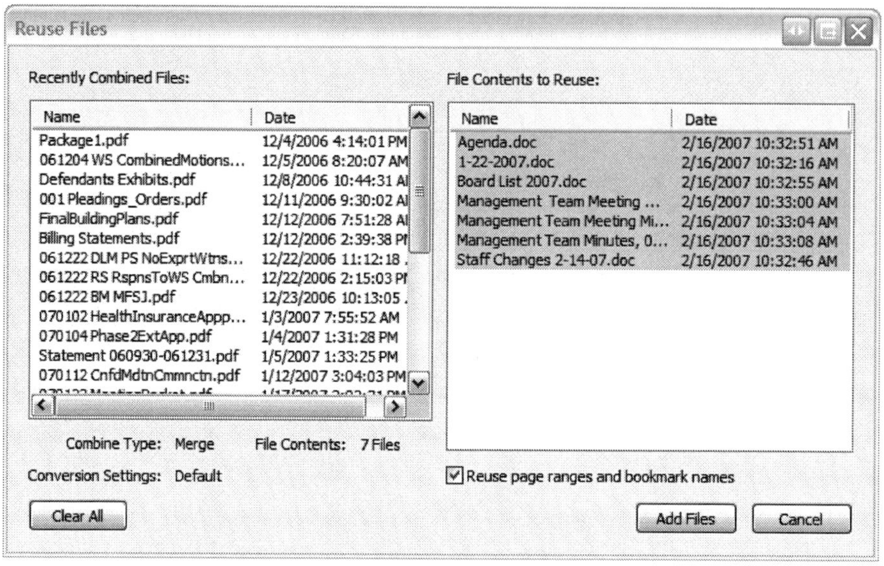

Figure 4.11

combined files that you want to reuse. Finally, if you click the **Add Open Files** button, the Open PDF Files dialog box appears (Figure 4.12).

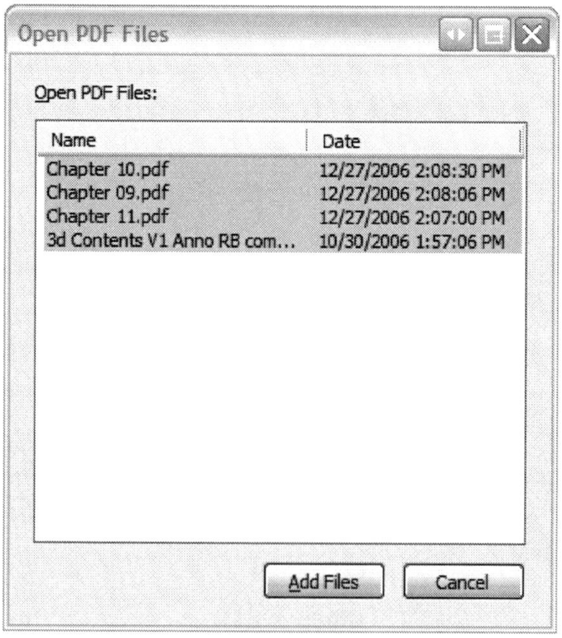

Figure 4.12

Notice that after files or folders have been selected, the Combine Files wizard allows you to arrange the order in which the files or folders will be combined (Figure 4.13). You may choose to combine files of many file types,

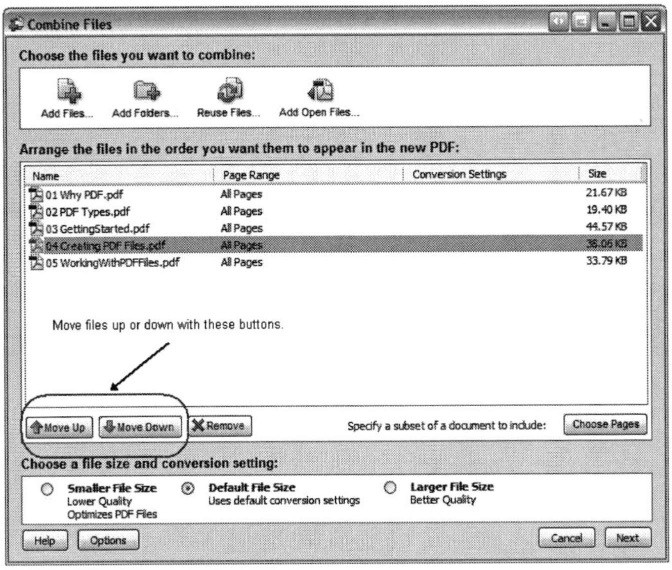

Figure 4.13

from .TIFF to .PDF to .DOC to .XLS, then sort, delete, and add documents. You can choose to add only certain pages of certain documents, from within the Combine Files wizard. When you click the **Next** button the Combine Files wizard moves to the next step, where you decide whether to create a single PDF file or a PDF Package (Figure 4.14). Notice that at this stage you still

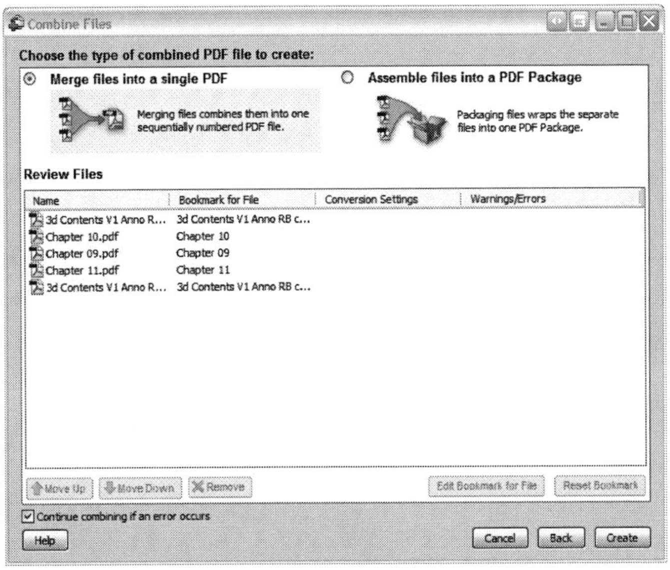

Figure 4.14

have the option to move files and folders up or down in the combination order or remove them. By selecting **Merge files into single PDF** and clicking **Create** the files are combined, converting as needed, in the order specified. When the combination has been completed you have the option to go back or save the resulting file (Figure 4.15). Clicking the **Save** button brings up a file window that allows you to navigate to the desired location before providing a file name and completing the process of combining files into a single PDF.

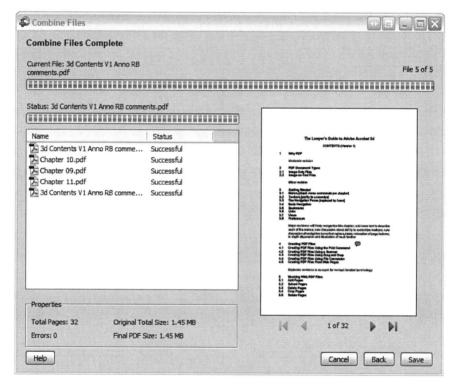

Figure 4.15

§ 4.5.2 Creating a PDF Package

The process to create a PDF package is primarily the same as creating a single PDF from multiple files. The benefits of the PDF package lie in the fact that the package, which appears as a single file with the extension ".PDF", is actually an envelope or container that can hold PDFs and other types of documents. The package offers a spreadsheet-like view that can be sorted and customized. Users can choose to create full-text indexes of packages, for optimal searching.

A PDF package collects existing PDF files or converts other file formats and assembles them into an integrated PDF unit. The original files retain their individual identities and characteristics while forming part of a single PDF package file. Each component file can be opened, read, edited, and formatted independently of the other files in the PDF package. You can create PDF packages when you use the **Combine Files** wizard (described above). In Windows, the Acrobat PDFMaker in Outlook and Lotus Notes can create PDF packages when you convert electronic mail messages to PDF or migrate PDF electronic mail archives created in earlier version of Acrobat.

Depending on the circumstances, PDF packages offer advantages over merging multiple files into single PDF file. You can add or remove component documents easily, without having to find and select all the pages that originated in that file. The component files do not open in separate windows, so users can quickly flip through them and make changes without having to pause for the Open or Save dialog boxes. You can make changes to individual PDF files within the PDF package without affecting the other component files. For example, you can change the page numbering within a given PDF file, digitally sign, select different security settings, and so forth, without those changes applying to the other component documents. You can rename components. Because the PDF Package is one file, you can share it with others and be sure that they are getting all the component parts. The component PDF files in a PDF package are listed under an assortment of categories that you can add to, delete, hide, and customize. Then, users simply click the category name to sort the list. The **Print** command on the Acrobat File menu includes commands for printing the currently open document, all the documents in the PDF package, or multiple component documents selected in the PDF package list. PDF packages allow for unattended batch printing. You can add non-PDF files to an existing PDF package without converting them to PDF. This can be done by a simple drag-and-drop process from the desktop, Microsoft Explorer, or Macintosh Finder to the list of components in the open PDF package, or by clicking the **Options** button in the Package window and choosing **Add File**. The source files of a PDF package, even existing PDF files added to the package, are not changed when added to the package. Changes made to the PDF files within the PDF package do not change the original files. You can move a PDF package anywhere on your computer, network, or to removable media, without any risk of losing or disconnecting its components.

To create a PDF package, select **Assemble files into a PDF Package** in the **Combine Files** wizard (Figure 4.16). When the **Package** option has been selected you have the option to use an Adobe template for the cover page or the first document. At this point you still have the option to move files and fold-

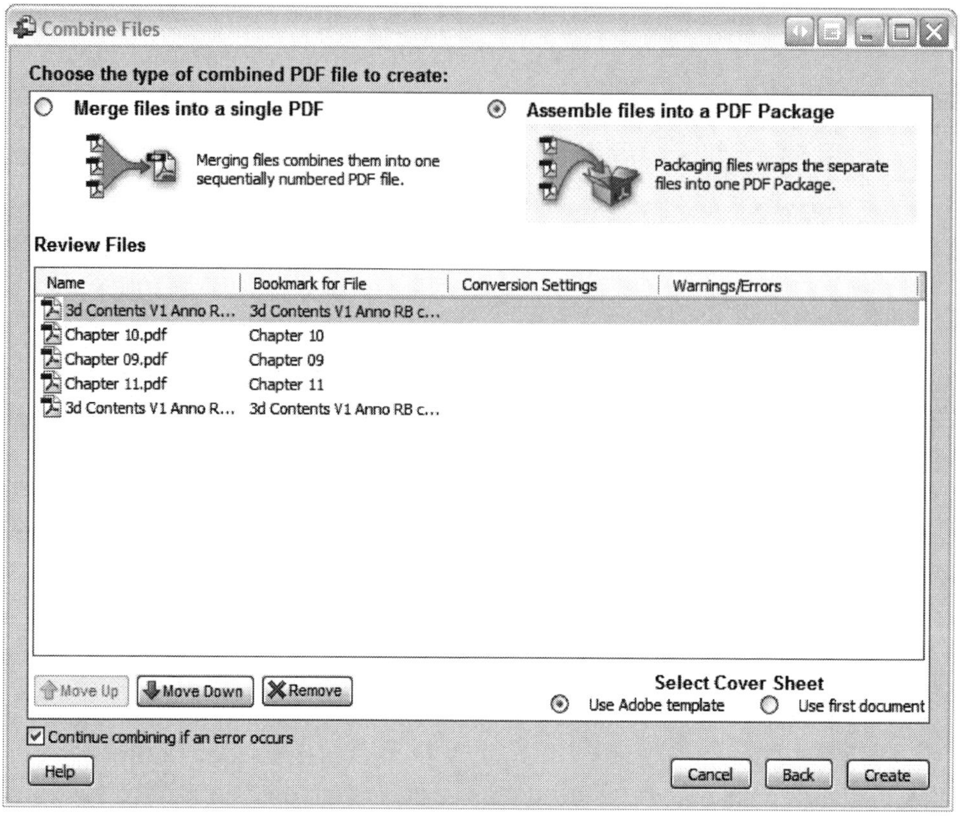

Figure 4.16

ers up or down in the package order or remove them. The PDF package can have an Adobe template cover sheet or you can use the first document. By selecting **Assemble files into a PDF Package** and clicking **Create** the files are combined, converted as needed, in the order specified. When the combination has been completed, you have the option to go back or save the resulting file. Clicking the **Save** button brings up a file window that allows you to navigate to the desired location before providing a file name and completing the process of combining files into a PDF package.

§ 4.6 Creating PDF Files from Web Pages

Creating PDF files from Web pages comes in handy when you want to capture an entire section of a Web site, such as a code section or reported decision. You can also save electronic statements, receipts, and Web orders directly to PDFs. Web pages can be converted to PDF directly from Internet Explorer with a single click. PDFs created from Web pages can include active links from the pages, depending on the number of levels captured (**Get Only *n* levels**). If the linked pages are not included in the PDF, Acrobat prompts the user to open the pages in a browser (in other words, connect to the Internet and open the page in your default browser). Web pages captured to PDF have their Macromedia Flash content preserved (those sometimes annoying moving elements in Web pages). This is possible because the PDF file format itself has been upgraded (to version 1.5). This new format supports JPEG2000 image compression and can fully embed multimedia content instead of linking to external audio and movie files. To create a PDF file from a Web page:

Click the **Create PDF** button (Figure 4.17) and select **From Web Page**; alternatively, use the menu or keyboard commands shown below:

Menu (Create PDF from Web Page): **File > Create PDF > From Web Page**

Keystroke (Create PDF from Web Page): **Alt+F-F-W;** or Keystroke (Create PDF from Web Page): **Ctrl+Shift+O**

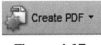

Figure 4.17

The **Create PDF from Web Page** dialog box appears with a space to enter the URL (Web address) for the desired Web page.

You may find it easiest to locate the Web page in the browser of your choice, then highlight the URL in the browser address window and copy it to the clipboard (**Edit > Copy** or **Ctrl+C**). Now you can paste the URL into the Acrobat **Create PDF from Web Page** dialog box. Notice that the dialog box has other options for you to select. You can specify the number of levels to convert or even select an entire site (use the latter with caution—telling Acrobat to convert the entire Thomas or ABA sites to PDF would be time consuming, bandwidth intensive, and produce a monstrously huge file).

§ 4.7 Creating PDF Files from Clipboard Images

You can create PDF files from screen captures and other images you copy from an image editing application. The Create PDF From Clipboard Image command appears only when there is an image copied to the clipboard. If the clipboard is empty or if text has been copied to the clipboard, the command does not appear. To create a PDF file from an image on the clipboard, first select and copy the displayed image to the clipboard either by using the **Copy** command in an image-editing application, such as Adobe Photoshop, using the **Ctrl+C** keyboard command, or by pressing the **Print Screen** key. Then switch to Acrobat, click the **Create PDF** toolbar button and select **From Clipboard**, or use one the following alternatives:

Menu (Create PDF from Clipboard Image): **File > Create PDF > From Clipboard**

Keystroke (Create PDF from Clipboard Image): **Alt+F-F-C**

Acrobat will insert the image into a blank page of a new PDF file that can be saved with an appropriate name.

§ 4.8 Creating PDF Files from Blank Pages

Acrobat 8 Professional introduces the PDF Editor feature. With it, you can create a PDF from a blank page rather than beginning with a file, a clipboard image, or scanning. The PDF Editor can be useful for creating relatively small files; for longer, more complex, or heavily formatted new documents, it's usually better to create the source document in an authoring application that offers more layout and formatting options. The PDF Editor can make changes in text only with PDFs created from blank pages. You can set preferences for the PDF Editor by selecting **Edit > Preferences** and selecting **New Document** in the list under **Categories**. You can specify the font family and font size that will be used by default for typing on a new, blank page; the default margins; paper size; and orientation. To create a new PDF file from a blank page:

Menu (New PDF From Blank Page): **File > Create PDF > From Blank Page**
Keyboard (New PDF From Blank Page): **Alt+F-F-B**

Begin typing the text you want to add to the blank page. Add any formatting to the text by selecting it and selecting options on the **New Document** toolbar (Figure 4.18). As needed, select other tools and options that you want to apply to the PDF file.

Figure 4.18

When the page is filled with text, the PDF Editor automatically adds a new blank page to the document. To edit text in a PDF file created from a blank page, locate and select the file created with PDF Editor (that is, one created from a blank page):

Menu (Edit PDF Created From Blank Page): **Document > Resume Editing**
Keyboard (Edit PDF Created From Blank Page): **Alt+D-U**

You can lock the text you have added to PDF files created from a blank page. This prevents anyone from adding or changing the text.

Menu (Prevent Edits): **Document > Prevent Further Edits**
Keyboard (Prevent Edits): **Alt+D-V**

In the message that appears, click **Prevent Further Edits** to confirm your choice. Note: there is no Undo for this process.

Working with PDF Files

5

 T hink of working with PDF files as working with a notebook full of paper documents. Just as with a notebook or file folder full of paper, you can add pages to PDF files (at the point of your choosing), remove pages (take them out, copy, and reinsert), and delete pages (take them out and discard) from PDF files. Beyond the basics of taking pages in and out, you can build an electronic table of contents using bookmarks and create links (you can build a link from virtually any point within a PDF file to many other types of digital information, not just other PDF files). Another aspect of working with PDF files involves settings that control how you want your PDF file to look when you or someone else opens it, including how the pages are numbered. When you set the look of your PDF file, you can also build in some identifying features so that your document can be found using Windows Explorer or other search software in case it ends up in the wrong place in your filing system.

From the very first day that you were a lawyer, you have probably worked with paper documents collected in file folders, notebooks, boxes, and various other means of keeping certain pages together and other pages apart. Whether the pages were client files organized in folders or notebooks, or boxes full of paper produced in discovery, you have basically dealt with paper. Paper documents consist of pages that can be organized in a myriad of ways. PDF files consist of pages, and like their paper counterparts, the pages can be organized in any number of ways. Sometimes the pages that exist as paper in a folder, notebook, or box are collected together as a single PDF file. Other times, those pages might be split into multiple files and may even be stored in various electronic file folders (directories). As you read the material in this chapter, think initially in terms of one large document such as a thousand pages of discovery or a hundred-page contract. That will provide a good mental framework for seeing the similarity between working with paper and working with PDF files.

The material in Chapter 16, "Acrobat in the Paper-Free Office," provides more information on working with and organizing large collections (such as all the files in your office). There you will learn some basic file-naming conventions and folder-organization tips that make working with multiple PDF files seem, again, much like working with paper documents. For now, we'll focus on what you can do with a single multipage PDF file. The next seven sections are about working with pages; keep in mind that you can preform all these tasks from the **Page** pane (click on the **Page pane** icon) by right-clicking on a particular page.

§ 5.1 Add Pages

Okay, you have a PDF file—whether one page or a thousand-plus pages—and you want to add more pages. New pages can be inserted at any point in the PDF file; you need only decide whether the page or pages are added before or after the insertion point. For example, in a ten-page document you need to add three new pages between the current pages 7 and 8. If you open the existing file and turn to page 7, then you would insert the new pages "after" the insertion point; if you were at page 8, the insertion would be "before" the currently displayed page. The pages to be added, or inserted, can be single-page or multiple-page PDF files. To add pages:

> Menu (Add Pages): **Document > Insert Pages**
> Keystroke (Add Pages): **Shift+Ctrl+I**

The "Select File to Insert" window will then appear (Figure 5.1), from which you can select the PDF file with the pages to be inserted.

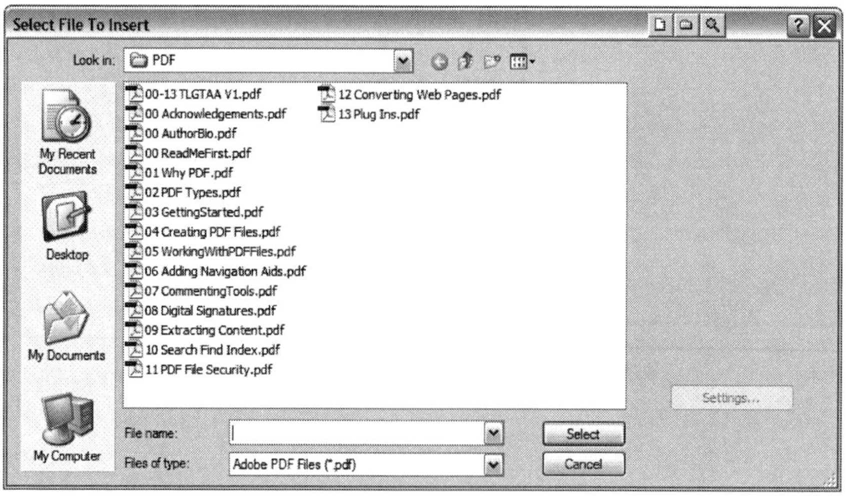

Figure 5.1

§ 5.2 Replace Pages

Okay, I've been using Acrobat on a daily basis for about six years and have never "replaced" pages. That said, you can replace one or more pages with others from another PDF file. Only the text and images on the original page or pages are replaced. Any interactive elements associated with the original page or pages, such as links, form elements and bookmarks, are not affected. Bookmarks and links that may have been previously associated with the replacement page or pages do not carry over. Comments, however, are carried over and are combined with any existing comments in the document. To replace a page or pages:

Menu (Replace Pages): **Document > Replace Pages**
Keystroke: (Replace Pages): **Alt+D-R**

After the menu or keystroke commands have been issued, a window opens from which you can select the file with the pages to use as replacements (Figure 5.2). Click on a file then click the **Select** button (or double click on the file to select it), and the **Replace Pages dialog** box appears (Figure 5.3). In the **Original** section of the **Replace Pages** dialog box, specify the page or pages to be replaced. In the **Replacement** section of the **Replace Pages** dialog box, select the page or pages to insert at replacements. In Figure 5.3, page 1 will be replaced by page 7.

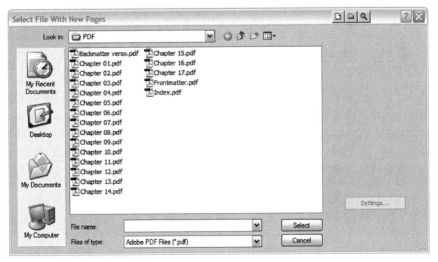

Figure 5.2

§ 5.3 Extract Pages

Extracting pages means taking pages out of a PDF file and saving them as a separate document (they may continue to exist as a separate document or

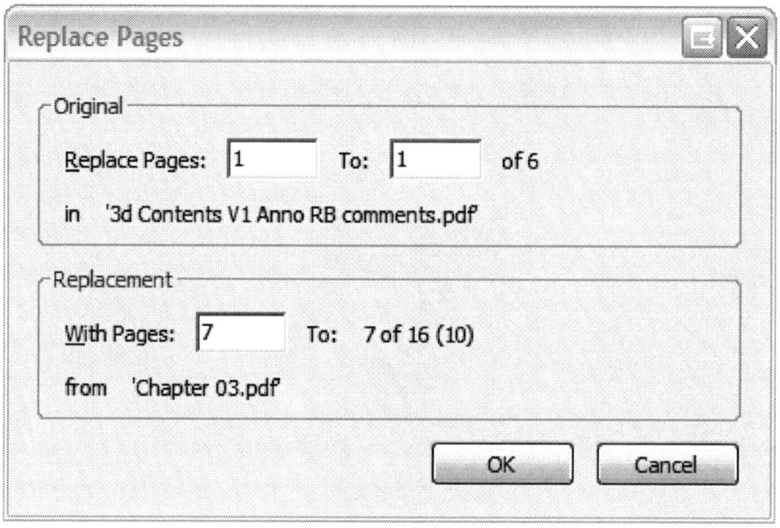

Figure 5.3

may be inserted into another document or documents). This is something that we do on a regular basis. To extract pages:

> Menu (Extract Pages): **Document > Extract Pages**
> Keystroke (Extract Pages): **Alt+D-X**

Extracting pages from a PDF file is equivalent to taking paper pages out of a folder, notebook, or box, making copies, and then putting the pages right back where they came from. The paper copies are the extracted pages. You can work with these pages, save them, or throw them away. For example, if you have a fifty-page contract and you only want to use page 3 (containing a legal description of real property) as an exhibit, then you would extract page 3 and save the extracted page with a new name (such as "001 Exhibit 1 LegalDescription.pdf"). The original fifty-page contract would not be altered in any way (unlike removing and copying pages from a paper document, there is no risk that you have put page 3 back in the wrong place). When you extract pages, the **Extract Pages** dialog box appears (Figure 5.4).

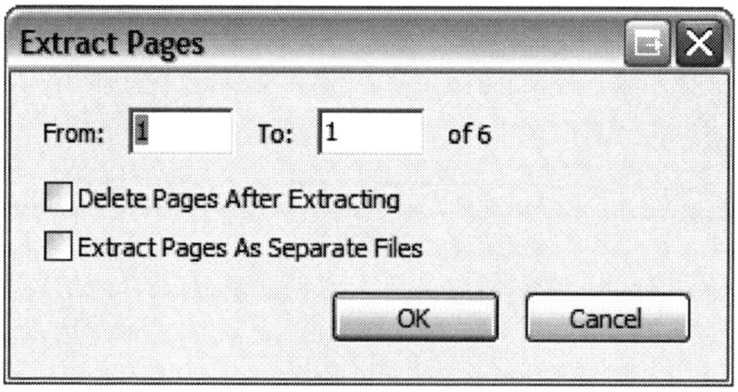

Figure 5.4

If you want to extract only the current page, tap the **Enter** key (or click on **OK**). If you want to extract a series of consecutive pages, specify the range in the **Extract Pages** dialog box. Notice that the current page is by default selected as the beginning point for the From-To range.

Notice the checkbox option that allows you to **Delete Pages After Extracting**. When you extract pages, the extracted pages appear in a new window. If the box is checked, the extracted pages are no longer in the original document—they have been deleted. The extracted pages that appear in the new window must be saved with a new file name if you want to keep them. Extracting pages with the **Delete Pages After Extracting** box checked is useful when reviewing a document for privileged material. As you go through the document you extract (and delete) the privileged pages; the extracted pages are then named and saved in a manner that reflects their privileged status. The original document exists, but without the privileged material.

§ 5.4 Delete Pages

"Deleting" takes the pages out of the current PDF file and throws them away. No, they do not go to the recycle bin so that you can retrieve them if you change your mind! This is taking pages out of a notebook and running them through the shredder; they are gone for good (so use with caution). This feature is handy for ripping out blank pages. To delete pages:

Menu (Delete Pages): **Document > Delete Pages**
Keystroke (Delete Pages): **Ctrl+Shift+D**

Notice that once you have told Acrobat to delete a page, the **Delete Pages** dialog box appears (Figure 5.5). If you want to delete only the current page, tap the **Enter** key (or click on **OK**), and it is gone (for good). If you want to delete a series of consecutive pages, specify the range in the **Delete Pages**

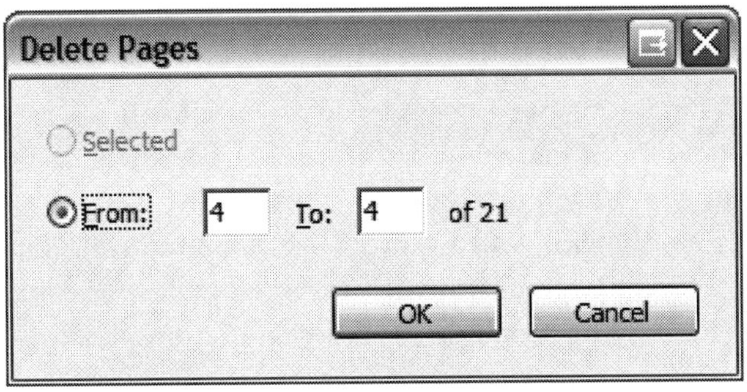

Figure 5.5

dialog box. Notice that the current page is by default selected as the beginning point for the From-To range.

Use **Delete Pages** with caution. Remember, this is not removing pages and putting them in the trash or recycle bin (from where you might get them back if you're lucky).

§ 5.5 Crop Pages

Sometimes the information on a page can be enhanced by removing extraneous materials from the edges (you know, those black borders from the photocopy process). This is also handy when someone scans in a bunch of pages to legal size when they should have been letter size. If you use Acrobat in display mode, **Crop Pages** can be used to carve out a portion of a document so that it can be displayed following a full-page display to create an effective zoom effect. To crop pages click the **Crop** tool (on the **Advanced Editing** toolbar) (Figure 5.6), or do one of the following:

Menu (Crop Pages): **Document > Crop Pages**
Keystroke (Crop Pages): **Shift+Ctrl+T**

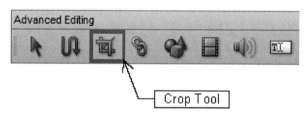

Figure 5.6

Once the menu or keyboard commands and have been issued, the **Crop Pages** dialog box appears (Figure 5.7), allowing the user to set the parameters for cropping. The current page, all pages, or a range of pages can be cropped.

As an alternative to the menu and keyboard commands, you can click on the **Crop** tool located on the **Advanced Editing** toolbar. The **Crop** tool is third from the left. Select the **Crop** tool with a left click then position the pointer to the area where you want to begin the selection for cropping. Hold down the left mouse button and drag a rectangle over the area to be retained (everything outside the box will be cropped). Now double click inside the box drawn by the Crop tool and the **Crop Pages** dialog box appears (Figure 5.7), just as when using the menu or keyboard commands, allowing you to select cropping options.

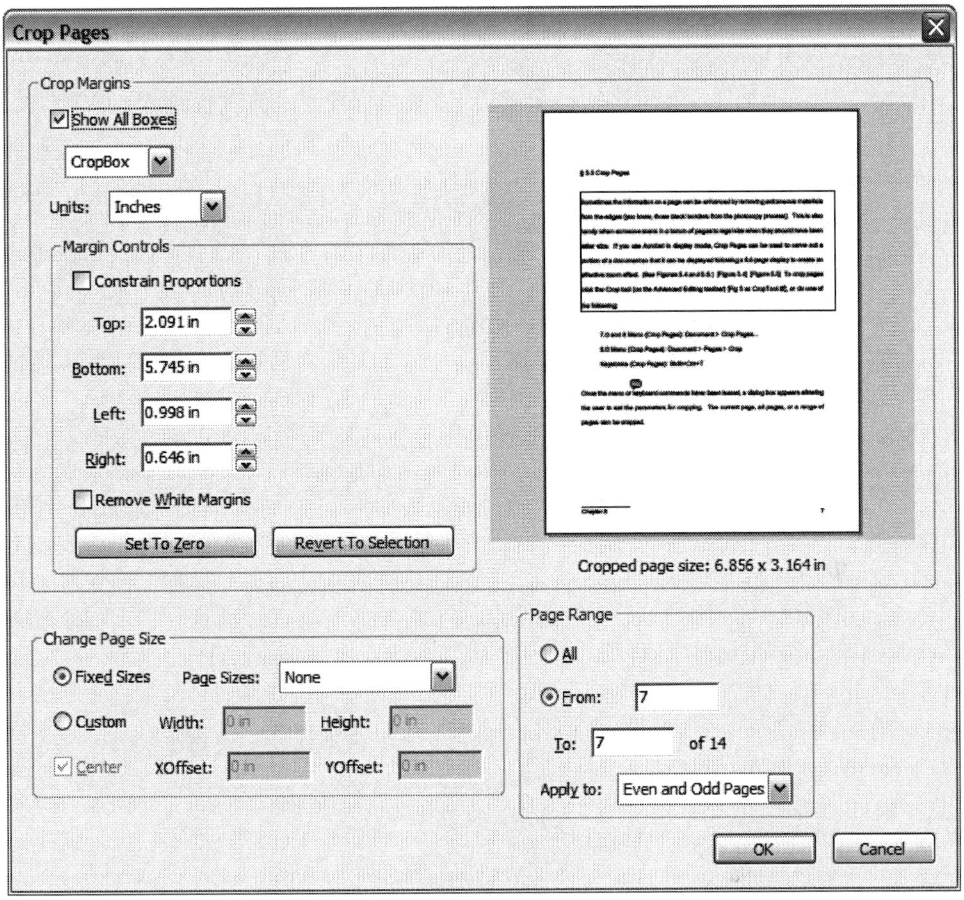

Figure 5.7

§ 5.6 Rotate Pages

Now this is something you cannot do in your paper notebook, or at least not with as good a result. You will find it particularly useful with scanned documents; by virtue of mechanics all documents go through the scanner in portrait orientation regardless of how the information was set on the physical page. It is also handy when someone places the pages in the scanner top down, so that the resulting images are upside down. To rotate single or multiple pages to correct the orientation:

Menu (Rotate Pages): **Document > Rotate Pages**
Keystroke (Rotate Pages): **Ctrl+Shift+R**

Once the menu or keyboard commands have been issued, a dialog box appears allowing you to set the parameters for rotating pages, including the direction and amount of rotation (clockwise 90 degrees, counter-clockwise

90 degrees, or 180 degrees) (Figure 5.8.). The current page, all pages, or a range of pages can be rotated. Note: Rotate View (**View > Rotate View**) is different; that function rotates the view for the entire document and cannot be saved.

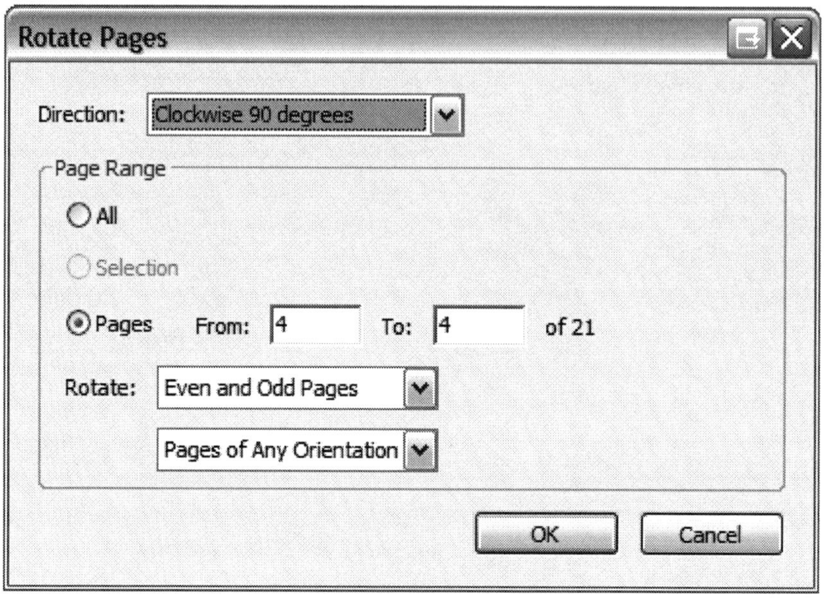

Figure 5.8

§ 5.7 Rearranging Page Order Using Pages Panel

You have added, extracted, deleted, cropped, and rotated pages—and now you want page 5 to come before page 3. To accomplish this, use the thumbnail view on the Pages panel to drag and drop pages to reorder them. To rearrange pages using thumbnails:

1. Select the **Pages** icon.
2. Left-click on the desired page, and while holding down the left button, drag the page to the desired location; multiple pages can be selected by holding down the **Control** key while then clicking on the desired pages. In Figure 5.9, pages 5, 6, and 7 have been "selected."
3. As the page or pages are moved by dragging, a vertical bar appears between the thumbnails displayed in the Pages window; when the desired destination has been reached simply release the left button on the mouse (pointer).

This feature works well for small documents, but the larger the document, the less practical it becomes (it's pretty hard to drag page 499 to the

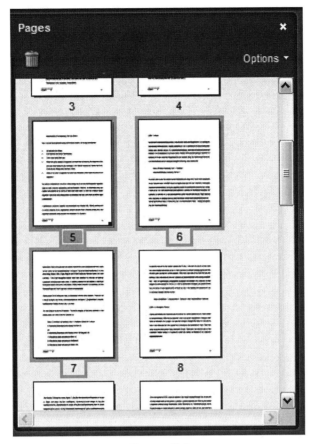

Figure 5.9

page 3 position). If faced with this situation, consider extracting the page or pages to be moved (with the **Delete Pages After Extracting** option checked; see the discussion in section 5.2 above), temporarily saving them as a new PDF file, then reinserting them (see section 5.1).

§ 5.8 Document Open Options

The way a PDF file appears when opened can be controlled by setting the initial view in the **Document Properties** window. If bookmarks have been created, then you may want anyone who opens your document to see, in the initial view, the **Bookmarks** pane. For example, when sending a lengthy document to a client for review, or submitting an electronic brief that contains various sections and exhibits, it helps to show the client or court that the document contains bookmarks. With a few clicks of the mouse and using the **Document Properties** window, you can establish how the document appears when others open it. To access the **Document Properties** window:

Menu (Document Properties Window Initial View): **File > Properties** (select **Initial View** tab)

Keystroke (Document Properties Window Initial View): **Ctrl+D** (select **Initial View** tab)

Once the menu or keyboard commands have been issued and the **Initial View** tab has been selected, options for how the document appears upon opening can be selected (Figure 5.10). The top section (**Layout and Magnification**) of the **Document Properties—Initial View** window contains the most salient features. First, you can select how the document appears with the **Navigator tab** drop-down menu:

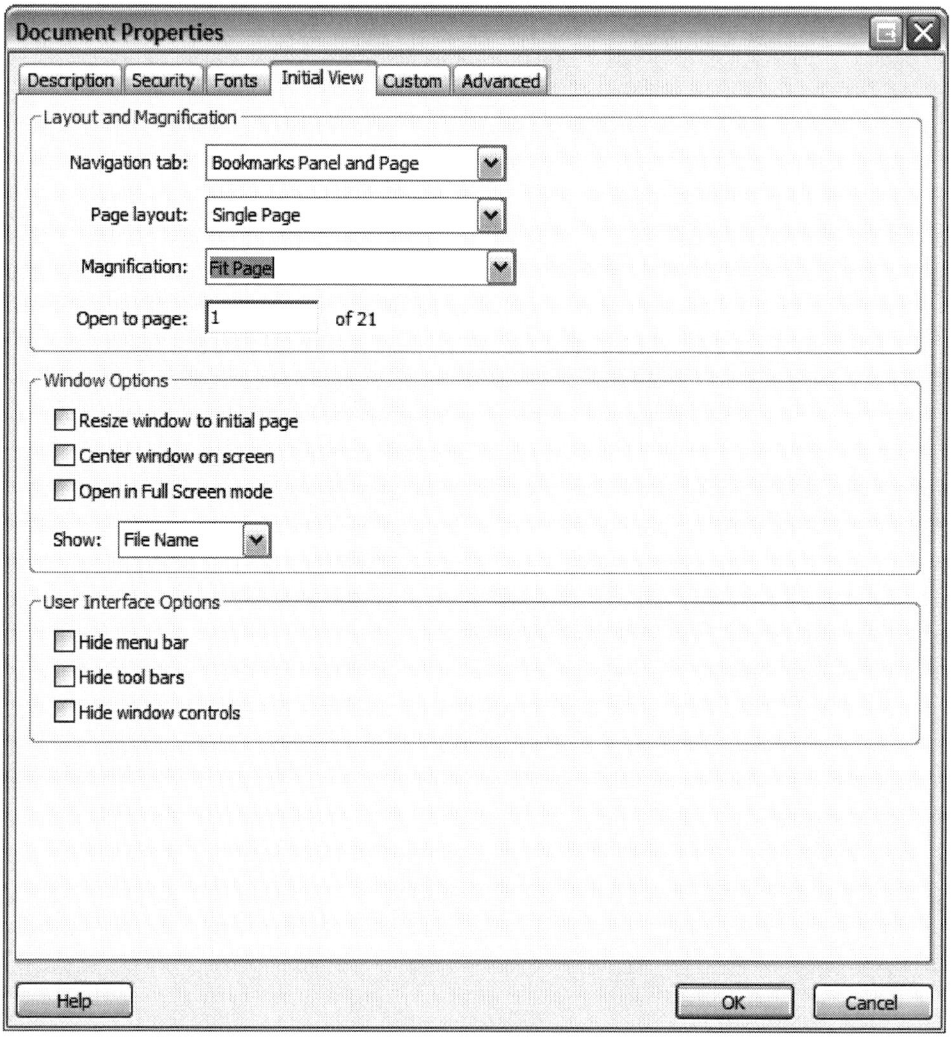

Figure 5.10

- Page Only
- Bookmarks Panel and Page
- Pages Panel and Page
- Layers Panel and Page

Next, you can specify how individual pages display with the **Page Layout** drop-down menu:

- *Default:* uses the individual user's default page display settings.
- *Single Page:* one page at a time appears on the screen (my preference).
- *Continuous:* pages scroll from one to the next.
- *Facing:* multiple pages appear on the screen and navigation occurs one page at a time.
- *Continuous Facing:* multiple pages appear on the screen and pages scroll from one to the next.

Next, you can specify how much of the display area the pages use by making choices from the **Magnification** drop-down menu:

- *Default:* uses the individual user's default page display settings.
- *Percentage views:* the document is magnified or reduced within the display area by the percentage selected.
- *Fit Page:* displays the entire page, full height and width in the work area (my preference).
- *Fit Width:* displays the page in full width; generally requires scrolling to see the bottom portion of each page but provides for a larger image.
- *Fit Visible:* provides a slightly wider view than Fit Width.

§ 5.9 Document Properties

Think of the Acrobat **Document Properties** as a card catalog entry for the current PDF file. Having card catalog information for image-only PDF files can make a world of difference finding documents using the search function in Windows Explorer or other file searching tools. Remember, image-only PDF files are just that—images only, just digital photocopies of paper documents. Without **Document Properties**, the location of a given image-only PDF file can be determined only by knowing its file name. Searching for the file by name can be narrowed down a bit using other criteria such as date range and file type. But in the end, finding image-only files by file name comes down to a manual search, just like rifling through a box of paper looking for a particular document. If an image-only file happens to be saved to the wrong folder (accidents do happen), the manual search to find it can be time-consuming and problematic.

The perils of a manual search can be avoided by using the **Document Properties** feature. With **Document Properties** the power of the computer can be harnessed to locate specific information. Information contained in the **Document Properties** can be found by Windows Explorer searches of files and folders containing certain text. To supply **Document Properties**:

Menu (Document Properties): **File > Properties**, select the **Description** tab
Keystroke (Document Properties): **Ctrl+D**, select the **Description** tab

Once the menu or keyboard commands have been issued, and **Description** tab selected, a dialog box appears for entering information to be contained in the **Document Properties** (Figure 5.11). Text entered in any of the

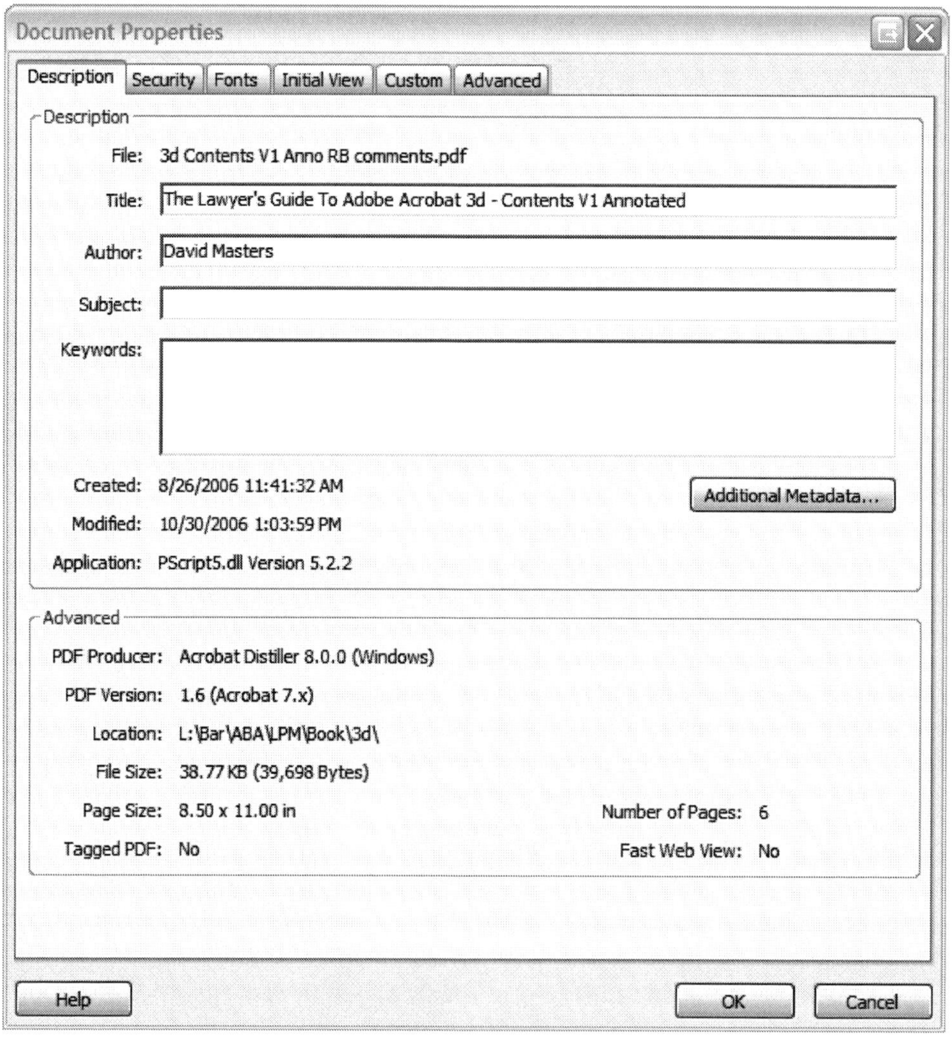

Figure 5.11

four fields (Title, Author, Subject, and Keywords) can be found using a Windows Explorer search for files containing the specified text.

The **Document Properties** is metadata. So, depending on what you include, you may want to edit or delete the contents of the **Document Properties** before sharing the PDF file with others (such as electronic court filings and discovery responses).

§ 5.10 Chapter 5 Wrap-up

If you read this chapter from start to finish, congratulations—it contains a lot of important information. Please don't think that you need to commit the information to memory. Instead, make a test copy of a medium-sized document (fifty to five hundred pages) and spend an hour adding, extracting, deleting, rotating, cropping, and moving pages. After an hour, working with PDF files will be second nature to you.

Adding Document Navigation Aids

6

Navigation aids, such as bookmarks, links and virtual page numbering, make PDF files more powerful than their paper counterparts. When bookmarks outline the major and minor divisions of a lengthy brief or contract, reference to each section is only a click away. A disparate stack of discovery documents can be quickly reviewed and each separate document within the collection marked with a bookmark. Bookmarks are the quick way to organize and provide navigation in PDF files (Figure 6.1). Think of bookmarks as an easily created hyperlinked table of contents.

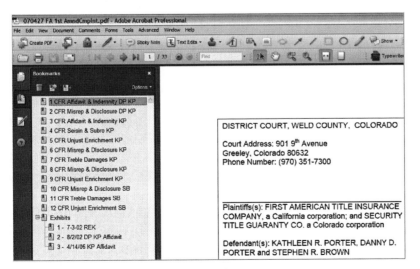

Figure 6.1

Links are similar to bookmarks in that they can take you, or any other viewer of a PDF file, from point A to point B with a click of the mouse. Unlike bookmarks, which appear in the navigation pane external to the document, links exist internally within PDF files. Links within PDF files are much like links within Web pages—click here (on the link) and go to a different page. Links can be used within PDF files to take the reader to other pieces of information, not just to other PDF files. Virtual page numbers make Bates numbers or record index page numbers correspond to physical document page numbers, thus enabling the reader to navigate by using the **Go To Page *n*** function.

§ 6.1 Bookmarks

Bookmarks are a powerful feature to aid navigation in PDF files, especially large documents. For little effort, bookmarks produce big returns in document organization and navigation. Again, think of bookmarks as an electronic table of contents that link each entry to the material referenced within the document. Clicking on a bookmark in the **Bookmarks** pane of the navigation window takes you directly to the referenced material. The table-of-contents elements created by some desktop publishing programs become bookmarks when those documents are printed (converted) to PDF. Bookmarks can be quickly added to image-only PDF files created by scanning. Adding bookmarks to a one-hundred-page image-only PDF can be accomplished in a matter of minutes; once done, this powerful hyperlinked table of contents exists for all other users of the document. Bookmarks can be nested to show a hierarchical order, color coded, revised, added, and deleted at any time (as long as document security settings permit).

§ 6.1.1 Using Bookmarks with Litigation Documents

Bookmarks can be used to organize and navigate document collections produced in litigation. For example, opposing counsel delivers 500 pages of medical records. These pages can be scanned to a single PDF file and bookmarks added. The bookmarks could be one for each discrete record, or grouped by treating physician. The initial review and bookmarking can be performed by staff or by a lawyer. This first quick trip through the documents to add bookmarks provides an opportunity for the lawyer to make a preliminary assessment of the content, and adding bookmarks provides a lasting organizational scheme to quickly navigate within the document.

While bookmarks look and act like a hyperlinked table of contents (a linear depiction of subject matter within a document), with a little imagination they can be used in a nonlinear fashion and consequently put to a slightly different purpose. Rather than creating bookmarks that describe the referenced materials linearly by subject, consider creating a set of bookmarks that reflect issues (liability, damages, and so on). (See Figure 6.2). The issue bookmarks would be the primary level of a bookmark hierarchy, with nested marks using content- or subject-descriptive titles to link each portion of a document to an issue. This arrangement would be nonlinear insofar as the issues need not be listed in the order of appearance within a document; the nested marks might even be coded and ranked by the power or weight with which the referenced material supports the parent issue.

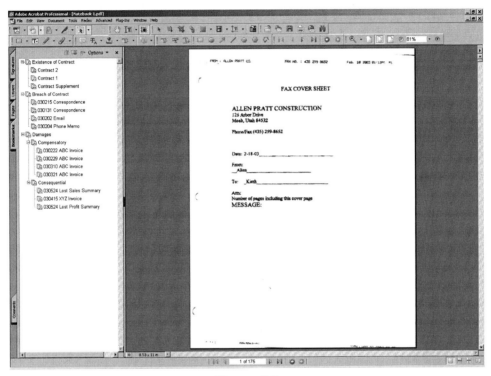

Figure 6.2

§ 6.1.2 Creating Bookmarks

Bookmarks can be created in a variety of ways, some more complicated than others. The preferred method is the simplest. To quickly create a bookmark:

1. Press **Ctrl+B**.
2. Type a short description.
3. Press **Enter**.

The simple command (**Ctrl+B**) opens the bookmarks pane and adds an "untitled" bookmark to the end of the list; typing a short description names the bookmark, and pressing the **Enter** key completes the process. Note that the first bookmark title text ("untitled") is not active and you need to right-click and select **Rename** before typing the description; after the first bookmark has been created the "untitled" text is active and you simply type to replace it. If you prefer working with the Acrobat user interface, display the bookmark pane by clicking on the bookmark icon then left-click the bookmark after which you want to place the new bookmark. If you don't select a bookmark, the new bookmark is automatically added at the end of the list. Next, select **New Bookmark** from the Options menu or click on the **New Bookmark** icon in the bookmark navigation pane. Note: after you have defined a bookmark's appearance, you can reuse the appearance settings by selecting the bookmark, right-clicking, and choosing Use **Current Appearance as New Default**.

§ 6.1.3 Bookmarking Selected Text or Image

In image-on-text PDF files, bookmarks can be targeted to specific text or graphics. Remember, image-on-text files are created by printing text-based documents to PDF or processing image-only paper files with an OCR application.

Bookmarks that link to selected text can be particularly useful to direct readers to specific passages within a document. For example, you might print a case to PDF and highlight a section that you want the court or opposing counsel to focus on. A bookmark linked to the selected text would take the reader to the highlighted passage.

Bookmarks to selected text take the reader directly to the referenced information. Recall that Acrobat has three standard page views: Actual Size, Fit Page, and Fit Width. When documents are displayed in the Actual Size or Fit Width view, only a portion of the current page appears in the work area. If you create a bookmark that links to a page and the information that you want the reader to see happens to be at the bottom of the page, the relationship may not be apparent. However, if you create a bookmark by selecting text, then clicking on the mark takes the reader to the exact location in the document where the text appears, and the relationship is apparent. Consider using **Select Text** to create bookmarks that correspond to headings in a contract, brief, or other long image-on-text PDF files. To create a bookmark that targets specific text:

1. Click on the **Select Text** tool on the toolbar.
2. Select the text.
3. Press **Ctrl+B** (the selected text becomes the label of the new bookmark; you can edit the label).
4. Press **Enter**.

If you prefer working with the Acrobat user interface, do the following to create a bookmark:

Select the **Select Text** tool on the toolbar and do one of the following:
   a) Drag to select the text (the selected text becomes the label of the new bookmark; you can edit the label).
   b) Right-click and choose **Add Bookmark.**

A process similar to that described above for creating bookmarks using the **Select Text** tool can be used for creating bookmarks that are linked to specific graphics or portions of graphics. The **Select Graphic** tool is used in place of the **Select Text** tool and the bookmark label must be typed (the graphic or portion of a graphic selected does not supply the bookmark label).

§ 6.1.4 Changing Bookmark Appearance

The appearance of bookmarks, including the name, font, and color, can be changed at any time. You may want to change the appearance of certain bookmarks for various reasons. For example, changes in appearance can be used to signify importance or to do issue coding. Using color to differentiate bookmarks (even a set of basic linear bookmarks—the table of contents) can produce rudimentary issue coding. To change a bookmark's name or appearance, do one of the following:

1. Select the bookmark in the **Bookmarks** pane, choose **Rename Bookmark** in the **Options** menu, and type the new bookmark name; or
2. Select the bookmark in the **Bookmarks** pane, right-click, and choose **Rename**; or
3. Select the bookmark, right-click, and select **Properties**; in the **Appearance** tab, change the color and style of the text.

Bookmark appearance and action can also be set using the **Bookmark Properties** dialog box (Figure 6.3). To set the appearance or action of a bookmark using the **Bookmark Properties** dialog box, first click on the bookmark to be altered, then:

Keystroke (Bookmark Properties): **Ctrl+I** (works only when the **Bookmarks** navigation pane is open and the active window; and no, **Bookmark Properties** cannot be invoked with the **Properties Bar** command, **Ctrl+E**)

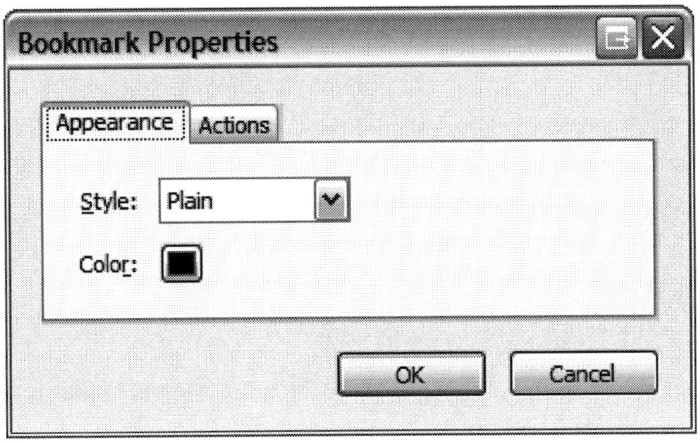

Figure 6.3

§ 6.1.5 Editing the Bookmark Destination

The destination or target of a bookmark can be changed at any time. To edit the destination of a bookmark:

1. Go to the page in the document that will be the new destination.
2. Right-click on the bookmark you want to edit and select **Set Destination**; a warning that you are about to make a change appears (Figure 6.4).
3. Click **Yes** to confirm the change of address.

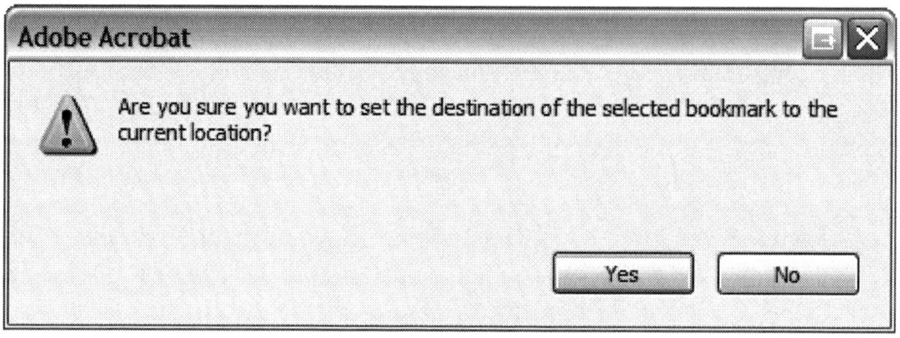

Figure 6.4

If you prefer working with the Acrobat user interface, to change the destination of a bookmark do the following:

1. Click the **Bookmarks** icon and select the bookmark.
2. In the document window, move to the location you want to specify as the new destination.
3. Choose **Set Bookmark Destination** in the **Options** menu or right-click and select **Set Destination**.
4. Click **Yes** to confirm the change of address.

§ 6.1.6 Deleting Bookmarks

Bookmarks, being the powerful and flexible tool they are, can be removed from documents at will. To delete a single bookmark:

1. Right-click on the bookmark to be removed and select **Delete**; or
2. Click on the bookmark to be removed and press the **Delete** key.

To delete multiple bookmarks:

1. Hold down the Control (**Ctrl**) key and left-click on the bookmarks to be removed.
2. Press the **Delete** key.

If you prefer working with the Acrobat user interface, to delete a bookmark do the following:

1. Click the **Bookmarks** icon.
2. Left-click on the target bookmark and do one of the following:
   a) Choose **Delete Bookmark** in the Options menu.
   b) Right-click and choose **Delete**.
   c) Drag the bookmarks to the trash can.

Caution: Deleting a bookmark deletes any bookmarks that are subordinate to it. However, deleting a bookmark does not delete any text or other file information.

Caution: Unlike changing the destination, you are not given an opportunity to confirm the deletion; when you select **Delete**, the bookmark disappears. Inadvertent deletions can be recovered immediately using the **Undo** command (**Ctrl+Z**).

To undo the deletion of a bookmark:

Menu (Undo Delete Bookmark): **Edit > Undo Delete Bookmark**
Keystroke (Undo Delete Bookmark): **Ctrl+Z** or **Alt+E-U**

The **Undo** command can be executed a number of times to undo a series of actions, including the deletion of bookmarks. The Acrobat help manual does not indicate how many levels of undo are available.

§ 6.1.7 Wrapping Long Bookmarks

Sometimes the name you give to a bookmark is just too long to be displayed in the **Bookmarks** pane. There are several ways to deal with this problem. First, rename the bookmark with a shorter name. If shortening the name is not an option, then the **Bookmark** pane can be resized to display more text; however, this option correspondingly decreases the size of the document window. If long bookmark names are a necessity, then the elegant solution is to wrap the text in the bookmark name. In Acrobat 8, you can select an option that wraps text (as necessary) in all bookmarks. To do this, simply right-click any Bookmark and select **Wrap Long Bookmarks** (Figure 6.5). Regardless of the method used to wrap the text in long bookmarks, this option is on when checked and off when not checked.

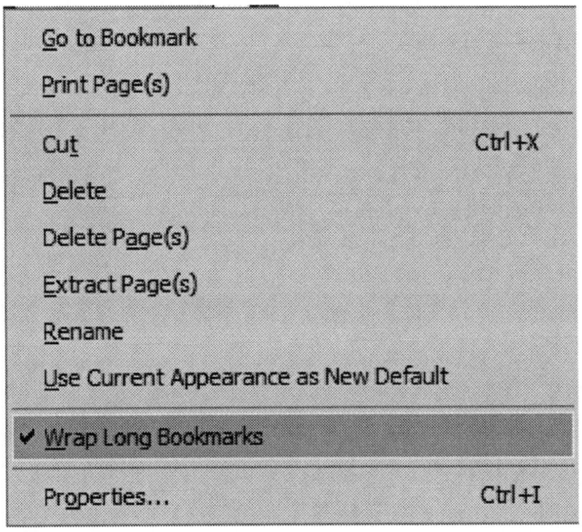

Figure 6.5

§ 6.1.8 Bookmark Hierarchy

You can nest a list of bookmarks to show a relationship between destinations or topics. Nesting creates an outline-like parent-child relationship. You can expand and collapse this hierarchical list as desired.

To expand and collapse the bookmark hierarchy, do one of the following:

1. Click the plus sign or next to the bookmark icon to show any children related to the bookmark; click the minus sign to collapse the list again; or
2. Select the bookmark, and choose **Expand Current Bookmark** from the **Options** menu; or
3. From the **Options** menu, choose **Expand Top-Level Bookmarks** to show all bookmarks; or
4. Choose **Collapse Top-Level Bookmarks** to collapse all bookmarks.

§ 6.1.8.1 Nesting a Bookmark Under Another Bookmark

To create a hierarchy after bookmarks have been created, it is necessary to move individual bookmarks or groups of bookmarks up or down (in and out) in the hierarchy. Moving a bookmark to a lower level in the hierarchy is accomplished by nesting. To nest a bookmark or group of bookmarks under another bookmark, do the following:

1. Select the bookmark or range of bookmarks to be nested.
2. Drag the icon or icons directly underneath the desired parent bookmark icon (a line shows the position of the icon or icons).
3. Release the bookmark and nesting is complete (the destination remains in its original location).

§ 6.1.8.2 Moving a Bookmark Out of a Nested Position

Just as bookmarks can be nested to create a hierarchy, so can they be "unnested" or moved out of nested position when necessary. To move a bookmark out of a nested position:

1. Select the bookmark or range of bookmarks to be moved.
2. Drag the icon or icons in an upward direction to position the small arrow directly under the label of the parent bookmark.
3. Release the bookmark.

§ 6.1.9 Bookmark Security

Now that you know how easy it is to change bookmark properties (name, destination, and so on), maybe you don't want other users to change your bookmarks. Basic PDF file security can be used to restrict the ability of others to make changes. In the **Password Security—Settings** dialog box, setting **Changes Allowed** (in the **Permissions** section) to **None** requires other users to enter the correct password before bookmark properties can be changed.

Password security can be applied to PDF files several ways. See Chapter 11, "PDF File Security." Password security can be implemented by selecting the **Security** tab in the **Document Properties** dialog box (Figure 6.6). Using the drop-down menu in the **Security Method** window select **Password Security**. The **Password Security—Settings** dialog box appears. Check the box, **Restrict editing and printing of the document**. In the **Changes Allowed** window, select **None**, supply the **Change Permissions** password, click **OK** and confirm the password. Persons who view the secured PDF file will be able to select text and print but not make changes.

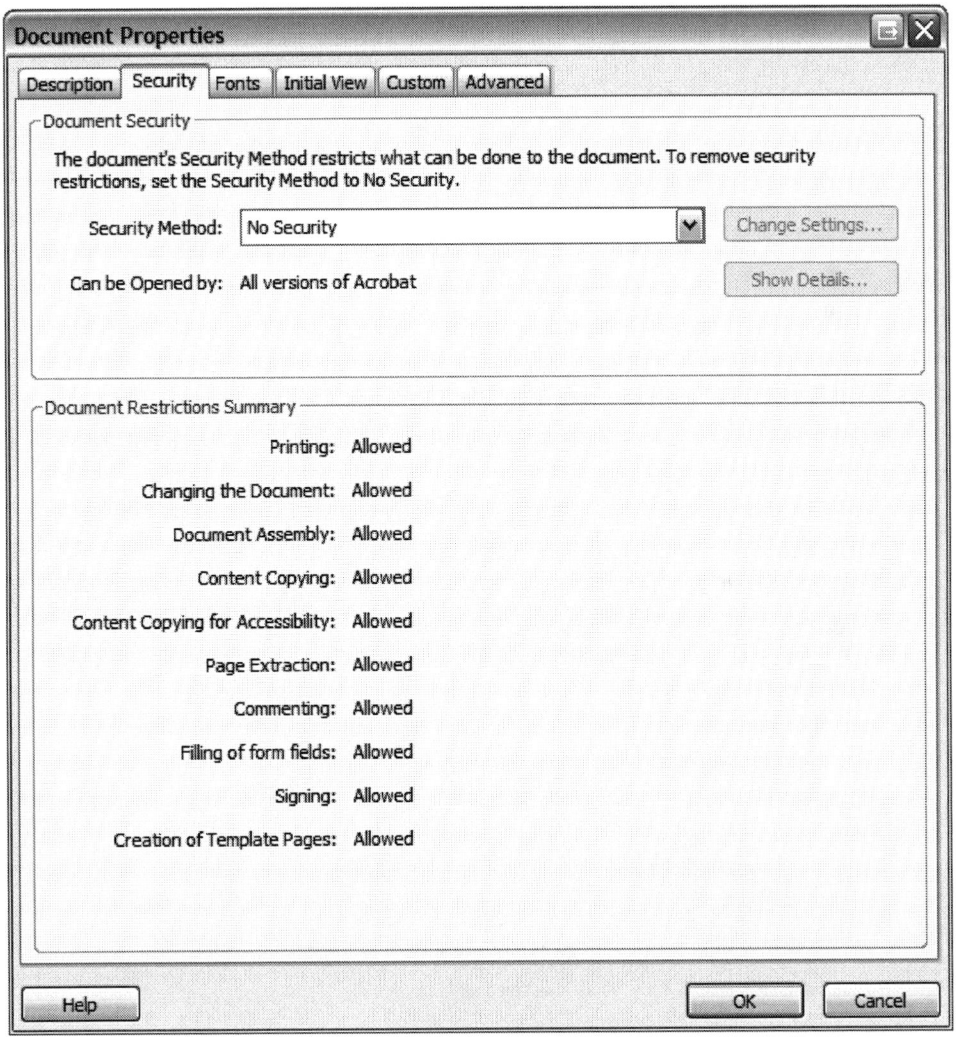

Figure 6.6

§ 6.2 Links

Links make PDF files interactive and truly powerful. In a transactional practice setting, think of a long contract with links built into it that take the reader to the various exhibits or schedules to the contract. Every reference to Exhibit A can be linked to that exhibit; a click on the link takes the reader to the exhibit. (Tip: Remember, the best way back to the original point of the link is the **Previous View** button at the bottom of the work area.) In the litigation context, links are the magic that add power to electronic briefs. When a citation to a case, statute, or other authority appears in your brief, it can be linked to the cited material so that with a click of the mouse the reader sees the authority you have cited. Links let you and other readers of the document jump to other locations in the same document, to other electronic documents, to Web sites, and more. Links can initiate actions, such as playing a sound or movie file. They can be visible or invisible (color-coded invisible links are the best).

Of the commonly used power features of Acrobat, links are probably the most difficult to master. That said, once mastered, links bring a level of interactivity to PDF files that simply cannot be matched in the paper world.

§ 6.2.1 The Link Tool

Links are created in PDF files using the Link tool. The Link tool looks like two links of connected chain (Figure 6.7); it resides on the **Advanced Editing** toolbar, so before you can use it you must display that toolbar (Figure 6.8). To display the **Advanced Editing** toolbar:

Menu (Display Advanced Editing Toolbar): **Tools > Advanced Editing > Advanced Editing Toolbar**

Keystroke (Display Advanced Editing Toolbar): **Alt+T-A-B** NOTE: Remember that in Acrobat 8 you can customize the toolbars to select the tools that appear on a particular bar; accordingly, the tools visible on a given toolbar will vary depending on how you have configured the toolbar.

Figure 6.7

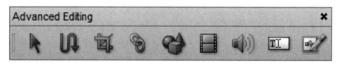

Figure 6.8

§ 6.2.2 Creating Links

Links can be created directly from text and images using the **Select Text** tool or the **Select Image** tool. Using the **Select Text** tool insures that links are matched to exact text and provides uniform link sizing. Links can also be created on any space in a PDF file; that means that you can build links within image-only documents. To create a link using the Link tool:

- Go to the location in the document where you want the link.
- Select the **Link** tool on the **Advanced Editing** toolbar (the pointer becomes a cross hair [+], and any existing links in the document, including invisible links, are temporarily visible).
- Drag the mouse to create a rectangle (this is the area in which the link is active).
- The **Create Link** dialog box will appear (Figure 6.9). Do one of the following:
  - In the **Link Appearance** section select a link appearance (**Visible Rectangle** or **Invisible Rectangle**) from the Link Type drop-down menu.
  - TIP: Invisible rectangle links are unobtrusive in that there is no "box" around the link, but the reader of the document will not know that a link exists at a given location without some other indication, such as a change in font color.
  - In the **Link Action** section select the desired action (Go to a page view, Open a file, Open a web page, or Custom Link); what you see when you click **Next** will depend on the type of action selected.
  - If you selected **Go to a page view**, the **Create Go to View** dialog box appears and instructs you to "Use the scrollbars, mouse and zoom tools to select the target view, then press Set Link to create the Link destination." Okay, this calls for a couple of TIPS.

    TIP 1: If you know you will be creating numerous links within a document (not linking to external documents), you can speed the link creation process by bookmarking the link destination pages be-

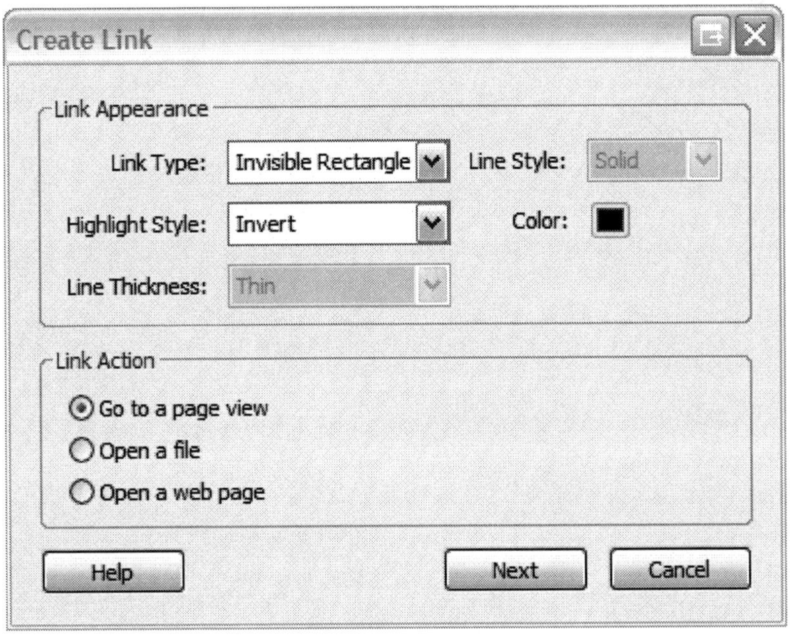

Figure 6.9

fore you start creating the links. With bookmarks in place, when the **Create Go to View** dialog box appears all you have to do is click on the bookmark for the desired destination and *presto!* you are there and ready to click the **Set Link** button (this eliminates lots of scrolling, page clicking, or guessing at page numbers).

TIP 2: In addition to using the scroll bars and mouse you can: Use the **next-page** and **previous-page** buttons to navigate to the desired page; Use the **Go To Page** command (Menu: **View > Go To > Page**, then specify page number; unfortunately the keystroke **Ctrl+Shift+N** does not work). If you chose **Open a File**, clicking **Next** brings up a file open dialog box that allows you to browse for the file to be opened by the link.

To create a link that connects to a Web page, perform the above steps, but rather than selecting **Go to a page view** or **Open a file**:

♦ Select **Open a web page**, click **Next** and provide the URL of the destination Web page.

To create a link using the **Select Text** tool or the **Select Image** tool:

♦ Select the **Select Text** tool or the **Select Image** tool.
♦ Drag to select the text or image from which you want to create a link.
♦ Right-click and choose **Create Link**, the **Create Link** dialog box will appear (Figure 6.10). From this point the procedure is the same as creating a link using the **Link** tool described above.

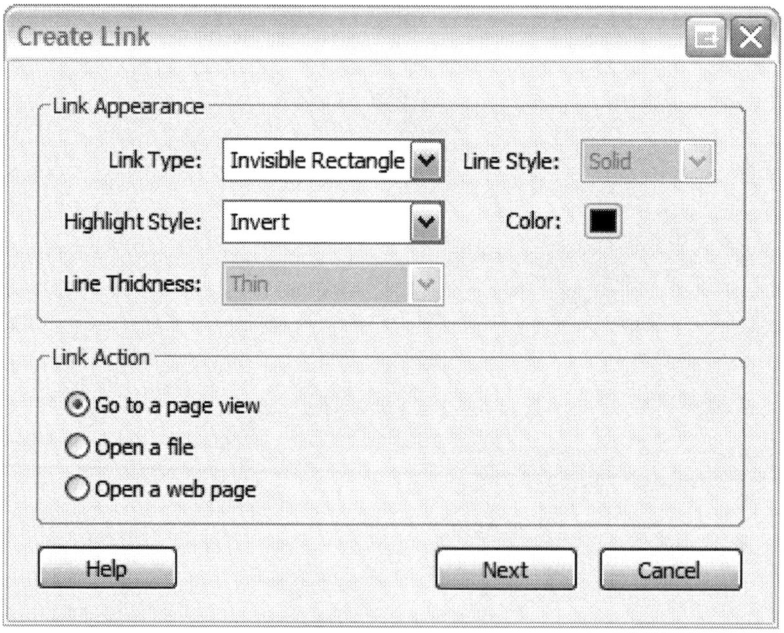

Figure 6.10

§ 6.2.3 Setting the Appearance of Links

You can set the link appearance before or after you create the link—you choose. You can set the appearance of links using the **Properties** bar or by right-clicking on the link, then selecting the **Appearance** tab in the **Properties** dialog box. To display the **Link Properties** bar, select a link, then:

> Menu (Display Links Properties Bar): **View > Toolbars > Properties Bar**
> Keystroke (Display Links Property Bar): **Ctrl+E**

You can reuse the appearance settings of a link for all subsequent Links in the document by right-clicking the link and selecting **Use Current Appearance as New Default**.

The **Properties** dialog box must be used to define the visibility of a link; the visibility of a link cannot be set in the **Properties** toolbar.

You can specify whether a link is visible or invisible, and lock the settings to prevent accidental changes:

- ◆ Select **Invisible Rectangle** for **Link Type** if you do not want users to see the link in the PDF file (invisible links are useful over photographs or graphics), or if you color code the text of the link.
- ◆ Select the **Locked** option in the **Appearance** tab of the **Properties** dialog box to prevent users from accidentally changing settings.

§ 6.2.4 Link Properties

Link properties are reused when you create new links until you change the properties again. You can edit a link at any time. You can change its appearance, hotspot area, or associated link action; delete or resize the link rectangle; or change the destination of the link. Changing the properties of an existing link affects only the currently selected link. You can change the properties of several links at once if you select the links using the **Link** tool or the **Select Object** tool.

§ 6.2.5 Moving and Resizing Links

To move a link rectangle:

1. Select the **Link** tool or the **Select Object** tool.
2. Move the pointer over the link rectangle (the cross hair [+] changes to an arrow when the cursor is over a corner).
3. Drag the link to the desired new location.

To resize a link:

1. Select the **Link** tool or the **Select Object** tool.
2. Move the pointer over the link rectangle (the cross hair [+] changes to an arrow when the cursor is over a corner).
3. Drag any corner point until the rectangle is the desired size.

§ 6.2.6 Deleting Links

Any link in a PDF file can be deleted, or all links can be deleted at once. To delete a single link:

> Select the **Link** tool or the **Select Object** tool, click on the link rectangle to be deleted, and then press the **Delete** key.

To delete all links in a document:

1. Select the **Link** tool or the **Select Object** tool.
2. Right-click on any link.
3. Select **Edit > Select All** (all links in the document will be selected), press the **Delete** key (all links in the document will be deleted).

§ 6.2.7 Link Destinations

A destination is the end point of a link represented by text in the **Destinations** tab (where the user goes when the link is clicked). Destinations allow you to set navigation paths across a collection of PDF files. Linking to a destination is recommended when linking across documents because, unlike a link to a page, a link to a destination is not affected by the addition or deletion of pages within the target document. The destinations of all links within a document can be displayed using the **Links Destination** list. To display the **Link Destinations** list:

> Menu (View Link Destinations List): **View > Navigation Panels > Destinations**
> Keystroke (View Link Destinations List): **Alt+V-N-D**

Opening the **Link Destinations** dialog box automatically scans the document for existing links. To sort the destinations, in the **Link Destination** list, do one of the following:

1. To sort destination names alphabetically, pull down the **Options** list and select **Sort by Name**; or
2. To sort destinations by page number, pull down the **Options** list and select **Sort by Page**.

To change or delete a destination using the **Links Destination** list, select a destination, right-click, and do one of the following:

1. To move to the target location, choose **Go to Destination**; or
2. To delete the destination, choose **Delete**; or
3. To reset the target of the destination to the page displayed, choose **Set Destination**; or
4. To give the destination a different name, choose **Rename**.

To create and link a destination in the same or another PDF file using the **Links Destination** list:

1. In the target document, click **Scan Document** under **Options** in the **Links Destination** list.
2. Navigate to the location where you want to create a destination.
3. Set the destination by doing one of the following:
   a. Choose **New Destination** from the **Options** menu; or
   b. Click the **Create New Destination** button at the top of the **Destinations** tab.
4. Type the name of the destination, and press **Enter** (Note: a destination name must be unique).
5. In the source document (the document you want to create the link from), select the Link tool.
6. Drag a rectangle to specify a source for the link.
7. In the **Create Link** dialog box, select **Custom Link** and click **OK**.
8. On the **Actions** tab of the **Link Properties** dialog box, select **Go to a page in this document** (if you're linking to a destination in the same document) or **Go to a page in another document** (if you're linking to a destination in another document) from the **Select Action** menu, and click **Add**.
9. If you are linking to another document, in the **Go to a page in another document** dialog box, select your target file (the file in which you defined the destination). In the **Open in** menu, specify how the target document should open.
10. Select **Use Named Destination**, and browse to select your named destination. Click **OK**, and click **OK** again.

§ 6.2.8 Link Security

Now that you know how easy it is to change link properties (name, destination, and so on), maybe you don't want other users to change your Links. Basic PDF file security can be used to restrict the ability of others to make changes.

Password security can be applied to PDF files several ways. See Chapter 11, "PDF File Security." Password security can be implemented by selecting the **Security** tab in the **Document Properties** dialog box (Figure 6.11). Using the drop-down menu in the **Security Method** window select **Password Security**. The **Password Security—Settings** dialog box appears. Check the box, **Restrict editing and printing of the document**. In the **Changes Allowed** window, select **None**, supply the **Change Permissions** password, click **OK** and confirm the password. Persons who view the secured PDF file will be able to select text and print but not make changes.

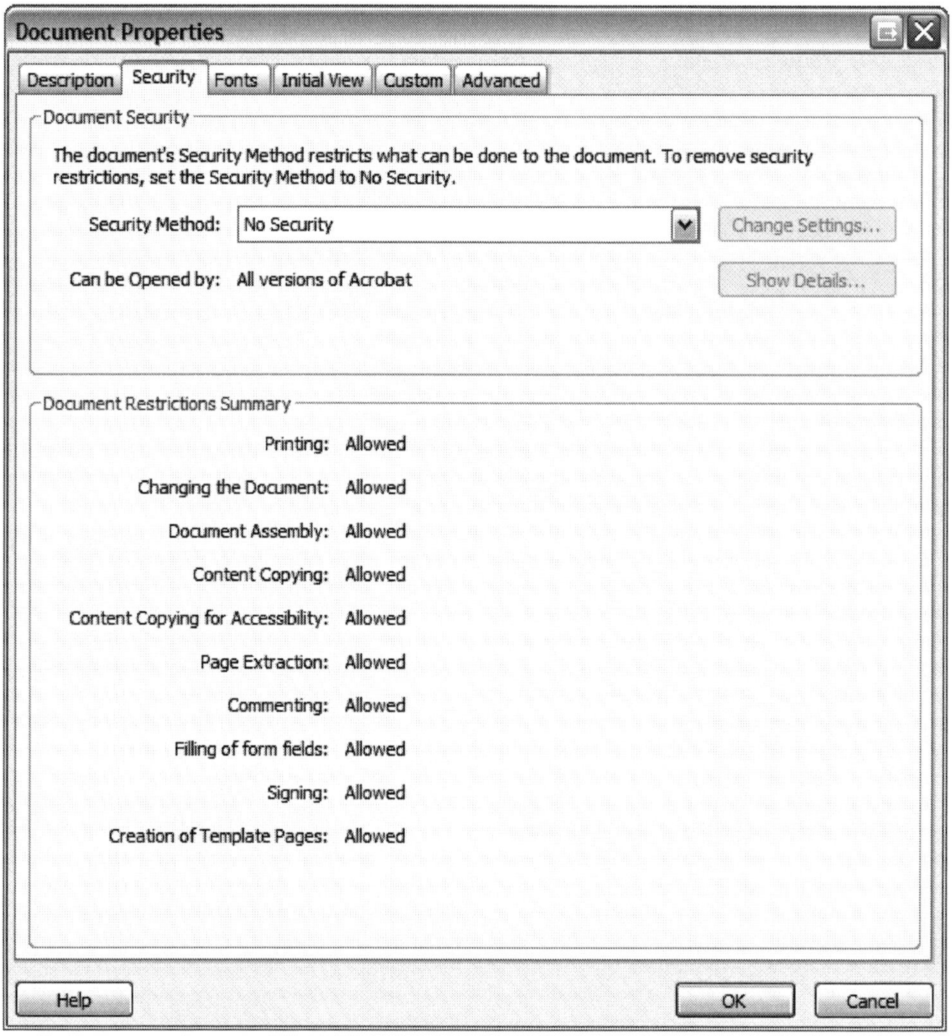

Figure 6.11

§ 6.3 Page Numbering

You may notice that the page numbers on the document pages do not always match the page numbers that appear below the page thumbnails and in the status bar. Pages are numbered with integers, starting with page 1 for the first page of the document, and so on. Because some PDF files may contain front matter, for example an appellate brief or motion for summary judgment may have a cover page, a table of contents, and a table of authorities, the body pages may not follow the numbering shown in the status bar. Or, you may want a PDF file to have page numbers that correspond to Bates numbers or record index numbers.

Acrobat uses two types of page numbers: actual page numbering; and virtual page numbering. By setting the virtual page numbers to correspond with record index pages or Bates numbers, **Go To** (**Ctrl+Shift+N**) can be used to navigate PDF files according to those number systems. An example illustrating the use of virtual page numbers might be helpful. Consider a matter where you have an appellate record (or appendix) that consists of five volumes. Each volume contains approximately five hundred pages. Thus, the pages in Volume III will be in the approximate range of 1,500 through 2,000. In order to be able to Go To page 1,665 in Volume III, the virtual page numbers in that document need to be reset to begin at 1,500—likewise for discovery documents. Assume five notebooks of documents, each containing approximately five hundred pages. Each notebook was scanned as a separate PDF file. Each page in all five files has been sequentially Bates numbered. In order to Go To page Bates number 1,776 in the file covering that page range, the virtual page numbers must be set to commence with the first Bates number in that document.

To set virtual page numbers to correspond to volume page numbers:

1. In the **Pages** pane, choose **Number Pages** from the **Options** menu (Figure 6.12).

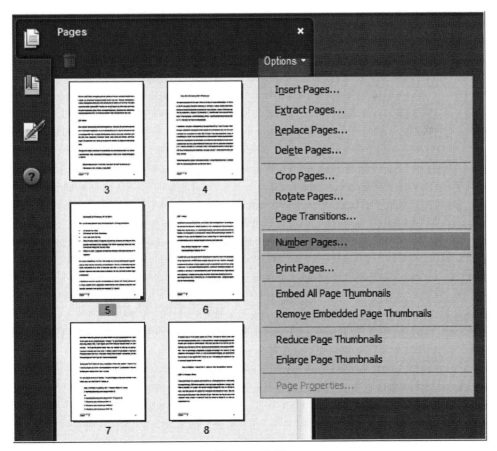

Figure 6.12

2. In the **Pages** section (top half of Page Numbering dialog box; see Figure 6.13), select **All**.

3. In the **Numbering** section (bottom half of the Page Numbering dialog box), do the following:

   a. Select **Begin New Section**.

   b. Choose a **Style** (1, 2, 3 works well).

   c. Type in a **Prefix**, if desired.

   d. Type the **Start number** (for example, 1552).

   e. Click **OK**.

To test the new virtual page number system, use the Go To function (**Ctrl+Shift+N**), type in an appropriate virtual page number, and press **Enter**; the destination should correspond to the appropriate Bates number or record index page number.

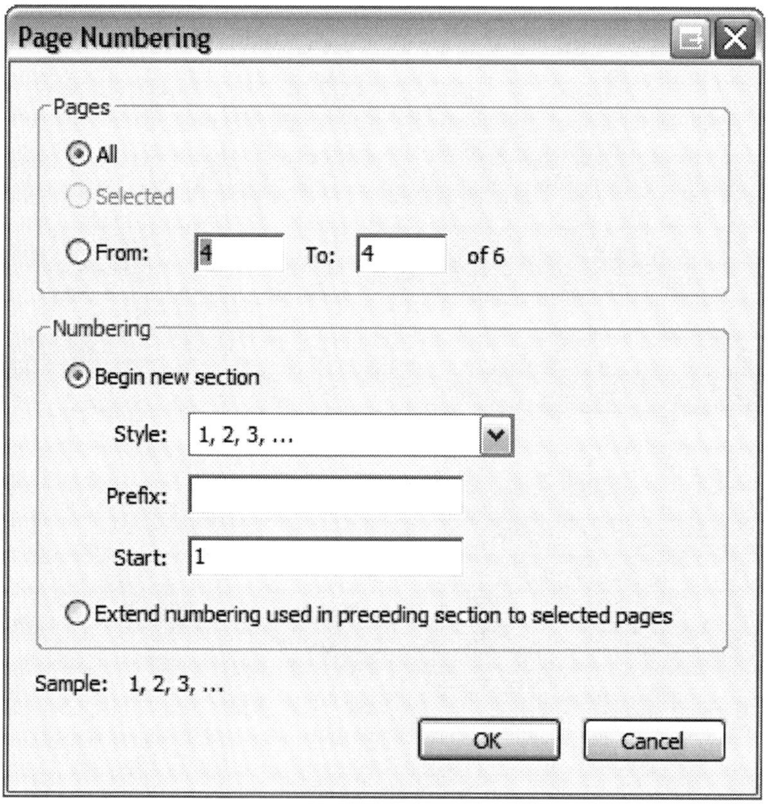

Figure 6.13

Commenting Tools 7

Information, information, information; lawyers process information (remember Chapter 1?). Historically, much of the information processed by lawyers existed in paper form. One of the barriers to working with information that has been converted from paper to digital form was the lack of familiar tools like highlighters and sticky notes. Acrobat removes this barrier with a full palette of commenting tools.

In Acrobat, a "comment" refers to a note, text box, callout, highlighting, drawing markup, or any other annotation added to a PDF file using one or more of the commenting tools. Sticky notes are probably the most useful and commonly used comment. Think of notes as electronic Post-it® Notes. The Sticky Note tool lets you add the equivalent of a sticky note to your PDF file just as you would with a paper document. Text box comments are a great way to annotate drawings and diagrams. You can also add stamps and draw shapes. Comments can be placed anywhere in the PDF file, and you determine the style and format of the comments.

If your comments are too long to fit in a note or text box, you can put lengthy remarks into an attached file. If you need to annotate with something more powerful than mere words, sound and video clips can be attached as well.

Sticky notes and text boxes differ in how they respond to search tools. The text added to sticky notes can not be located by the Find or Search features in Acrobat. However, the text in sticky notes can be found with the search feature found on the menu bar that appears above the Comments window and using the search for files containing text feature in Windows Explorer. On the other hand, the content of text boxes can be located by both the Find and Search tools in Acrobat, or with the search feature found on the menu bar that appears above the Comments window, as well as the search feature in Windows Explorer. Additionally, because sticky notes and text boxes are comments, they appear in the Comment pane at the bottom of the work area with a simple click on the **Comment** icon. If you want to review the comments that have been added to a thousand pages of discovery documents, simply open the PDF file in Acrobat and click on the **Comment** icon, and a list of all comments appears at the bottom of the work area (Figure 7.1). Use the "Show" menu to hide or show comments in the currently displayed PDF file. Use the "Sort" menu to change the order of the comments in the comments list. Use "Search" to find specific comments based on the author, subject, or contents (Figure 7.2). If you see a comment in the comments window and want to go to the page in the document, simply double-click the comment and the location of the comment is displayed.

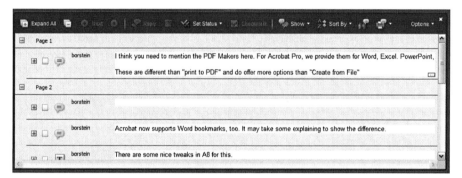

Figure 7.1

§ 7.1 Commenting Toolbars

To add comments to a PDF file, you begin with the Comment & Markup toolbar. The Comment & Markup toolbar is shown in Figure 7.3.

To display the Comment & Markup toolbar:

Menu (Display Comment & Markup Toolbar): **View > Toolbars > Comment & Markup**

Keystroke (Display Comment & Markup Toolbar): **Alt+V-T-C**

To select a commenting tool, click the desired tool, or click the down-arrow next to a tool and then select a tool from the menu. Remember that in Acrobat 8 you can customize the toolbars to select the tools that appear on a

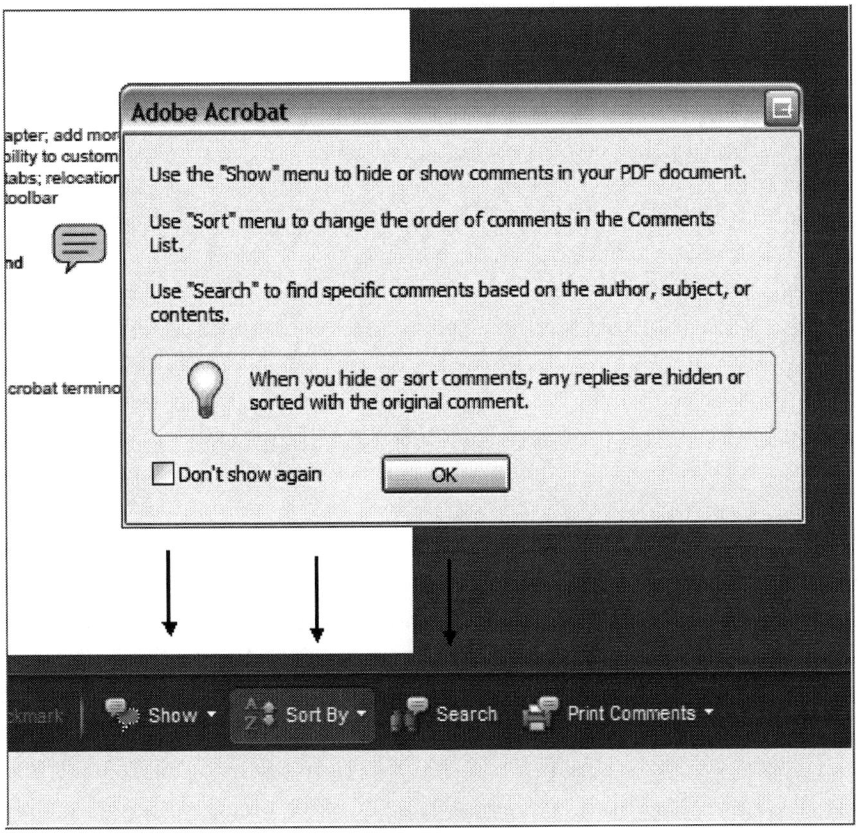

Figure 7.2

Figure 7.3

particular bar; accordingly, the tools visible on a given toolbar will vary depending on how you have configured the toolbar.

§ 7.2 Sticky Notes

Sticky notes are the most commonly used comment. You can use the Sticky Note tool to add notes on any page in a PDF file, you can position them anywhere on the page, and you can add as many notes to each page as you want. When you add a note, an icon and a pop-up window appear. You can add bold, italics, and other attributes to the text in the pop-up window, similar to formatting text in a word processing application. If you enter more text than fits in the pop-up window, the text wraps. You can also resize the window, if desired.

§ 7.2.1 Adding Sticky Notes

To add a Sticky Note:

1. Select the **Sticky Note** tool on the Comment & Markup toolbar.
2. Click the location where you want to place the note.
3. Type the text for the note in the pop-up window (You can use the **Select Text** tool to copy and paste text from an image-on-text PDF file into the Note).
4. If desired, click the **Close** box in the upper-right corner of the pop-up window to close the note (closing the pop-up window does not delete the Note).

§ 7.2.2 Sticky Note Properties

With Acrobat you can set various characteristics of notes by right-clicking a note and selecting **Properties** or, with a note as the active element in the work area, invoke the **Properties** toolbar by pressing **Ctrl+E**. The Sticky Note Properties dialog box has three tabs: Appearance; General; and, Review History (Figure 7.4). On the **Appearance** tab you can select an icon that will appear in the document where you insert a note. The color selection changes the color of both the note and the icon that marks the note location. Use the slider to adjust the opacity of the note and icon from 0 to 100%.

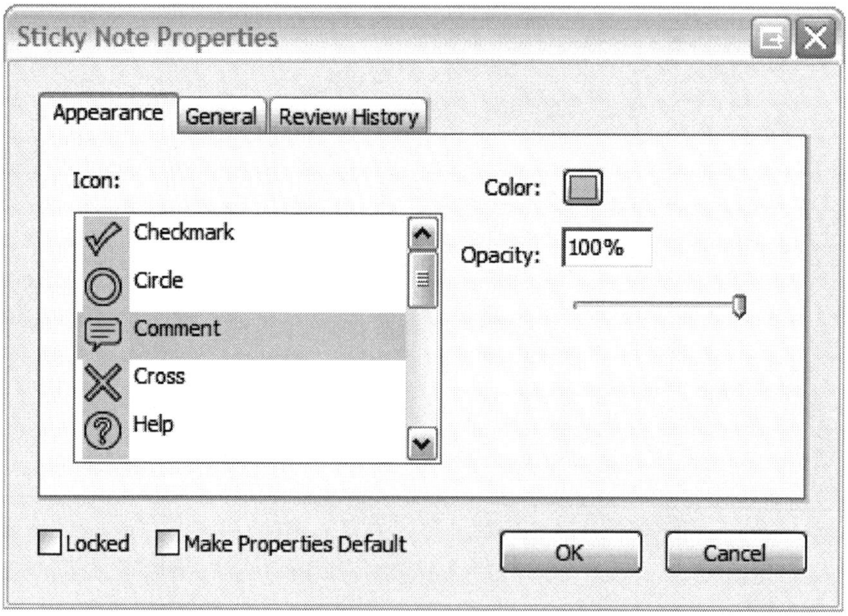

Figure 7.4

§ 7.2.3 Editing Sticky Notes

To edit a note:

1. Click or double-click the note icon to open the pop-up window.
2. Edit the text as needed. When finished, click the **Close** box in the upper-right corner of the pop-up window, or click anywhere outside the pop-up window.
3. Use the **Properties** toolbar (**Ctrl+E**) to change the text formatting, note color, and other note properties.

To resize a pop-up window, drag the lower-right corner of the window to the appropriate size. Use the **Commenting** panel in the **Preferences** dialog box to change the font size, default pop-up behavior, and other settings for creating and viewing Comments.

To delete a note, select the **Sticky Note** tool or the **Hand** tool, and do one of the following:

1. Click on the note icon, then press **Delete**; or
2. Right-click the note icon or the title bar of the pop-up window, and select **Delete**; or
3. Right-click the text area of the pop-up window, and select **Delete Comment**.

The properties that you set for a sticky note can be selected as the default properties for all future notes. So, if you want your sticky notes to be yellow, your paralegal's notes to be green, and your associate's to be blue, this can be quickly and easily accomplished. Right-click on the note and select **Make Current Properties Default** (Figure 7.5).

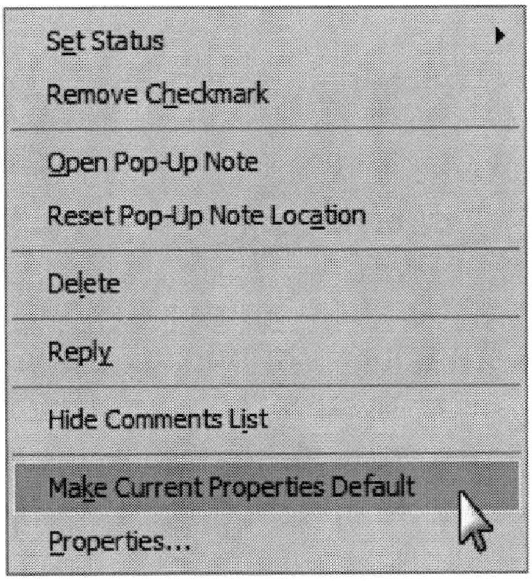

Set Status ▶
Remove Checkmark
Open Pop-Up Note
Reset Pop-Up Note Location
Delete
Reply
Hide Comments List
Make Current Properties Default
Properties...

Figure 7.5

§ 7.3 Text Boxes

Text boxes differ from sticky notes in their appearance and function. Text boxes are useful for annotating drawings and diagrams, or adding labels (think exhibit stickers) to documents. Because exhibit stickers can be a frequent use of text boxes, we'll take a minute to provide an example.

You have assembled all your trial exhibits into a single PDF file; it may be a few pages or a few hundred. An example of a text box exhibit label appears in Figure 7.6. To speed up the process of applying the exhibit labels, first go through the file and bookmark the first page of each exhibit. Now, go to the first page of the first exhibit and create an appropriate exhibit label text box (include the information required in the particular jurisdiction such as the case number). Select the desired background color. Next, copy the label (text box) that you applied to the first exhibit (left-click the edge of the text box, then copy it by pressing **Ctrl+C** or **Menu > Edit > Copy**). Click on the bookmark for

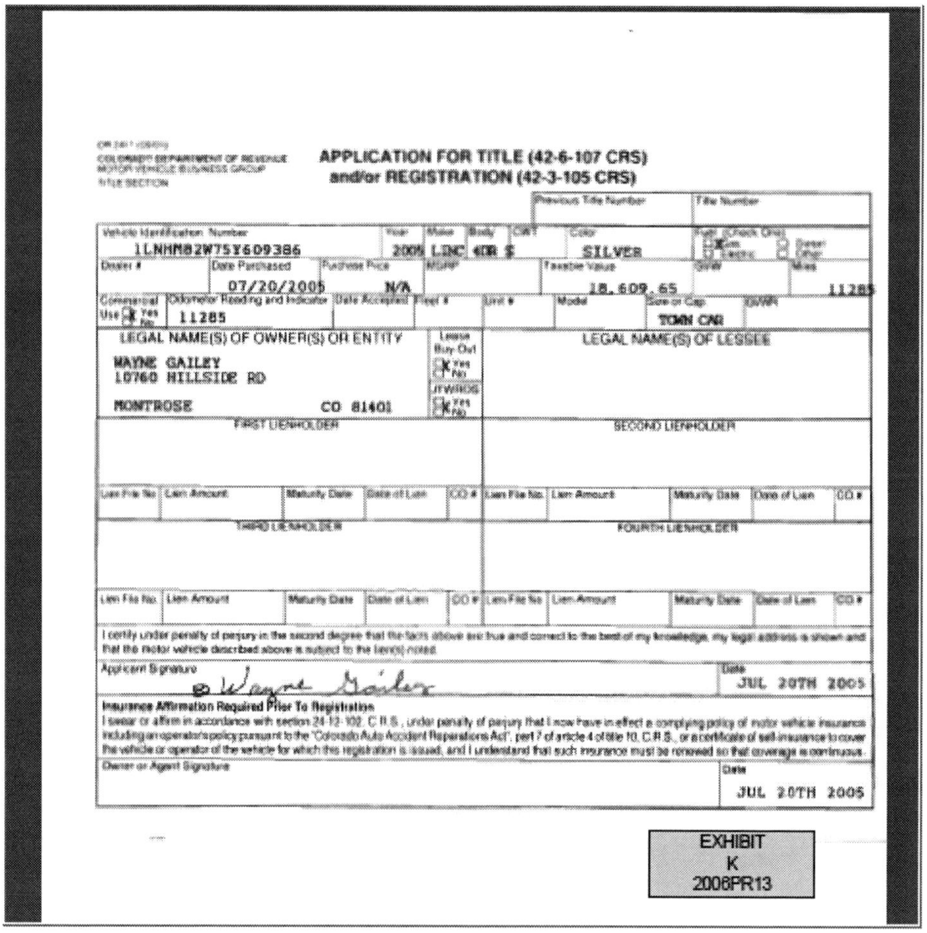

APPLICATION FOR TITLE (42-6-107 CRS)
and/or REGISTRATION (42-3-105 CRS)

1LNHM82W75Y609386 2005 LINC 4DR SILVER
07/20/2005 N/A 18,609.65
11285 TOWN CAR

LEGAL NAME(S) OF OWNER(S) OR ENTITY
WAYNE GAILEY
10760 HILLSIDE RD
MONTROSE CO 81401

LEGAL NAME(S) OF LESSEE

FIRST LIENHOLDER SECOND LIENHOLDER
THIRD LIENHOLDER FOURTH LIENHOLDER

Applicant Signature Date JUL 20TH 2005

Insurance Affirmation Required Prior To Registration

Owner or Agent Signature Date JUL 20TH 2005

EXHIBIT
K
2006PR13

Figure 7.6

the next exhibit (you should now be at the first page of the next exhibit); click on the page and paste the exhibit label (**Crtl+V** or **Menu > Edit > Paste**). Left click on the exhibit label (text box), hold down the button, and drag the box to where you want it on the page. Double-click in the exhibit label (text box) and change the text as appropriate to specify the proper exhibit number. Finally, click anywhere on the current page outside the exhibit label (text box). You're now ready to click on the bookmark for the next exhibit and repeat the process until all exhibits have labels (this may sound complicated and cumbersome but once you try it you'll see how quick and easy it is to apply exhibit labels)

You can create a text box on any page in a PDF file and position it anywhere on the page. Text boxes remain visible on the page; they do not close like notes. Text boxes are created using (you guessed it) the **Text Box** tool. When you click a text box to select it, you can use the options on the **Properties** toolbar to format the fill and border of the text box. When you double-click a text box, you can use the options on the **Properties** toolbar to format the text inside the text box.

To add a text box, select the **Text Box** tool on the Comment & Markup Toolbar.

1. Click the location for the text box (alternatively, drag a rectangle to define the boundaries of the text box).
2. Use the **Properties** toolbar to change the color, alignment, and font attributes of the text, and then type the text (to display the Properties toolbar, right-click the toolbar area and select **Properties**).

As with notes, the properties that you set for a text box can be selected as the default properties for all future text boxes. So, if you want your text boxes to be yellow with black text, the text boxes added by your paralegal to be dark green with white text, and the text boxes of your associate to be light blue with black text, this can be quickly and easily accomplished. After setting the desired properties, right-click on the text box and select **Make Current Properties Default**. To resize a text box, select the box using the **Hand** tool or the **Text Box** tool, and then drag one of the corners to the desired size.

Remember, the content of text boxes can be located using the Find and Search tools in Acrobat, while sticky note content cannot (you can search for sticky note content with the tool on the Comment window).

§ 7.4 Callout Text Boxes

Callout text boxes are great for annotating documents for use as exhibits, or for creating charts and drawings. Callout text boxes are really just text boxes that you connect to an area of the document with an arrow. To create a callout text box simply click on the **Callout** tool (Figure 7.7), located on the Com-

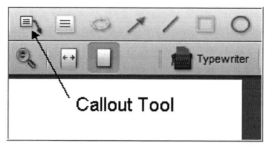

Figure 7.7

ment & Markup toolbar, move your pointer to the approximate location on the page where you want the arrow to be and click. A callout text box will be created. You can now insert text in the box, drag the box to a new location, and drag the pointer end of the arrow to a new location (the connecting lines will automatically adjust) (Figure 7.8). Callout text boxes can be placed anywhere on the page. Both the "box" and the "pointer" can be moved and the connecting lines automatically adjust.

and mechanics

7	Commenting Tools
7.1	Commenting Toolbar [renamed]
7.2	Notes
7.3	Text Boxes
7.4	Callouts
7.5	Text Markup
7.6	Comment Summaries
7.7	Lines and Shapes [Drawing Markups]

Insert text in the box, drag the box to a new location, and drag the pointer end of the arrow to a new location

Figure 7.8

§ 7.5 Text Markup

The Highlighter tool, Cross-Out Text tool, and the Underline Text tool do what their names suggest. The functions of the text markup tools come within Adobe's definition of comments, so their use and attributes are much like Notes and Text Boxes. However, unlike notes and text boxes, these markup tools work only with image-on-text PDF files. This type of comment may be used independently or in conjunction with notes. For example, you may want to highlight a section of text, and then double-click the highlighting to add a note window.

To highlight, cross out, or underline text:

1. On the **Comment & Markup** toolbar select a tool (**Highlighter, Cross-Out Text,** or **Underline Text**).

2. Move the cursor to the beginning of the text to be marked up, then click and drag (use **Ctrl+** while dragging to mark a rectangular area of text; this is especially useful to mark up text in a column).

To associate a note with the highlighted or underlined text, select the **Hand** tool and double-click the markup. Type the text in the pop-up window that appears. To delete a highlight, cross out, or underline markup, do one of the following:

1. Right-click the markup and select **Delete**.
2. Select the **Hand** tool, click the markup, then press **Delete**.

§ 7.6 Measuring Tools

Acrobat includes three measuring tools (distance, perimeter, and area), located on the Measuring toolbar (Figure 7.9). If you use the line, box, or other shape drawing tools to create diagrams, then you may find the dimensioning tools helpful.

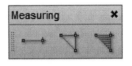

Figure 7.9

§ 7.6.1 Distance Measuring Tool

Click on the **Distance Measuring** tool, click and drag the pointer between the points that you want to show dimensions for. When you stop dragging and release the button on your pointing device, the **Distance Tool** box appears showing the measurement, cursor location, and the units and markup settings (Figure 7.10). Fill in the desired distance measurement in the "Label" window and that text will appear with the distance line drawn on the document (the actual distance may be 2 inches but may in fact represent 2 feet, 500 feet, 1.3 miles, etc.). You can edit the label or change the properties of the measurement markup by right-clicking and choosing an action from the menu (Figure 7.11).

§ 7.6.2 Perimeter and Area Measuring Tools

Select the **Perimeter** tool to measure a set of distances between multiple points. Click each point you want to measure. When have gone all the way around the object to be measured, double-click the last point, or hold the

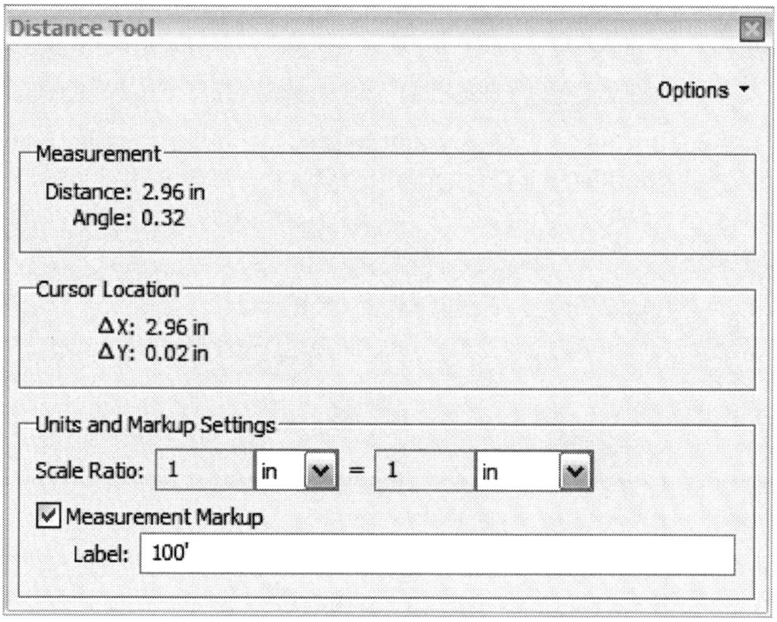

Figure 7.10

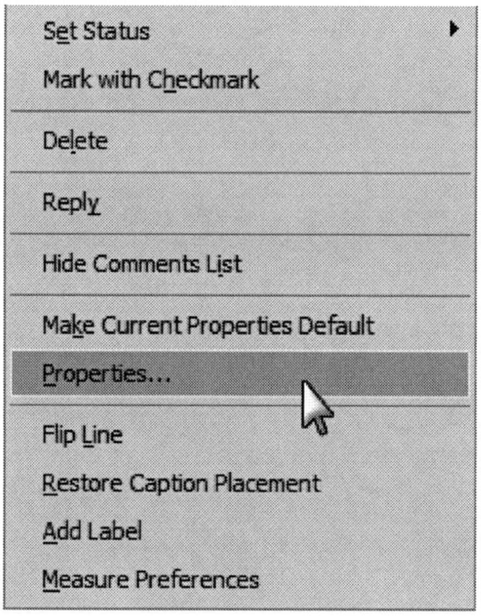

Figure 7.11

pointer over the last point, and click. Select the **Area** tool to measure the area within the line segments that you draw. Click each point you want to measure. After you have clicked at least two points, click the first point to complete the area measurement. You can also finish a measurement by right-clicking and choosing **Complete Measurement** from the context menu.

§ 7.7 Comment Summaries

The ability to summarize comments using Acrobat is a powerful tool for lawyers. Think of a thousand or ten thousand pages of discovery documents. No, they are not in notebooks or boxes; these pages have been scanned and exist as one or more PDF files. Start turning the pages and adding notes or text boxes as you go. Now, after reviewing those thousand or ten thousand pages and adding a hundred or a thousand comments, all of the text in every note or text box can be extracted in a matter of seconds to a new PDF file.

When you summarize comments, you can either create a new PDF file with comments that can be printed, or you can print the summary directly. The summary is not associated with or linked to the PDF file that the comments come from. If **Print Comment Pop-ups** is selected in the **Commenting** panel of the **Preferences** dialog box (see Section 7.10), note pop-ups appear on the printed pages when you select **File > Print**. The **Print with Comments** command provides more control over how the comments are printed than the **Print** command.

To create a comment summary:

Menu (Summarize Comments): **Comments > Summarize Comments**
Keystroke (Summarize Comments): **Alt+C-Z**

To print a comment summary:

Menu (Print Comments): **File > Print with Comments**

Whether creating or printing a comment summary, the **Summarize Options** dialog box appears (Figure 7.12). In this box you can:

- ◆ Specify how to lay out the comments on the page.
- ◆ Choose how to sort the comments.
- ◆ Select whether you want all comments to appear in the summary, or only the comments that are currently showing.

If you created a summary, a separate PDF file appears. You can save or print this document. If you want to summarize the comments again, switch back to the original document using the Windows menu or typing **Ctrl+F6**. Comments can be printed or summarized directly without opening the **Summarize Options** dialog box by selecting **Print Comments Summary** or **Create PDF of Comments Summary** from the **Print Comments** menu in the Comments list. Choose **More Options** from this menu to specify the summary settings to be used.

Comment summaries work best for notes, text boxes, and marked-up text because these summaries contain text. Because the drawing markup tools (graphic shapes) are also comments, those markups are also included in

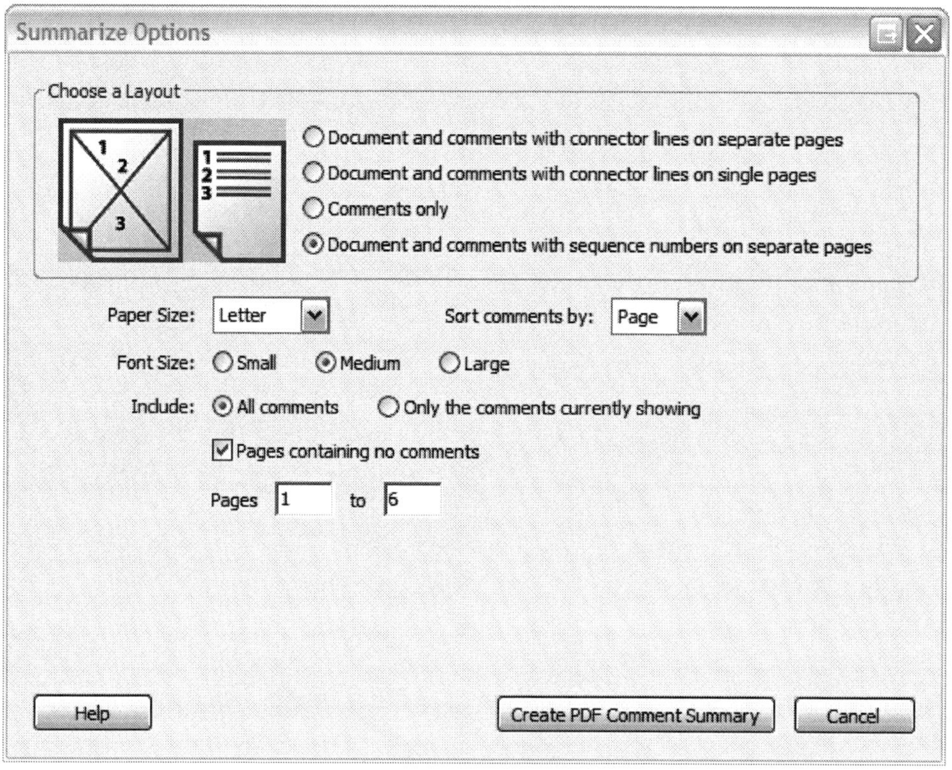

Figure 7.12

the comment summary. If you use the drawing tools to mark up image-only files (e.g., using a translucent shape as a highlighter), the Comment summary provides a list of where you drew lines and shapes.

§ 7.8 Lines and Shapes

The drawing tools are used to mark up PDF files with lines, circles, and other shapes; these are called drawing markups. Why would you want to draw on your documents? (You're a lawyer, after all.) Well, recall the different types of PDF files: image-only and image-on-text. When working with image-only files (think discovery documents that have been scanned to PDF) there is no text to select for marking up. With the drawing tools you can draw lines around portions of an image; in other words, you can draw lines (round, rectangular, polygonal) over, under, beside, and around the picture of the text. While there may be no text to highlight, you can draw a line over, under, or around what looks like text (or any other portion of the image). The drawing tools are really powerful when working with image-only files. You can make them even more powerful by adding text or a note to any drawing markup.

Acrobat includes a number of drawing tools. At the risk of stating the obvious, here is what they are and what they do:

- *Cloud:* same as the Polygon tool, but the segments turn into a cloud shape when you finish drawing.
- *Arrow:* draws straight lines with arrows on either or both ends.
- *Line:* draws straight lines.
- *Rectangle:* draws rectangles (hold down **Shift** while using this tool to draw squares).
- *Oval:* draws ovals (hold down **Shift** while using this tool to draw circles).
- *Polygonal Line:* creates an open shape (line) with multiple segments.
- *Polygon:* creates a closed shape with multiple segments (great for sketching odd shaped objects).
- *Pencil:* creates free-form drawings.
- *Pencil Eraser:* removes lines drawn with the Pencil tool.

To use the drawing tools, display the **Comment & Markup** toolbar (remember, you can customize the toolbars to select the tools that appear on a particular bar; accordingly, the tools visible on a given toolbar will vary depending on how you have configured the toolbar). With the toolbar in place, select a drawing tool.

- To draw a cloud, left-click a starting point (note: left-click only, not left-click and drag), move the mouse pointer and click to create a segment of the cloud shape, then continue moving the mouse pointer and clicking to create additional segments of the cloud.
- To draw an arrow, left-click and drag across the area where you want the line with an arrow to appear (note: the arrow pointer appears where you begin drawing).
- To draw a line, left-click and drag across the area where you want the line to appear (TIP: If you hold down the **Shift** key will dragging the line will be forced to be either horizontal, vertical or forty-five degrees, whichever is closest to the orientation of the line you are drawing).
- To draw a rectangle left-click and drag across the area where you want the drawing shape to appear.
- To draw an oval left-click and drag across the areas where you want the shape to appear (TIP: Hold down the **Shift** key while dragging with the Oval tool to draw a circle)
- To draw a polygon or polygon line, left-click a starting point (note: left-click only, not left-click and drag), move the mouse pointer and click to create a segment of the polygon, then continue moving the mouse pointer and clicking to create additional segments of the polygon. You'll be surprised at how useful the polygon tools are.

- ◆ When finished drawing a polygon, click the starting point or double-click to close the shape.
- ◆ Double-click to end a polygon line.

You may find the polygon tool very helpful to highlight the fill in non-rectangular shapes on maps, plats, and the like. Figure 7.13 shows an area from a plat that was "highlighted" using the polygon tool set at 50% opacity.

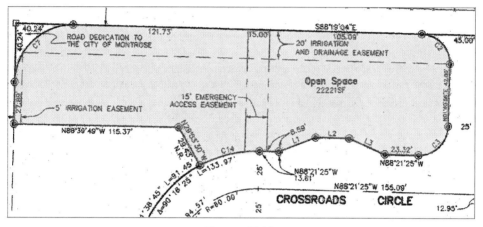

Figure 7.13

To delete a drawing markup:

- ◆ Right-click the drawing markup, and select **Delete**.

To change the appearance of a drawing markup:

- ◆ Right-click the drawing markup, select **Properties**, then change options on the **Appearances** tab.

You can use the drawing tools to create charts and diagrams on a blank page. To create a blank page:

Menu (Create PDF Blank Page): **File > Create PDF > From Blank Page**
Keystroke (Create PDF Blank Page): **Alt+F-F-B**

Tip: After the first use of a drawing tool, right-click the drawing to set the properties as desired. Then right-click again, this time selecting **Make Current Properties Default**.

Tip: Setting the opacity of the drawing markup tools to 50 percent allows them to be used as a highlighter on image-only PDF files. This can be a hugely powerful tool for lawyers working with image-only PDF files. You may come across a lot of paper that was scanned to PDF that cannot be OCR'd. Handwritten diaries, calendar entries, accident reports, medical notes; if they were handwritten they cannot be OCR'd. There will be no "text" to highlight, but with the drawing tools you can "highlight" image-only PDF files. For example, draw a rectangle, then right-click on it and select **Properties**. Now set the color for both the line and fill to yellow and set the opacity at 50%. Check the box to Make Properties Default and the rectangle drawing tool can now be used to highlight image-only files.

§ 7.9 Deleting Comments

Comments (whether notes, text boxes, shapes, highlighting, and so on) can be deleted about as easily as they can be added. To delete a single comment, do one of the following:

- ◆ Right-click the comment and select **Delete**, or
- ◆ Select the **Hand** tool, click the comment, and press **Delete.**

To delete multiple Comments:

1. Click the **Comment** icon to display the **Comment** pane at the bottom of the work area.
2. Select the comments to be deleted (hold down the **Ctrl** key to click on and select **Multiple Comments**).
3. Click the **Trash** (delete) icon.

When deleting Comments, note the following:

- ◆ If comments are placed on top of one another, deleting a comment may appear to do nothing, because the next item in the stack is still visible. You may need to delete several comments before they are all removed.
- ◆ If a comment is locked, you cannot delete it until you unlock it. To unlock a comment, right-click the comment, select **Properties**, deselect **Locked**, then click **Close**.

§ 7.10 Comment Properties

All of the comments described in this chapter (sticky notes, text boxes, callout text boxes, text markups, lines, shapes, and stamps) have properties. Those properties can be modified for each individual comment by right-clicking, selecting **Properties**, and making adjustments. Many comment properties can be set universally to affect all comments by working with commenting preferences on the **Edit** menu. For example, comments can be made easier to read by selecting a larger font size.

To set preferences for comments:

Menu (Edit Comment Preferences): **Edit > Preferences** (select **Commenting** in the left window)

Keystroke (Edit Comment Preferences): **Alt+E-N** (select **Commenting** in the left window) Keystroke (Edit Comment Preferences): **Ctrl+K**

Once the **Edit Comment Preferences** dialog box appears (Figure 7.14), there are a number of default settings that can be established. The dialog box is divided into three parts, each of which corresponds to a section discussed below.

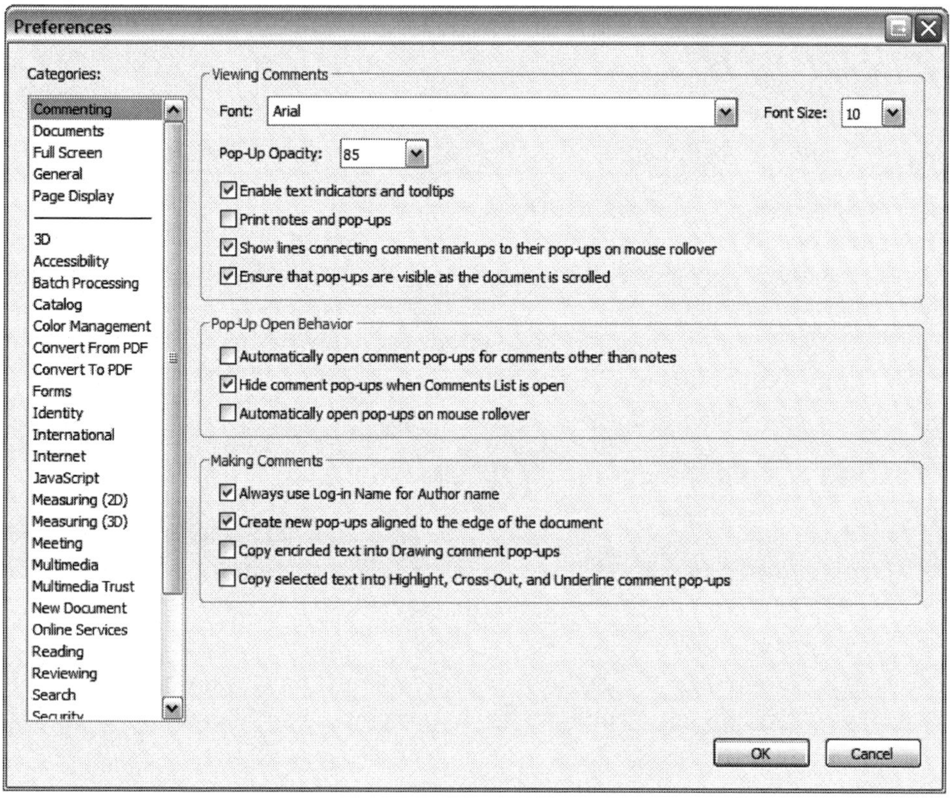

Figure 7.14

§ 7.10.1 Viewing Comments

◆ Font and Font Size. These determine the font and the size of text in pop-up windows. This setting applies to all new and existing comments.

◆ Pop-up Opacity. The value (between 0 and 100) determines the opacity of the comment popup windows. When the pop-up window is open but not selected, an opacity value of 100 makes the window opaque, while lower values make the window more transparent.

- Enable text indicators and tooltips. Shows the author name, comment status, and two lines of the text when you place the pointer over a comment that includes a pop-up note.
- Print notes and pop-ups. The pop-up windows associated with comments are printed. You may prefer using the **Print with Comments** command.
- Show lines connecting Comment markups to their pop-ups on mouse rollover. When the mouse pointer moves over a Comment markup (such as highlighting or a note icon), the shaded connector line between the comment and the open pop-up window appears.
- Ensure that pop-ups are visible as the document is scrolled. When the mouse pointer is placed over a Comment of any type, including drawing markups and Stamp, the pop-up window opens.

§ 7.10.2 Pop-Up Open Behavior

- Automatically open comment pop-ups for comments other than notes. A pop-up window appears when you create a new comment using a drawing tool, the Text Box tool, or the Pencil tool. This can be useful for adding commentary when using the drawing tools to highlight portions of image-only files.
- Hide comment pop-ups when Comments List is open. Pop-up windows do not appear when the comments list is displayed. This option helps reduce screen clutter when a page includes many Comments.
- Automatically open pop-ups on mouse rollover. When you place the pointer over a Comment of any type, including drawing markups and Stamp, the popup Note opens.

§ 7.10.3 Making Comments

- Always use the Log-in Name for author name. Determines which name appears in the pop-up note you create. If this option is selected, the login name in the Identity panel of the Preferences dialog box is used. If this option isn't selected, the default name you specify for author in a Comment Properties dialog box is used.
- Create new pop-ups aligned to the edge of the document. Aligns pop-up notes with the right side of the document window, regardless of where the comment markup (such as a note icon or highlighting comment) is added. You may prefer to uncheck this option so that pop-up notes appear next to the comment markup.
- Copy encircled text into Drawing comment pop-ups. The pop-up windows associated with drawing comments, such as those created by the Rectangle tool, include any text within the comment if this option is selected.

◆ Copy selected text in Highlight, Cross-Out, and Underline comment pop-ups. The pop-up window associated with proofreading markup comments, such as those created by the Highlighter tool, includes any text to which the comment is applied if this option is selected.

§ 7.11 Stamps

Stamps can be handy for marking PDF files as "DRAFT," "CONFIDENTIAL," "RECEIVED," and so on. Acrobat comes with a set of ready-made Stamps, both static and dynamic. An example of a static stamp is one that applies "RECEIVED" to a document. The dynamic RECEIVED stamp includes the user's name (derived from the Identity section of the Preferences dialog box) along with the date and time when the stamp is applied. Acrobat allows you to create custom stamps that can contain text or images. A custom stamp that applies a facsimile of your signature can be especially useful (see Section 7.11.3).

§ 7.11.1 Ready-Made Stamps

To use the ready-made stamps that come with Acrobat you need to first select the desired stamp (the last used stamp remains as the default selection). To select a specific stamp, click on the drop-down arrow on the right next to the Stamp tool, navigate to the desired category (Dynamic, Personal, Sign Here, or Standard Business), then highlight the desired stamp. The Stamp tool is on the **Comment & Markup** Toolbar (Figure 7.15). This becomes the selected stamp; place the pointer where you want to apply the stamp and left-click. To use the same stamp again, click on the Stamp tool on the **Comment & Markup** Toolbar, point and click; the last used stamp remains selected until you select a different stamp.

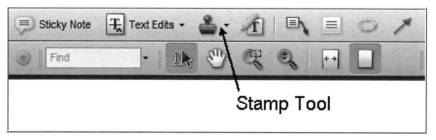

Figure 7.15

§ 7.11.2 Custom-Made Stamps

You can create custom stamps for a variety of purposes; think of all the rubber stamps in your office and you'll begin to see the possibilities. Custom stamps can be created from PDF files or from any common graphic format.

When you select the file to be used for the stamp, you can add it to an existing category or you can create a new one.

To create a Custom stamp follow the steps described below. While the steps described below may appear inconsistent with the menu choices in Acrobat, they will provide guidance for creating Custom stamps. If you pull down the **Tools** menu, select **Commenting**, then select **Stamps**, and then select **Create Custom Stamp**, you will be presented with a dialog box that does not offer the option to "create" a new Stamp. The same result follows if you use the pull-down menu on the **Stamp Tool** button and select **Create Custom Stamp**. As you will see, and as described below, when you select **Manage Stamps** the dialog box has a button (option) to "create" a new custom stamp.

Before you begin the process of creating a custom stamp, you will need the artwork that will be applied by the stamp. The artwork should be an image file (JPEG, TIFF, etc.) or an existing PDF file. Don't let the term "artwork" fool you. If you want to create a custom stamp that contains text, create the text in an image editing application (e.g., Adobe Photoshop, Gimp, etc.). It goes without saying that you need to know where the artwork file resides on your computer or network, so if you create many stamps it may be helpful to create a folder where all stamp artwork will be located.

With these preliminaries out of the way, to create a custom stamp:

Menu (Create Custom Stamp): **Tools > Comment & Marketing > Stamps > Manage Stamps**

Keystroke (Create Custom Stamp): **Alt+T-C-T-M**

Or, use the pull-down menu located next to the **Stamp Tool** on the Comment & Markup toolbar and select **Manage Stamps**. Then:

1. Click **Create.**
2. Click **Browse**, and double-click the file to be used as the stamp art (if the file has more than one page, select the page to use for the stamp).
3. Click **OK.**
4. For **Category**, select an existing category, or type a name to create a new category.
5. For **Name**, type the name that will appear on the Stamp menu on the Comment & Markup toolbar.
6. Click **OK.**

Once applied to a PDF file, stamps can be resized, moved, or have their properties modified.

The Acrobat stamp feature can be used to create a simple signature stamp. This signature, just like its real-world rubber-stamp counterpart, cannot be verified or secured. However, until we reach a point where courts and opposing counsel require verification of signatures, digital-stamp signatures present a quick and convenient alternative to secure digital signatures.

§ 7.11.3 Creating a Stamp of Your Signature

To create a signature stamp:

1. Sign your name on a piece of paper about a dozen times (or at least until you have created one exemplar that you like enough to use as your stamp signature).
2. Scan the page of exemplars to PDF (if you want your stamp signature to appear in color (for example, in blue ink), scan in color mode; this increases the size of the stamp file but it's pretty small to start with).
3. Use the **Crop** tool to draw a box around the desired exemplar.
4. Double-click inside the box and click **OK**.
5. **Save** the resulting PDF file to a convenient location, such as C:\Program Files\Adobe\Acrobat 8.0\Acrobat\Plug_Ins\Annotations\Stamps\Signatures. You may need to create the Signatures folder; the rest of the path should already exist.
6. Open a PDF file that you want to apply the signature stamp to.
7. From the **Tools** menu select **Commenting > Stamps > Manage Stamps**.
8. In the category box, type Signature. In the name box, type a name for the stamp (such as your initials).
9. Click **Select** and find where you saved the signature; click **OK**; click **OK** again.

To sign a document with your signature stamp: Click on the **Stamp** tool, select your signature stamp, then move the pointer (now your signature) to the desired location on the page and left-click. Or,

Menu (Sign Document with Stamp): **Tools > Comment & Markups > Stamps > Signatures** and select your signature stamp.

If you create a custom stamp for your signature, you'll find it useful for signing documents to be sent via electronic mail or facsimile transmission from your computer. If you use the forms feature of Acrobat Professional, you can scan any paper document that needs to be filled in and create form boxes for the areas where information needs to be supplied. When you are done, you simply stamp your signature on the dotted line. Once it is signed, you can send the document from the comfort of your desktop via electronic mail or facsimile transmission.

§ 7.11.4 Transparent Signature Stamps

Most stamps are opaque; that is, they cover up anything below them where they are placed in a PDF file. Creating a custom stamp from an image of your signature provides a great way to sign documents, such as letters and pleadings, that have been printed to PDF. Creating a custom stamp from an image of your signature, where the background has been rendered transparent means that your John Hancock can be placed over text or signature lines.

To create a transparent signature stamp you will need an image editing application that has the ability to create layers and transparencies. For our purposes, the following description was developed using Adobe Photoshop Elements™. Sign your name on a piece of white paper about a dozen times (or at least until you have created one exemplar that you like enough to use as your Stamp signature).

- Using Adobe Photoshop Elements (these instructions can probably be extrapolated to other image editing applications), scan the page of exemplars to an image file, the default Photoshop .psd file format works well. **File > Import > [Select your scanner]** (if you want your stamp signature to appear in color (e.g., blue ink), scan in color mode; this will increase the size of the stamp file but it's pretty small to start with).
- Use the **Crop** tool to draw a box around the desired exemplar, then select **Menu: Image > Crop**
- Save the resulting .psd file to a convenient location (Example: C:\Program Files\Adobe\Acrobat 8.0\Acrobat\Plug_Ins\Annotations\Stamps\Signatures; you may need to create the Signatures folder, the rest of the path should already exist).
- Using the "Magic Wand" tool to select all parts of the signature image (including the dots above the "i"s (set the tolerance close to or at 100 and uncheck the **Contiguous** box—this will result in all of the signature being selected with a single click).
- Use the **Layer** menu to create a new layer via cut: **Layer > New via cut** (after the first selection hold down the **Shift** key while making additional selections).
- Click on the **Layers** tab, click on the "background" layer and drag it to the trash bin (you now have a signature image with no background).
- Save the .psd file as a .tif (**File > Save As > (Format TIFF)**), check the **Layers** box, and in the TIFF options dialog box be sure to check the **Save Transparency** box.

Now that you have an image file of your signature against a transparent background, proceed with the steps to create a Custom Stamp described above.

§ 7.11.5 Signature Stamp Security

Now that you have created your own digital signature stamp and realize how easy it is to copy or delete that stamp from a PDF file, you should give some thought to securing the document and your signature. It is important to note that a signature stamp is not the same thing as applying a secure digital signature to a document.

You can use password security to prevent changes to PDF files that contain your signature stamp. Password security can be applied to PDF files several ways (see Chapter 11, "PDF FIle Security"). Password security can be implemented by selecting the **Security** tab in the **Document Properties** dialog box (Figure 7.16). Using the drop-down menu in the **Security Method** window select **Password Security**. The **Password Security—Settings** dialog box appears. Check the box "**Restrict editing and printing of the document.**" In the **Changes Allowed** window, select **None**, supply the Change Permissions password, click **OK** and confirm the password. Persons who view the secured PDF file will be able to select text and print but not make changes.

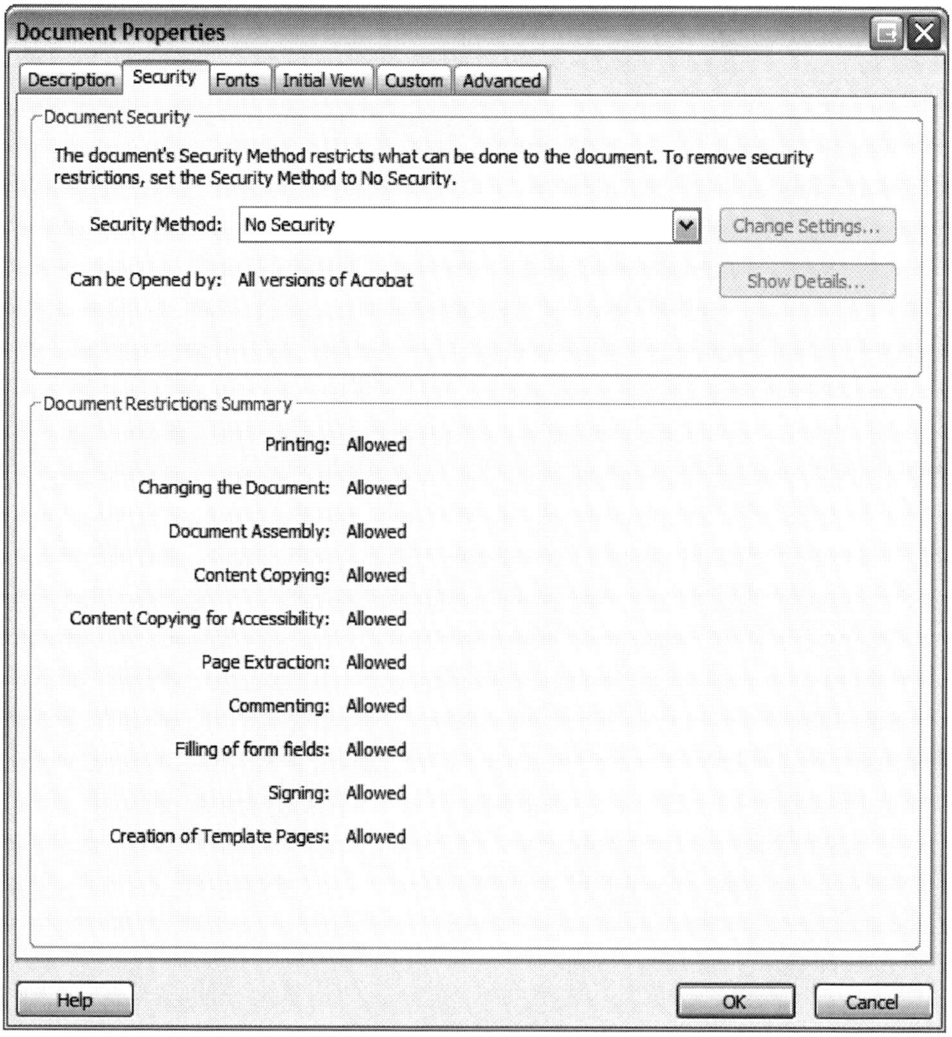

Document Properties

Description | Security | Fonts | Initial View | Custom | Advanced

Document Security

The document's Security Method restricts what can be done to the document. To remove security restrictions, set the Security Method to No Security.

Security Method: No Security

Can be Opened by: All versions of Acrobat

Change Settings...
Show Details...

Document Restrictions Summary

Printing: Allowed
Changing the Document: Allowed
Document Assembly: Allowed
Content Copying: Allowed
Content Copying for Accessibility: Allowed
Page Extraction: Allowed
Commenting: Allowed
Filling of form fields: Allowed
Signing: Allowed
Creation of Template Pages: Allowed

Help | OK | Cancel

Figure 7.16

§ 7.12 Final Comment on Comments

The ease of use and power of comments in Acrobat will likely be the feature to convince you that working with digital documents beats dealing with paper hands down. The ability to search for text in comments, not to mention the ability to summarize them, brings the power of your computer to bear on what has been at best more paper to keep track of. Remember, the text you add to PDF files, whether image-only or image-on-text PDF files, is included in searches performed and indexes maintained by third-party applications such as Windows Explorer. If you previously prepared written summaries of documents, you then had two documents to keep track of—the original and the summary. With Acrobat, comments can be part of the document, and they can be searched or summarized. And a digital document won't fall behind your desk or blow away with a gust of wind.

Digital Signatures 8

When you move beyond using Acrobat to simply organize, review, and comment on documents and start using it for the delivery or exchange of original work product, the time has come to sign your documents. Most court-approved e-filing systems accept pleadings that are signed with a typed statement as simple as "Signed by David L. Masters" or "/s/ David L. Masters." Not very professional or secure. There are basically two ways to use digital signatures with Acrobat: (1) secure digital signatures using Acrobat self-sign security or third-party digital signature applications, or (2) use an Acrobat custom stamp consisting of an image of your signature (See Sections 7.11.3 and 7.11.4). The signature image used for a custom stamp can be used (displayed) in Acrobat self-sign secure digital signatures.

A digital signature, like a conventional handwritten signature, identifies the person signing a document. Unlike traditional signatures on paper, however, a true digital signature (as opposed to simple signature stamps) stores information "behind the scenes" about the person signing a document.

As a lawyer you may have concerns about the security of digital signatures. True digital signatures can be more secure than traditional handwritten signatures. After all, anyone can pick up a pen and sign your name to a document. Worse still, anyone can pick up your rubber stamp and apply your signature to a document. In other words, if someone wants to put your signature on a document, paper or electronic, they can probably do it. If you are among the truly paranoid, then you will want to use a secure third-party digital signature application or plug-in.

§ 8.1 Using Acrobat Digital Signatures

An Acrobat digital signature can appear as a logo or other image, or as text explaining the purpose of the signing. A digital signature can be either visible or invisible (Figure 8.1).

Figure 8.1

A visible signature appears in both the document and the Signatures panel. To view the Signatures panel click on the **Signatures** icon. An invisible signature appears only in the Signatures panel (Figure 8.2).

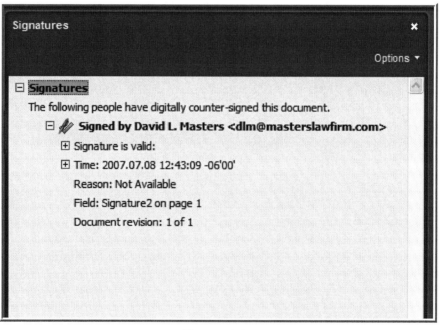

Figure 8.2

Before you can sign a document using an Acrobat digital signature, you must create or select a digital ID, which contains the signature information that you can share with other users in a certificate. A certificate confirms your digital ID and contains information used to protect data. You can create more than one digital ID if you sign documents in different roles or with different certification methods. When a digital signature is applied, a unique fingerprint with encrypted numbers is embedded in the document. The recipient needs the signer's certificate to validate that the digital signature and certificate match the signer's digital ID. Certificates can be sent via electronic mail to recipients who require the ability to validate signatures. Secure digital signatures have one major drawback that might persuade you to use a less secure method such as a simple signature stamp. If you sign and send many documents to people who don't have your certificate, the signature will probably appear on their computer screen or the printed page with a question mark or message indicating that the signature has not been verified or validated. Compare Figure 8.3 (validated signature) to Figure 8.4 (unvalidated signature). Figure 8.3, shows the validated signature on the computer right after the document was signed. Figure 8.4 shows the signature as it appears when the document was opened on another computer. The question mark may raise questions about the validity of the signature.

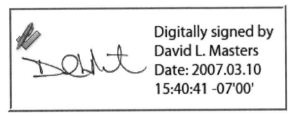

Digitally signed by
David L. Masters
Date: 2007.03.10
15:40:41 -07'00'

Figure 8.3

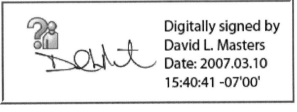

Digitally signed by
David L. Masters
Date: 2007.03.10
15:40:41 -07'00'

Figure 8.4

If you routinely digitally sign correspondence sent to clients or opposing counsel, or digitally sign pleadings filed with the courts, you can expect that some recipients of your documents may question the validity of the signature or even reject the document. In contrast, if you use a custom stamp that applies a facsimile of your signature to documents, it will probably go unquestioned. Distributing certificates to validate your digital signature and explaining to the recipients how to save and use the certificate may be all it takes to convince you that a signature stamp is probably no more insecure than your pen-and-ink signature on paper.

§ 8.1.1 Creating a Secure Digital Signature

To create a digital signature go to the **Preferences** dialog box (Figure 8.5).

Menu (Create Digital Signature): **Edit > Preferences** [select **Security** in the left-hand panel]

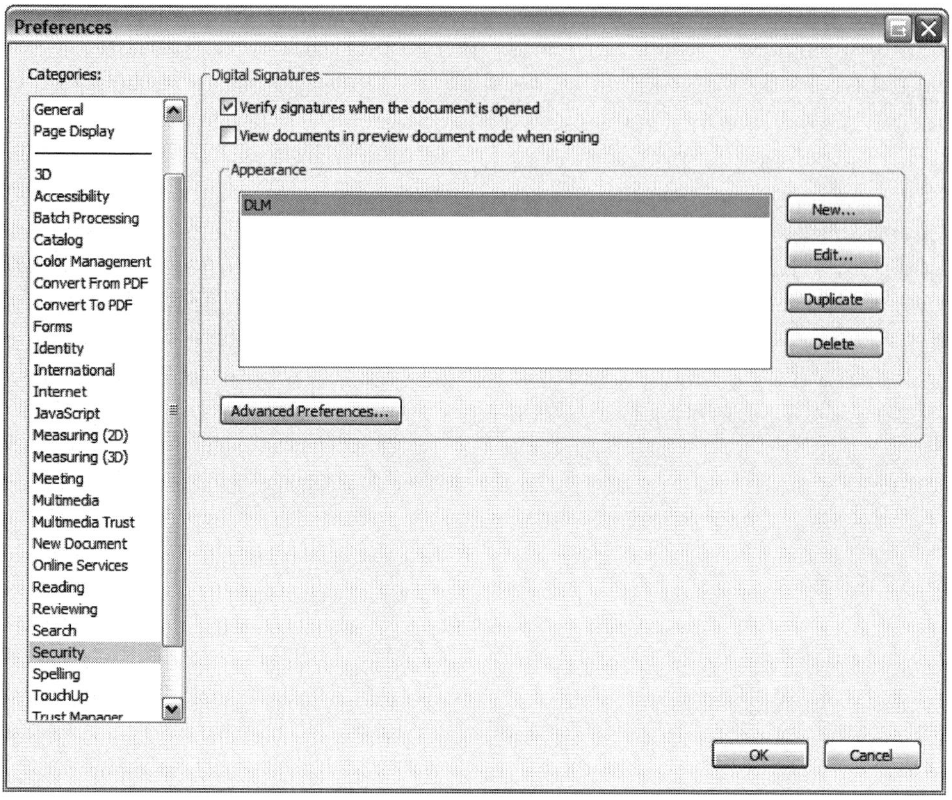

Figure 8.5

Keystroke (Create Digital Signature): **Ctrl+K** [select **Security** in the left-hand panel]

Keystroke (Create Digital Signature): **Alt+E-N** [select **Security** in the left-hand panel]

If you have not previously created a digital signature the **Appearance** window will be blank. Click the **New** button and the **Configure Signature Appearance** dialog box appears (Figure 8.6). Here, you supply a name for the digital signature that you are creating (your initials works well). The **Configure Graphic** section allows you to select a graphic file to be displayed next to the text (sample text appears in the Preview window above the Configure Graphic section). Note that the graphic image of your signature must be a PDF. You can use the image file of your signature created for a custom stamp, or follow the instructions in Chapter 7 on how to scan and save your signature as an image file. Convert the TIFF file of your signature to PDF. Now you can select the PDF file of your signature image to be displayed with your digital signature. The **Configure Signature Appearance** box, in the **Configure Text** section, allows you to select what text items will appear as part of your digital signature.

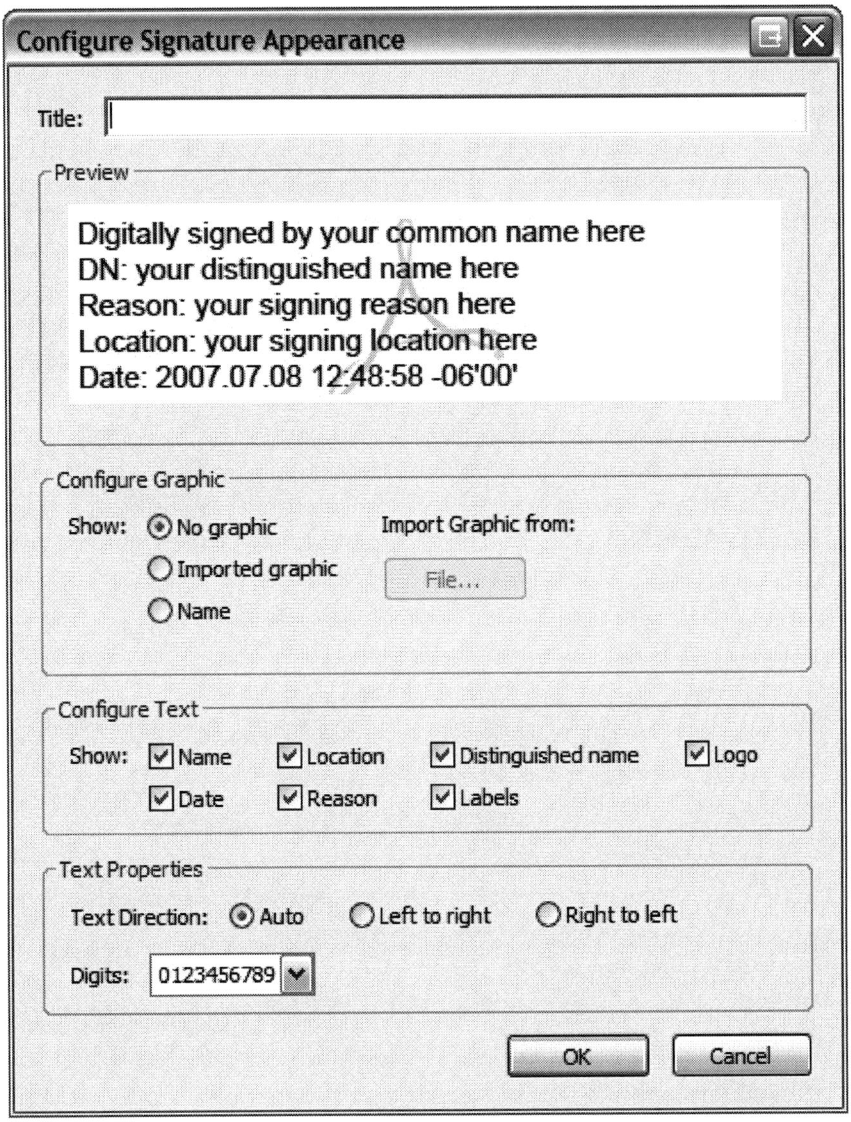

Configure Signature Appearance

Title: |

Preview

Digitally signed by your common name here
DN: your distinguished name here
Reason: your signing reason here
Location: your signing location here
Date: 2007.07.08 12:48:58 -06'00'

Configure Graphic

Show: ⦿ No graphic   Import Graphic from:
      ○ Imported graphic   File...
      ○ Name

Configure Text

Show: ☑ Name   ☑ Location   ☑ Distinguished name   ☑ Logo
      ☑ Date   ☑ Reason   ☑ Labels

Text Properties

Text Direction: ⦿ Auto   ○ Left to right   ○ Right to left

Digits: 0123456789 ▾

OK   Cancel

Figure 8.6

When you have made all your selections, click the **OK** button and return to the **Digital Signatures** dialog box. You can left-click on a signature then click the **Edit** button to make changes.

§ 8.1.2 Signing a Document with a Digital Signature

To apply your digital signature to a PDF file, click the **Sign** button on the **Tasks** toolbar and select **Place Signature.** The pointer turns into a cross, left-click, drag and draw a rectangle of the size and at the location where you want your signature to appear. The **Sign Document** dialog box appears (Figure 8.7). Supply the password and choose the desired appearance from the drop-down list

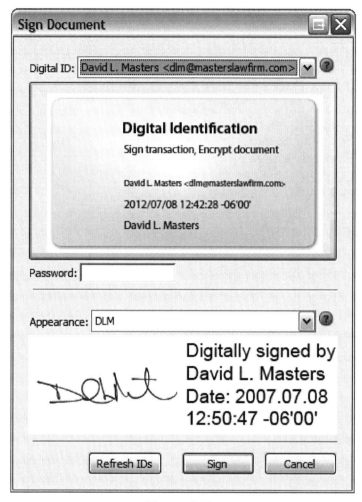

Figure 8.7

(the last used appearance will be selected as the default). Click the **Sign** button and presto, you have applied a secure digital signature.

Adding a signature does not affect the validity of existing signatures in the document. However, if you make changes to the saved PDF file, you may invalidate the signature. When you sign a document, your signature and the related information can be stored in a signature field embedded on the page. A signature field is an Acrobat form field. You can add a signature field to a page as you sign, or you can use the **Signature** tool to create an empty signature field that can be signed later. Sign documents only after making final changes. If changes are made to a PDF file after it has been signed, the signature may still be valid, but a caution triangle appears in the signature field and in the signature tab, indicating that changes were made after the signature was added.

§ 8.2 Validating Someone Else's Signature

When you receive a PDF file signed by another person, you can validate the signature to ensure that the document was indeed signed by that person and hasn't changed after it was signed. In order to validate someone's self-signed digital signature, you must have their certificate. You will obtain their certificate by electronic mail; save the certificate file in a location where you can find it.

Acrobat has simplified the process of obtaining a trusted certificate from someone else. To begin the process of obtaining another person's trusted certificate, open the **Manage Trusted Identities** dialog box (Figure 8.8).

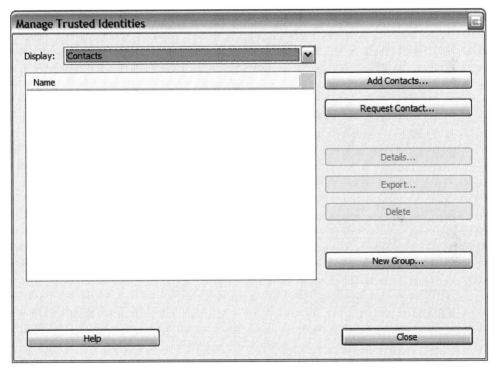

Figure 8.8

Menu (Manage Trusted Identities): **Advanced > Trusted Identities**
Keystroke (Manage Trusted Identities): **Alt+A-I**
Click on the **Request Contact** button and the **Email a Request** dialog box opens (Figure 8.9).

Fill in or confirm your name, e-mail address, and contact information, then decide whether you want to send your certificate to this person as part of your request for their certificate (check or uncheck the **Include my Certificates** box accordingly).

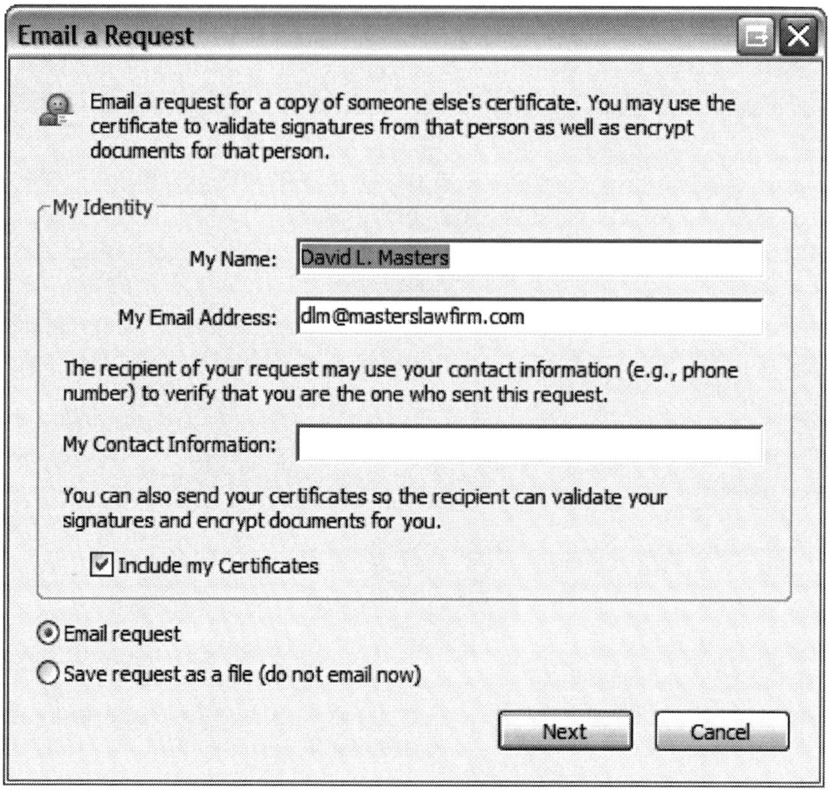

Figure 8.9

Click **Next** and select your digital ID to send to the other person (Figure 8.10). Click **Select**, then fill in the address of the person to send the e-mail to (the person who you are requesting a trusted certificate from (Figure 8.11).

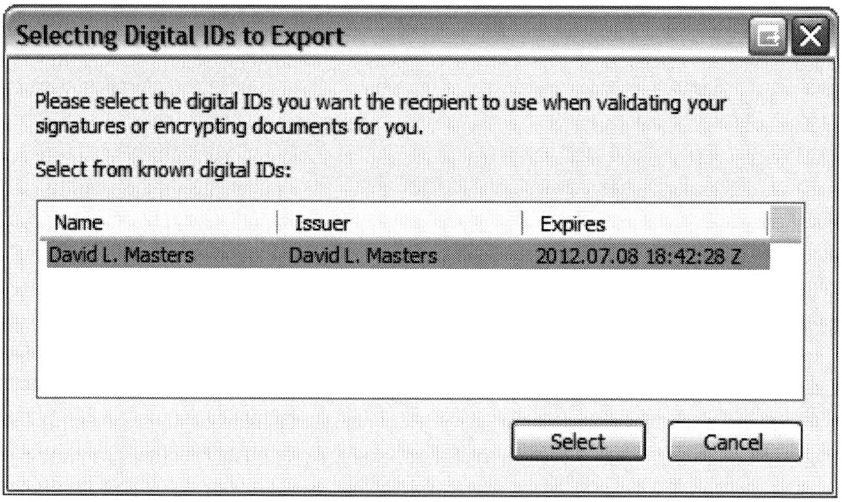

Figure 8.10

Figure 8.11

Acrobat has composed a message requesting the other person's certificate; clicking on the **Email** button transfers the message to your e-mail client software.

§ 8.2.1 Storing Someone Else's Certificate

To store someone else's self-signed digital signature certificate after you have received it via electronic mail:

Menu (Storing Someone Else's Signature Certificate): **Advanced > Manage Trusted Identities**

Keystroke (Storing Someone Else's Signature Certificate): **Alt+A-I**

The **Manage Trusted Identities** dialog box appears (Figure 8.12). Click on **Add Contacts**. Click the **Browse** button and navigate to the folder where you store other people's digital signature certificates. Double-click on the file to add it to your trusted contacts list. The certificate needs to be stored and added to the contacts list only one time; after it has been added, the other person's signature can be quickly validated.

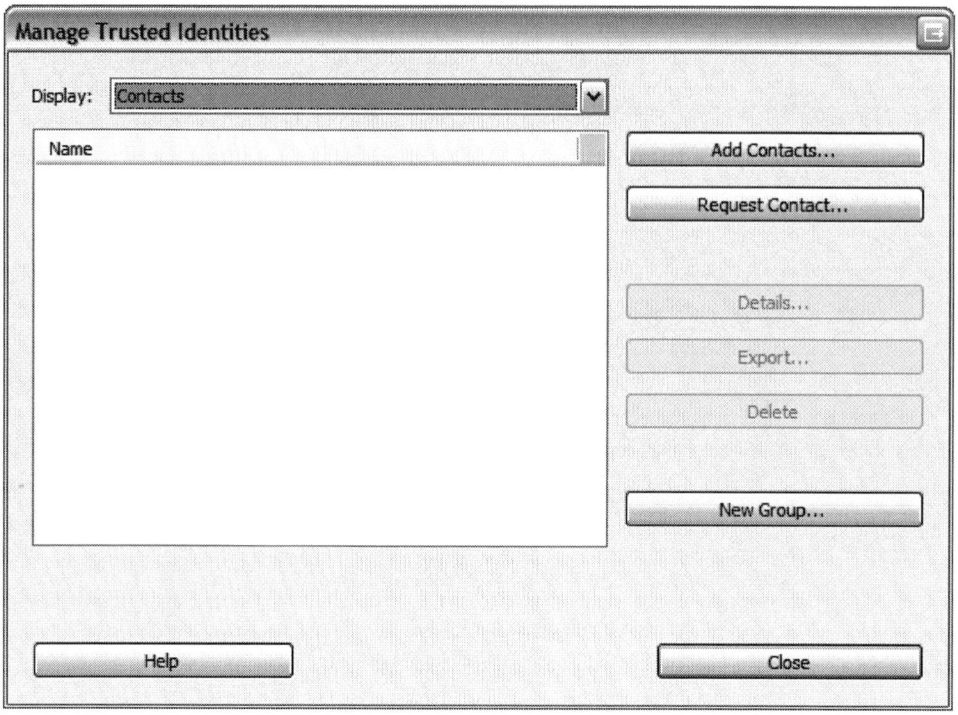

Figure 8.12

§ 8.2.2 Validating the Signature

To validate someone else's signature for whom you have stored a digital signature certificate:

Menu (Validating Someone Else's Signature): **Advanced > Sign & Certify > Validate All Signatures**

Or,

Click the **Sign** button on the toolbar and select **Validate All Signatures**

Extracting Content from PDF Files

9

The time will come when you want to extract the content from a PDF file to use in another application. If it happens to be an image-on-text PDF file, then you're part way there. It may be a set of discovery requests, a contract, or some other document that you have scanned, and now you want to use the text in your own work product. When that day comes, there are several options available. Be forewarned, the results may not be particularly pretty.

Of course text can only be extracted from image-on-text files; image-only files contain no text to extract. If the PDF file that you want to extract text from is an image-only file, it needs to be converted to an image-on-text file using an optical character recognition (OCR) application. If you use a third-party OCR application, you may be able to generate a text file directly from the PDF file; otherwise the process is to first create an image-on-text PDF file, then extract the text. The first two sections of this chapter discuss methods for extracting text from image-on-text PDF files. The last section covers extracting images. In image-only PDF files the image may look like text, but can only be extracted as a graphic image.

§ 9.1 Using Copy to Extract Text

To extract short sections of text, use the **Edit-Copy** function:

1. Select the **Select** tool (the Select tool is located on the **Select & Zoom** toolbar) (Figure 9.1).
2. Click and drag to select text.
3. **Ctrl+C** or **Edit > Copy** to copy.

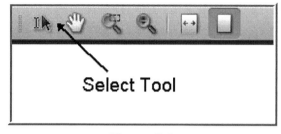

Select Tool

Figure 9.1

Switch to the application where you want to use the selected text and use the Windows paste function (**Ctrl+V** or **Edit > Paste**). When the Single Page layout is selected (**View > Page Display > Single Page**, or by clicking on the **Single Page** icon on the **Status Bar**), only the text on the current page can be selected. When the Continuous Page layout is selected (**View > Page Display > Single Page Continuous** or by clicking on the **Continuous Page** icon on the **Status Bar**), text can be selected over multiple pages.

Regardless of which method you use to select the text to be copied, be ready to do some editing after you paste it into the other application. This is especially true if the image-on-text PDF file was created by using optical character recognition. You may want to try using Paste Special in the destination application to see if that produces better results.

Note: The **Select** tool (on the **Select & Zoom** toolbar) looks just like the **Select Object** tool located on the **Advanced Editing** toolbar. The **Select Object** tool will not select text in image-on-text files that were created by printing to PDF, so if you're having problems make sure you have picked the right tool. The **Select Object** tool will select text in image-on-text files that were created by OCR of an image-only PDF file.

Tip: Objects are things like links, certain images, vector graphics, and other Adobe elements that lawyers will rarely, if ever, come across. Accordingly, if you display the **Advanced Editing** toolbar (and you should to have easy access to the **Crop** tool and **Link** tool), deselect (uncheck) the **Select Object** tool so that it is not displayed.

§ 9.2 Extracting Text Using Save As

To extract large amounts of text, such as the text from an entire document, such as a set of interrogatories, use the **Save As** function to save the file to a text format such as RTF (Rich Text Format—"rich" because it allows for some text formatting such as bold, underline, and italics). To save an image-on-text PDF file as an editable text file:

Menu (Save As): File > **Save As**
Keystroke (Save As): **Alt+F-A** or **Ctrl+Shift+S**

When the **Save As** dialog box appears (Figure 9.2), name the file, choose an appropriate location, and then select an editable text format from the **Save as type** drop-down menu (Rich Text Format works well).

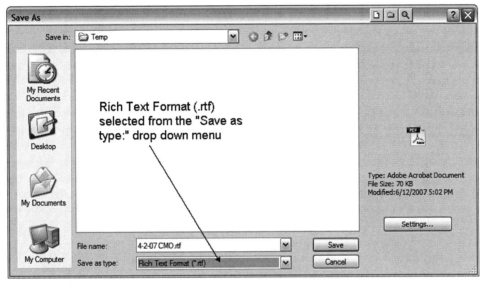

Figure 9.2

If **Save As Rich Text Format** produces intolerable formatting problems, select **Text (Plain) (*.txt)** (Figure 9.3). Saving to plain text format removes all formatting, but sometimes it's easier to add the desired structure than it is to remove unwanted formatting.

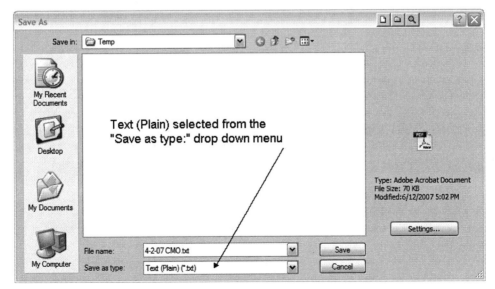

Figure 9.3

If you use Microsoft Word you can **Save As** directly to that format. Again, formatting might be an issue.

Tip: Try various methods for extracting text until you obtain the best result. It only takes a few minutes to Save As to RTF, .TXT or Microsoft Word format. If you use WordPerfect X3, try opening the image-on-text PDF file in that application.

§ 9.3 Extracting Text with WordPerfect X3

WordPerfect X3 allows users to open image-on-text PDF files directly into WordPerfect. In other words, the extract text process happens in WordPerfect and not in Acrobat. Depending on the complexity of the text structure (formatting, outlining, font characteristics, etc.) the results can be impressive or frustrating. The more complex the text structure the poorer the results.

§ 9.4 Extracting Graphic Images

Extracting graphics from PDF files might be more useful than you think. You may want to select the graphic image of what looks like a text document if it is important that an exact image of the text be reproduced in another application. For example, you may want to copy the portion of a letter that includes the closing paragraph and author's signature. Then again, there may be no text at all to be captured, such as when you want to paste a portion of a handwritten note into another application (Figure 9.4). Extracting images is not just

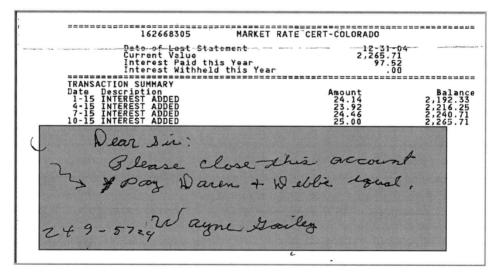

Figure 9.4

about "words." If you have a PDF file that is a picture, for example a JPEG or TIFF file that was converted (printed) to PDF, you may want to strip the PDF envelope and retain the picture format that can be opened in an image editing application (e.g., Adobe Photoshop).

Note: The "image" of the text in an image-on-text file that was created by printing a file to PDF cannot be selected. The "image" of text in an image-on-text file that was created by OCR can be selected, copied, and pasted.

Note: If you have applied Bates numbers using the StampPDF plug-in, or the PDF file has other stamped text information (such as the header applied by the federal court electronic filing system) you cannot select images—period. This is another reason to always keep a clean set of documents in addition to a numbered set.

Tip: If you run into the problem of not being able to select an image because of text that has been added, such as Bates numbers, extract the page that you want to copy the image from. Then crop the page to cut off the stamped text. Now you can select the image.

§ 9.4.1 Using Copy to Extract Images

To select and copy an image:

1. Select the **Select** tool (Figure 9.5).
2. Click and drag to draw a box around the desired image or portion of an image.
3. Use **Ctrl+C** to copy or **Edit > Copy**.

Select Tool

Figure 9.5

Switch to the application where you want to use the selected image and use the Windows paste function (**Ctrl+V** or **Edit > Paste**). The selected portion of the PDF file is pasted into the other application (this assumes that the other application can handle inserting and manipulating graphics). If you are selecting images from within PDF files remember that the **Select** tool is configured to select text before images, but switches automatically to select graphics when the area selected contains no text. Also, remember that the **Select** tool (on the **Select & Zoom** toolbar) looks just like the **Select Object** tool located on the **Advanced Editing** toolbar. The **Select Object** tool will not select an area of an image-only PDF file, so if you're having problems make sure you have picked the right tool.

§ 9.4.2 Using Save As to Extract Images

The **Save As** function may be used to convert an image-only PDF file to another graphic format (such as TIFF or JPEG).

To save a PDF file in another graphic format:

Menu (Save As): **File > Save As**
Keystroke (Save As): **Alt+F-A** or **Ctrl+Shift+S**

When the **Save As** dialog box appears, name the file, choose an appropriate location, and then select a format from the **Save As Type** drop-down menu (TIFF and JPEG work well) (Figure 9.6). Acrobat uses the original file name and appends a description of each extracted page using the following format: _Page_0X, where X represents the page number (Figure 9.7).

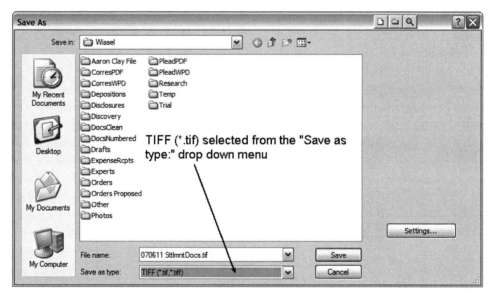

Figure 9.6

020703 Contract_Page_1.tif	.tif	29,568
020703 Contract_Page_2.tif	.tif	39,850
020703 Contract_Page_3.tif	.tif	36,978

Figure 9.7

§ 9.4.3 Using Export to Extract Images

With Acrobat, all images in a PDF file can be exported in a single operation. This may be useful when a PDF file contains several high-quality graphic images. To extract all images from a PDF file:

Menu (Export Images): **Advanced > Document Processing > Export all Images**

Keystroke (Export Images): **Alt+A-D-X**

When the **Export All Images** dialog box appears, navigate to an appropriate location; Acrobat saves each image with a new name in this location. Acrobat uses the original file name and appends a description of each image extracted using the following format: _Page_0X_Image_000Y where X represents the page number and Y represents the sequential number of each image from a particular page. You can use **Export All Images** to break a multipage image-only PDF file into as many separate image files as there are pages in the document. You can then convert all those image files back to PDF so that you end up with a separate PDF file for each page. If you're wondering why you would ever want to do this, here's one possible scenario. You have a long document that you want to use as an exhibit at trial. However, you expect that the judge or opposing counsel will only allow the use of about half the pages. Rather than extracting the pages that might be allowed, it may be easier to extract all pages as images, and then convert them back to individual PDF files.

Search, Find, and Indexing 10

Now here's something you can't do with paper documents. Okay, sure, you can read through a document looking for particular word or words, or even read through several documents looking for words or phrases, but you can't do it as fast as your computer can. Searching and indexing are potent features exclusive to digital documents. PDF files, being digital documents, allow for searching and indexing. Image-on-text PDFs are digital documents that can be searched and indexed. As you might expect, image-only PDF files cannot be searched or indexed; however, comments added to image-only PDF files can be searched and are included in catalog indexes. Searching, finding, and indexing are different functions described in this chapter, but first we need to make sure that we have text that can be found, searched, and indexed.

Lawyers and paralegals often think that because they have a collection of digital documents, those documents can now be searched. Not so fast; remember, not all PDF files are created equal. Image-only PDF files contain no text; without text there is nothing to search. On the other hand, image-on-text PDF files contain text behind an exact image of the original document. Image-on-text files can be indexed and searched.

The quality of the text behind the image in image-on-text PDF files depends on several factors. With image-on-text PDF files created by scanning and OCR, the quality of the underlying text file depends on the quality of the original scanned document. Large, clean, easily recognizable fonts produce nearly 100 percent accuracy. Small or faint text produces less-accurate results.

Hand writing, no matter how neat, cannot be recognized. Documents printed to PDF have exact text behind the image. The results produced can be substantially different; try the experiment in section 10.2 below. This may seem like a lot of work (it probably takes at least ten minutes), but you will likely learn a lasting and important lesson about OCR.

§ 10.1 Creating Image-on-Text Files

To convert scanned pages (image-only files) to ones with searchable and indexable text (image-on-text files), open an image-only PDF file. Use the **Recognize Text Using OCR** feature to generate a text layer that essentially converts an image-only PDF file to an image-on-text file.

Menu (OCR): **Document > OCR Text Recognition > Recognize Text Using OCR**
Keystroke (OCR): **Alt+D-C-R**

The **Recognize Text** dialog box opens (Figure 10.1). Specify the pages to be captured (all, current, or a range of pages), then click **OK** to start the

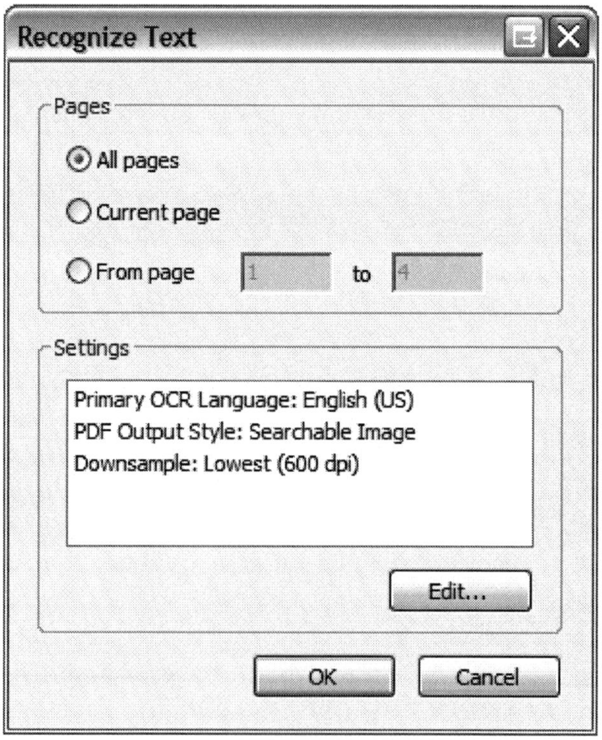

Figure 10.1

process. Note: if you use StampPDF or IntelliPDF BATES Pro to apply Bates numbers to image-only PDF files, you may not be able to use Acrobat to OCR the content (some third-party OCR applications, such as OmniPagePro, will OCR stamped image-only PDF files). Adobe has attempted to resolve this issue by telling the OCR engine to ignore text printed within a certain distance of the edge of the page.

§ 10.2 OCR Quality Experiment

1. Open a document in a word processing application.
2. Set the font to a **sans serif type** (Arial, Universal, and so on), and make it at least **12 points in size**.
3. Format the text for **double spacing**.
4. **Print** a page or two of this document.

Once you have printed a page or two of this document, scan it to PDF. While you're at it, e-mail it to a colleague and have them print it and fax it back to you. Now take the faxed copy and scan it to PDF (give each file a unique name such as Test1 and Test2). For the next step in the experiment, use the **Capture Pages** feature in Acrobat or an OCR application that can create image-on-text PDF files. After the two test files have been saved, run each through an OCR application (the following description assumes you do this within Acrobat using the **Capture Pages** function).

Menu (OCR): **Document > OCR Text Recognition > Recognize Text Using OCR**
Keystroke (OCR): **Alt+D-C-R**

When the OCR process completes, save and close each file. Now, open the PDF test file that you created by scanning a pristine original, select all of the text on the page (**Ctrl+A**), copy it (**Ctrl+C**), switch to a word processing application (**Alt+Tab**) and paste the text into a new document (**Ctrl+V**). Look at the result for typographical errors that were not present in the original. Now open the PDF test file that was received as a fax, select all of the text on the page (**Ctrl+A**), copy it (**Ctrl+C**), switch to a word processing application (**Alt+Tab**) and paste the text into a new document (**Ctrl+V**). Did you have more typographical errors in the second (scanned) test file? How did it compare to the scanned pristine original? Remember this when you OCR scanned documents with the idea that this will produce a perfect text file that can be searched.

In addition to the quality of OCR results, keep in mind that sometimes the most important information on a document may not be printed text that can be "recognized." For example, handwritten notes on a bank statement might be what you need to focus on, rather than the printed text that shows the date, account number and balance (Figure 10.2).

```
================================================================
          162668305          MARKET RATE CERT-COLORADO
          Date of Last Statement                    12-31-04
          Current Value                            2,265.71
          Interest Paid this Year                     97.52
          Interest Withheld this Year                   .00
================================================================
TRANSACTION SUMMARY
Date   Description                              Amount
 1-15  INTEREST ADDED                            24.14
 4-15  INTEREST ADDED                            23.92
 7-15  INTEREST ADDED                            24.46
10-15  INTEREST ADDED                            25.00
```

Dear Sir:

Please close this account

↳ # Pay Daren + Webbie equal,

Figure 10.2

§ 10.3 Searching Image-on-Text PDF Files

Image-on-text PDF files can be searched for words or phrases. Use the **Search PDF** feature to find a word, series of words, or part of a word in the active PDF file or in all PDF files in a particular folder. To search for words in a document, open an image-on-text PDF file, click the **Search** tool on the **File** toolbar (Figure 10.3), or use one of the following commands:

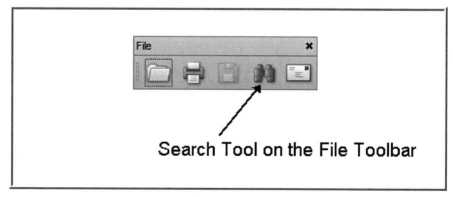

Figure 10.3

Menu (Search): **Edit > Search**
Keystroke (Search): **Alt+E-S**
Keystroke (Search): **Ctrl+Shift+F**

The **Search** window will open (Figure 10.4). Type the word, words, or part of a word that you want to look for in the space provided in the search window and click **Search**. The results appear in page order, showing a few words of the context in which the search term appears (Figure 10.5). Click an item from the list to jump to that search result; continue clicking items in the results list, or use the keyboard command **Ctrl+G** to go to the next occurrence in the document.

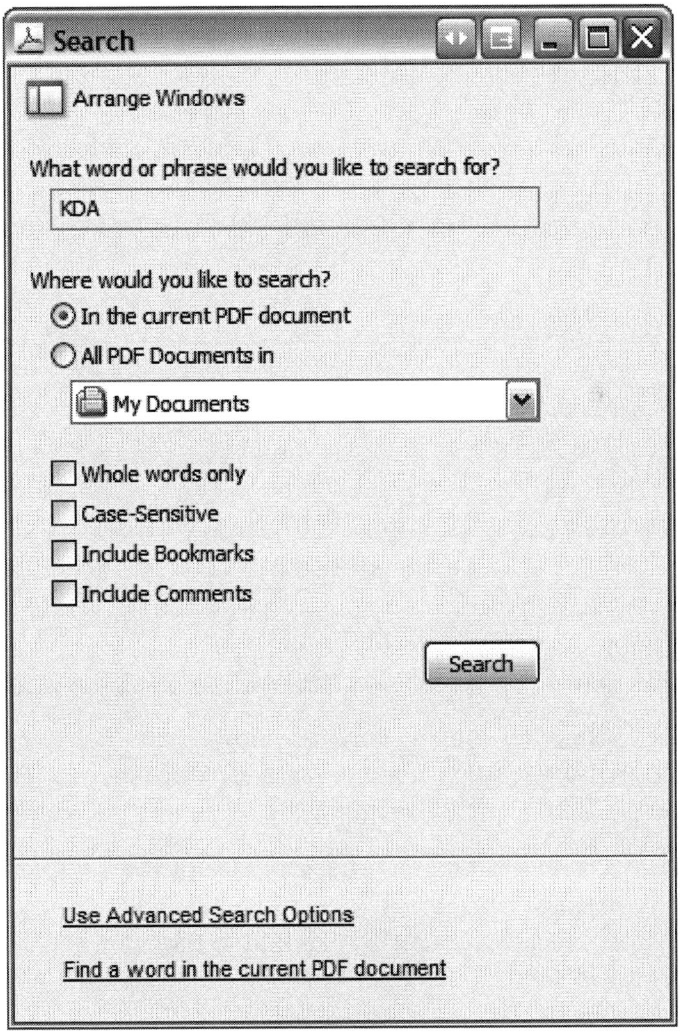

Figure 10.4

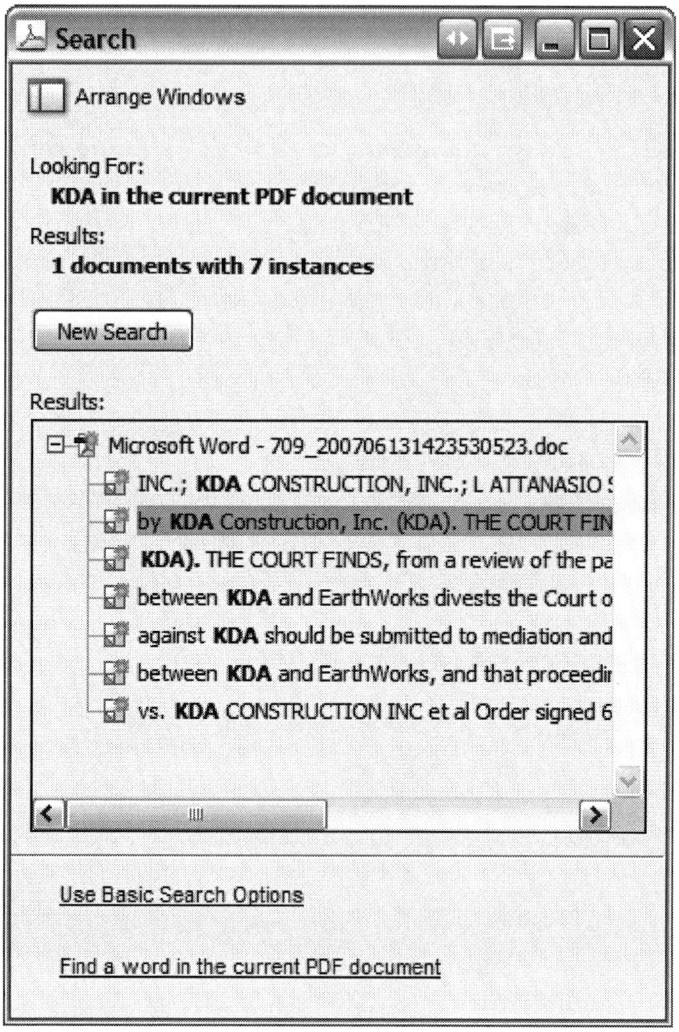

Figure 10.5

§ 10.4 Refining Searches

Searches can be refined by looking for whole words only, making search terms case-sensitive, or by including bookmarks and comments in the text to be searched. You can select any of the following to refine your search:

- *Whole Words Only* finds only occurrences of the complete word you enter in the text box. For example, if you search for the word "legal," the words "illegal" and "legally" are not found.
- *Case-Sensitive* finds only occurrences of the words that are in the case that you typed.
- *Include Bookmarks* searches the text in the Bookmarks pane as well as the text in the document. Occurrences in the Bookmarks pane appear

at the top of the list and are identified with a different symbol than occurrences in the document

◆ *Include Comments* searches the text in the comments and in the document text. Instances in the comments text are listed in the search results with a comment icon, the search word, and a word or two of context, and so on. The order in which the occurrences appear is related to their location on the document pages.

§ 10.5 Find

Acrobat 8 includes the simple "find" function found in most Windows applications (it went missing in Acrobat 6.0). When you just want to browse through a document quickly looking for a single word, or, for that matter, any character or string of characters (which might be more than one word), you issue the command **Ctrl+F**. The **Find** function has its own toolbar; put it in your toolbar collection for ready use (Figure 10.6).

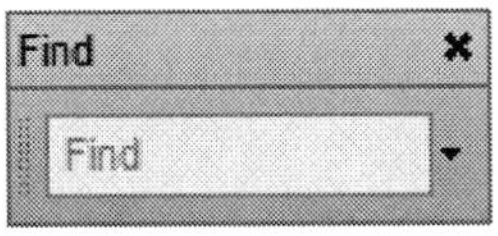

Figure 10.6

Menu (Find): **Edit > Find**
Keystroke (Find): **Alt+E-F**
Keystroke (Find): **Ctrl+F**

When the command has been issued the **Find** toolbar appears (unless you already have it displayed in your collection) where you type the word or characters to be found (Figure 10.7). If the **Find** toolbar is in your collection, then pressing **Ctrl+F** moves the cursor to the window where you enter the

Type what you want
to "Find" here.

Figure 10.7

word or characters that you want to find. Pressing the **Enter** key finds the first occurrence; continue to press the **Enter** key to browse through the document to find each occurrence of the word or characters entered in the window on the **Find** toolbar. If you prefer, you can use the arrows on the **Find** toolbar to find the next or previous occurrence (Figure 10.8).

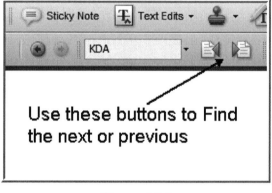

Figure 10.8

The **Find** tool has a drop down menu that allow you to refine this simple search tool (Figure 10.9). You can restrict the Find criteria to whole words or make it case sensitive. You can choose to include bookmarks and comments for Find to look for the specified text.

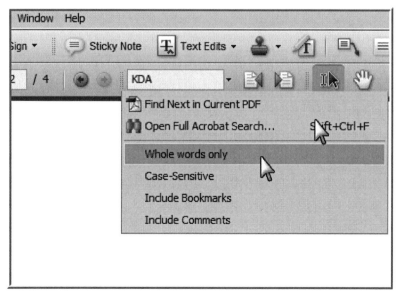

Figure 10.9

§ 10.6 Indexing Using Catalog

In Acrobat Professional, you can use the **Catalog** feature to create a full-text index of PDF files or document collections (**Catalog** is not available in Acrobat Standard). This can be helpful if large PDF collections of discovery documents, pleadings or contracts need to be searched repeatedly. Note that information contained in comments and document descriptions related to image-only PDF files are included in the index and found using the **Search** function. To create an index:

Menu (Create an Index): **Advanced > Document Processing > Full Text Index with Catalog**

The **Catalog** dialog box appears (Figure 10.10). Click the **New Index** button and the **New Index Definition** dialog box appears (Figure 10.11). Type a name for the index, select the folders (directories) that contain the PDF files to be included in the index (you can also select subdirectories to be excluded), and click **Build**.

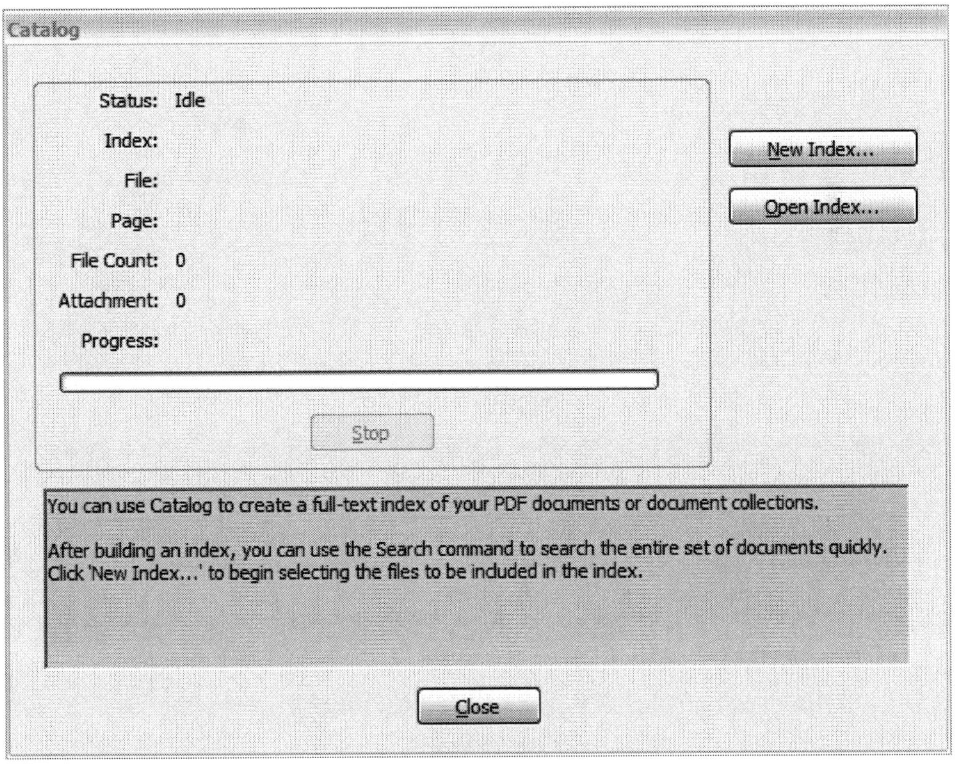

Figure 10.10

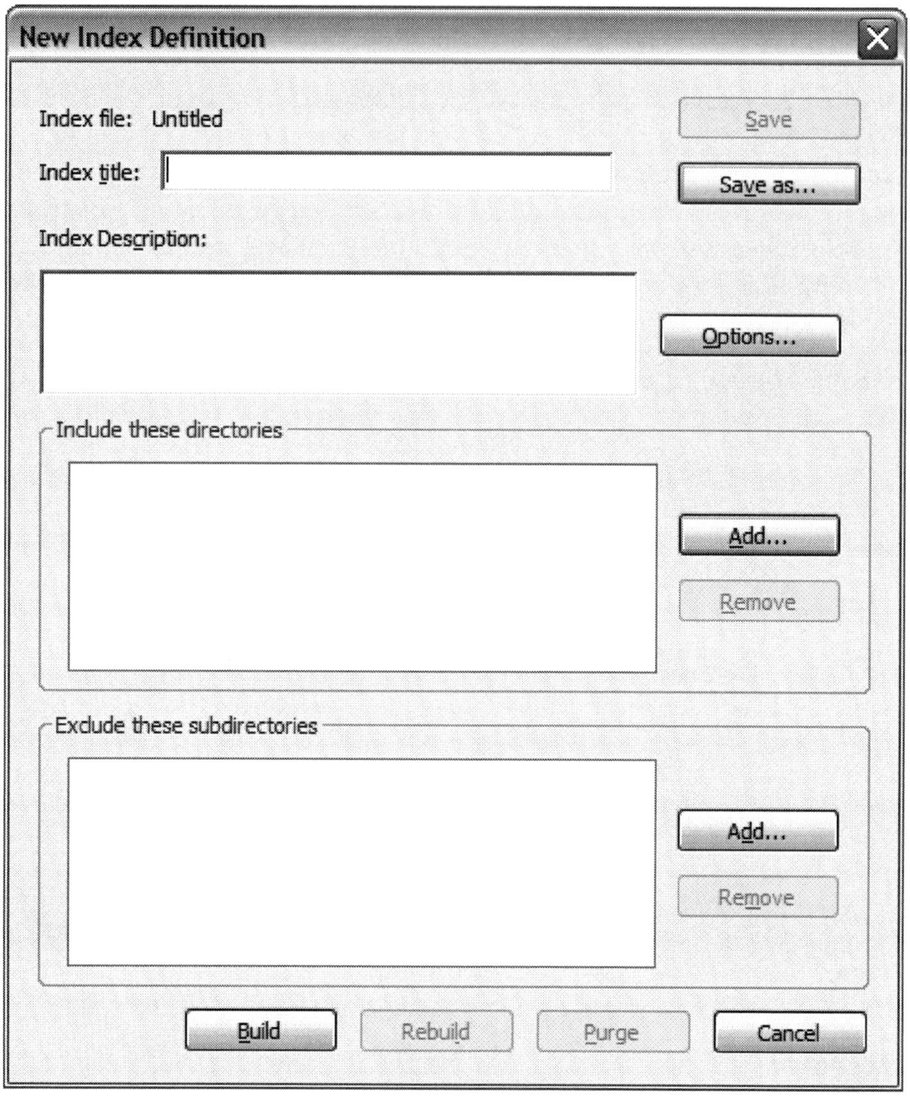

Figure 10.11

When you build a new index, the results are a new .pdx file and a new folder (named **Index**) that contains one or more .idx files. The .pdx file, which is small, makes the information in the .idx files available to the search function. The .idx files contain the index entries that a user finds in the index, so their file sizes—individually or collectively—can be large. All of these files must be available to users who want to search the index. In other words, if you catalog (index) a large collection of PDF files (documents) and put them on CD-ROM, be sure to include the .pdx file and index folder on the disk.

If you use Catalog to index large collections of documents that will be added to from time to time and accessed by multiple users, you should explore the advanced features of this function. For example, you can schedule indexes to automatically update or rebuild. For more information on using Catalog, see the Complete Acrobat Help online manual.

Menu (Help): **Help > Complete Acrobat Help**
Keystroke (Help): **Alt+H-H**

The help manual opens as a separate document. Select **Searching and Indexing** from the list of contents then choose **Creating PDF Indexes**.

PDF File Security **11**

Many legal professionals view paper documents as inherently more trustworthy than digital documents. Correspondence, contracts, and pleadings often bear original signatures, but just as often are only photocopies. Every day, however, lawyers distribute electronic versions of documents and ask others to accept and act upon them with the same confidence that they have in paper. Relying on electronic documents instead of paper can speed up processes, improve the distribution of information, and lower costs for lawyers, clients, and courts. Unfortunately, electronic documents—like their paper counterparts—can be tools for fraud, making some people wary of trusting and using electronic documents. Just as methods and systems developed over time for justifying trust in paper documents, so to have processes evolved to give credence to electronic documents. One method for improving the security, and thereby trustworthiness, of electronic documents comes from using PDF files.

Acrobat provides a level of security for PDF files not available for paper or other electronic documents created and shared in their original word processing format. If you worry about the metadata that accompanies word processing files that you share with clients and opposing counsel, Acrobat provides relief. Printing a word processing document to PDF removes all metadata, at least for now. As software developers (Adobe and Microsoft included) work to integrate products, it could be that metadata will be included in files converted from one format to another.

But there is more to document security than just metadata. For example, PDF files can be set to prevent viewers from selecting text or printing. This can be useful when sending documents to clients for review if you are concerned about sharing your work product before you have been paid. If you're really paranoid, you can set security so that PDF files can only be opened by persons with trusted certificates. Both basic security and certificate security use 128-bit encryption (strong stuff). For password protection, Acrobat supports 128-bit RC4 and 128-bit AES (Advanced Encryption Standard) security methods. You choose the method to use when securing documents. For digital signatures and document encryption, Acrobat supports public-key cryptography. Public-key cryptography uses two keys: a public key, stored in a certificate that can be shared with other users, and a private key, called a Digital ID, which you do not share with others. The public key certificate works to encrypt (scramble) documents or verify digital signatures, and the Digital ID functions to decrypt (unscramble) encrypted documents or to create digital signatures.

You can apply Acrobat encryption and permissions to PDF files. The ease and convenience of assigning security parameters to PDF files keeps information private and confidential. Protected PDF files can be viewed using free Adobe Reader software. Adobe Reader users can also validate digital signatures and verify document certification.

Perhaps the easiest way to use Acrobat's security features is to specify "permissions" that establish what a user can do with a document. If you send discovery documents to opposing counsel and do not want him or her to be able to remove or insert pages, then permissions protection fits the bill. If you send a prospective client sample or draft documents and don't want them to be able to print them or copy the content (before you receive the retainer), then a permissions password will do the trick.

You can limit access to PDF files by setting passwords and by restricting certain features, such as printing and editing. Acrobat can secure PDF files with two kinds of passwords: a **document open password** and a **permissions password**. When you set a document open password, anyone who tries to open the PDF file must supply the password you specified. A permissions password limits what can be done with a PDF file (print, copy, change, etc.) without the password. If you apply a permissions password, say to restrict printing and editing, you can also apply a document open password to enhance security.

You can create security policies that standardize and simplify the process of applying permissions passwords to PDF files. A permissions password security policy can include any combination of the following restrictions:

- ◆ Printing allowed (none, high resolution, low resolution—choose none to prohibit printing).
- ◆ Changes allowed (none; inserting, deleting and rotating pages; filling in form fields and signing existing signature fields; commenting, filling

in form fields and signing existing signature fields; any except extracting pages—choose none to prohibit any of the foregoing changes).

◆ Enable copying of text, images, and other contents.

Keep in mind that the permissions password also controls basic PDF file security. Accordingly, when you set a permissions password, the people who have the permissions password can change the security settings. If the PDF file has both types of passwords (document open password and permissions password), it can be opened with only the open password, and users can set or change the restricted features only with the permissions password. If the PDF file has a permissions password, and a user opens the file using the document open password, the password prompt appears if the user tries to change security settings.

§ 11.1 Applying Document Open Security Through Document Properties

Document open security (users must supply password to open the file) can be applied from the **Security** tab in the **Document Properties** window (Figure 11.1). To open the **Document Properties** window:

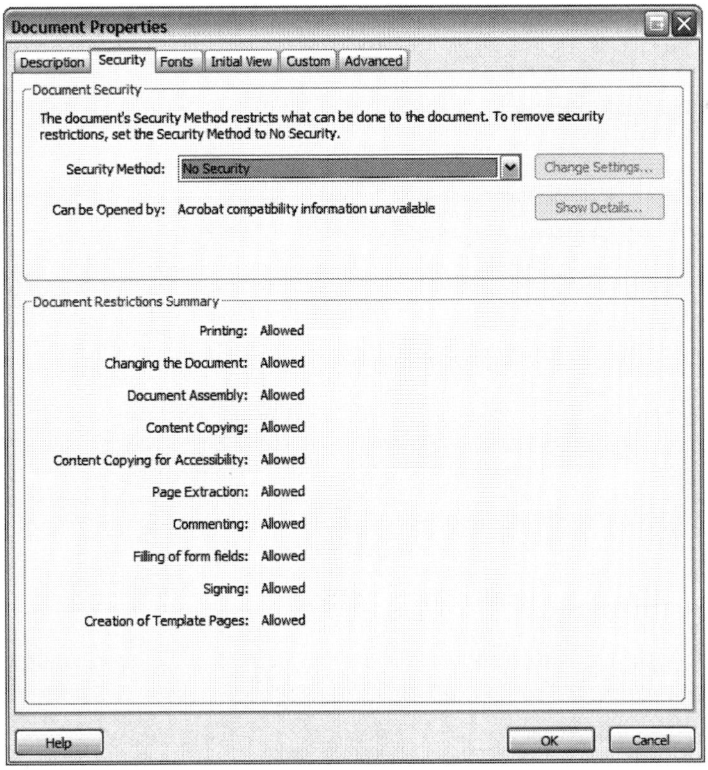

Figure 11.1

Menu (Document Properties): **File > Properties**
Keystroke (Document Properties): **Ctrl+D**

In the **Document Properties** window, click on the **Security** tab. Next, select **Password Security** from the **Security Method** drop-down menu (Figure 11.2). The **Password Security—Settings** window opens. Check the **Require a**

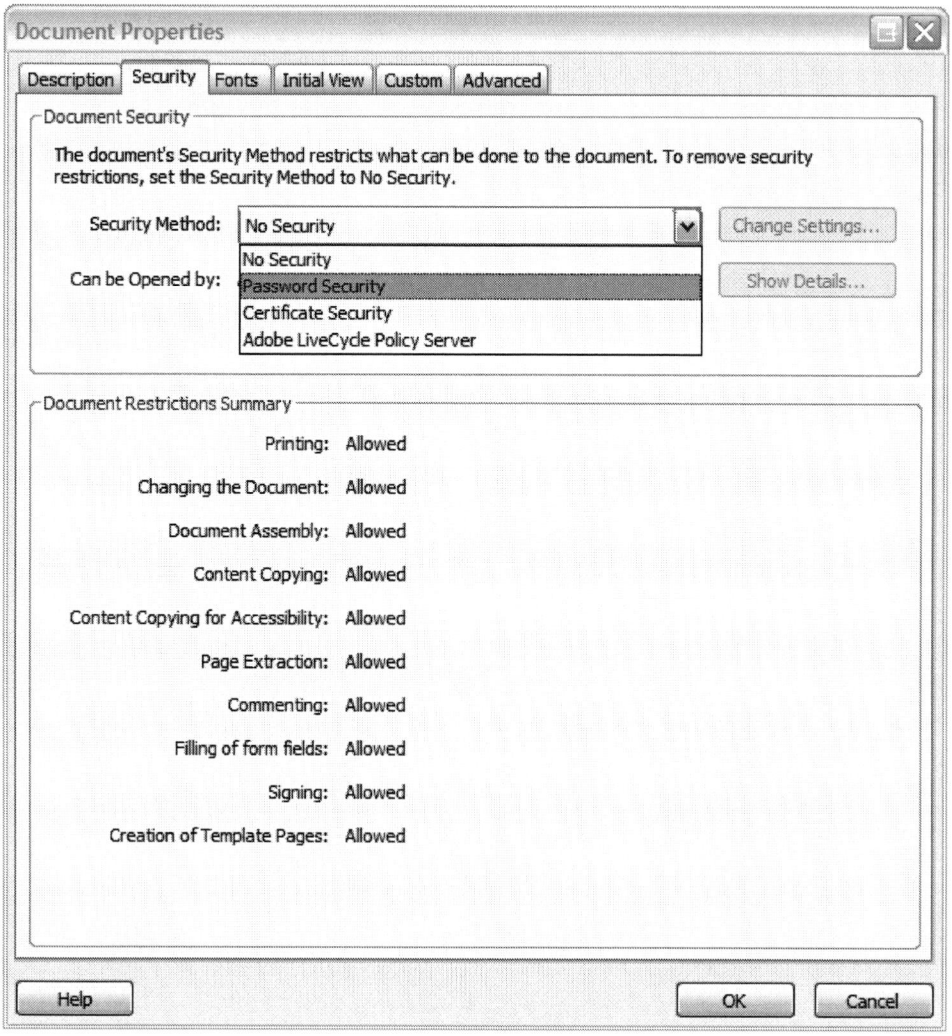

Figure 11.2

password to open the document box, then type the desired password in the **Document Open Password** box (Figure 11.3).

You will be asked to confirm the password (Figure 11.4).

Finally, you will be warned that the security settings will not be applied until you save the document (Figure 11.5).

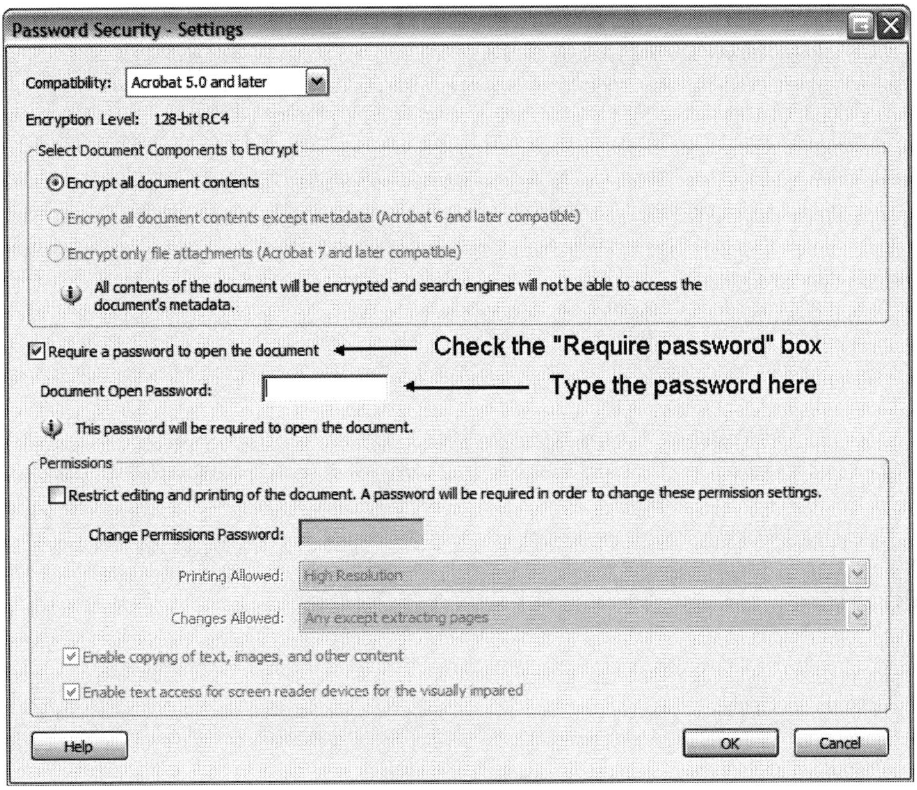

Figure 11.3

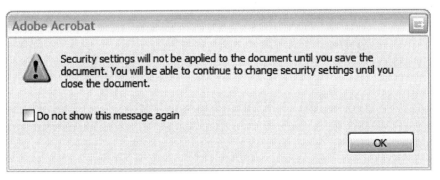

Figure 11.4

Adobe Acrobat

Security settings will not be applied to the document until you save the document. You will be able to continue to change security settings until you close the document.

☐ Do not show this message again

OK

Figure 11.5

§ 11.2 Applying Permissions Security Through Document Properties

Permissions security (restricting what users can do with the file) can be applied from the **Security** tab in the **Document Properties** window. The process follows the same pattern as that described for applying document open security through the **Document Properties** window above. To open the **Document Properties** window:

> Menu (Document Properties): **File > Properties**
> Keystroke (Document Properties): **Ctrl+D**

In the **Document Properties** window, click on the **Security** tab (Figure 11.6). Next, select **Password Security** from the **Security Method** drop-down

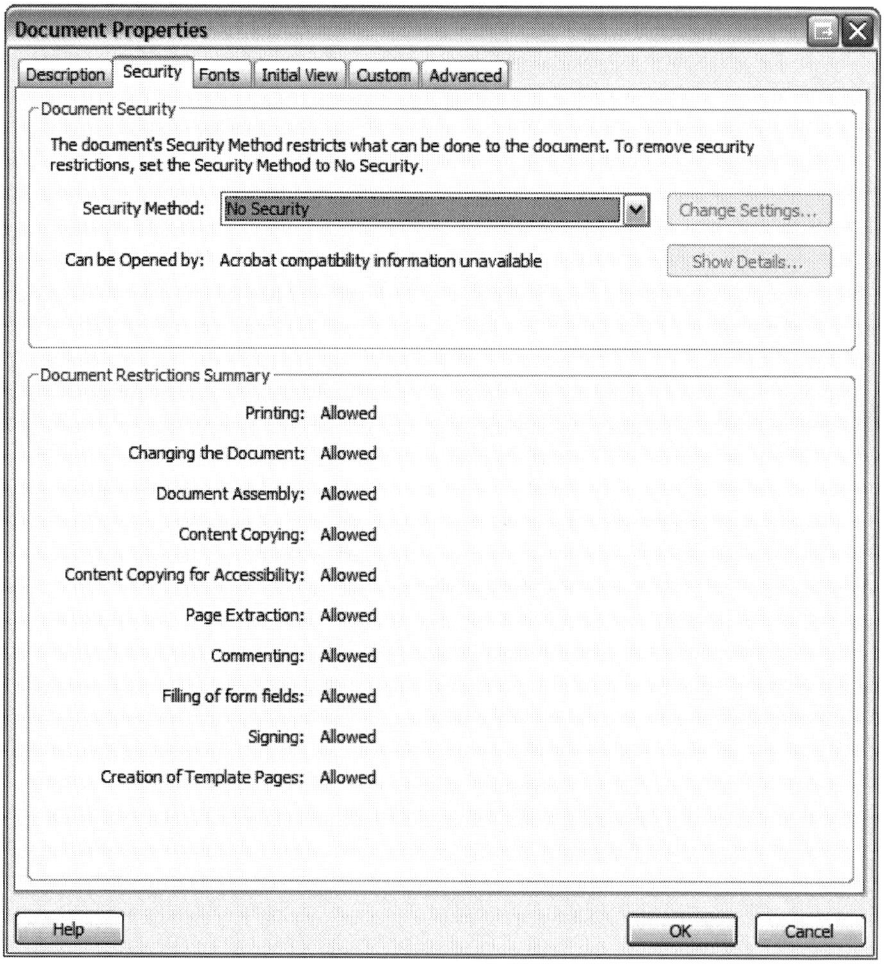

Figure 11.6

menu (Figure 11.7). The **Password Security—Settings** window opens. In the **Permissions** section, check the box to **Restrict editing and printing of the**

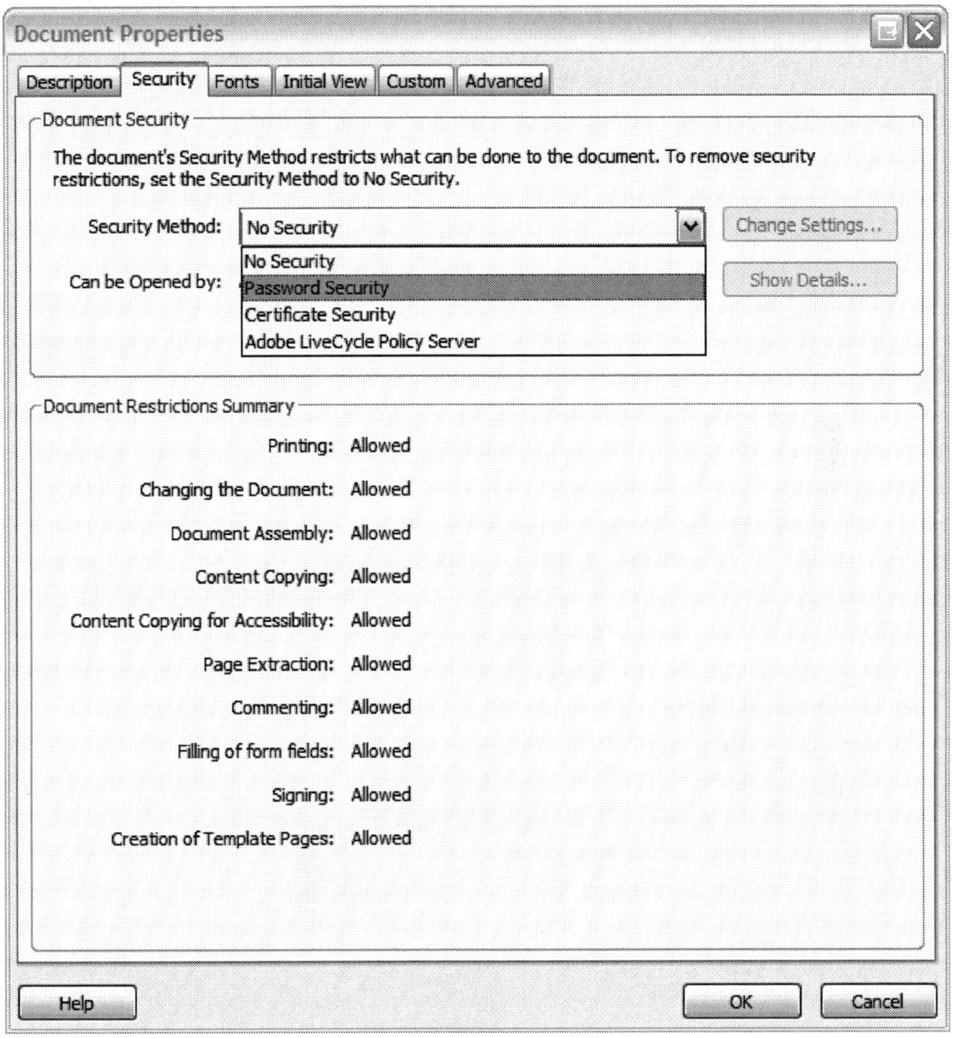

Figure 11.7

document, type the desired password in the **Change Permissions Password** box and make choices from the two drop-down menus ("Printing Allowed" and "Changes Allowed"). If you don't check the **Enable copying** box, users will not be able to copy any content from the file (Figure 11.8).

You will be asked to confirm the password (Figure 11.9).

Finally, you will be warned that the security settings will not be applied until you save the document (Figure 11.10).

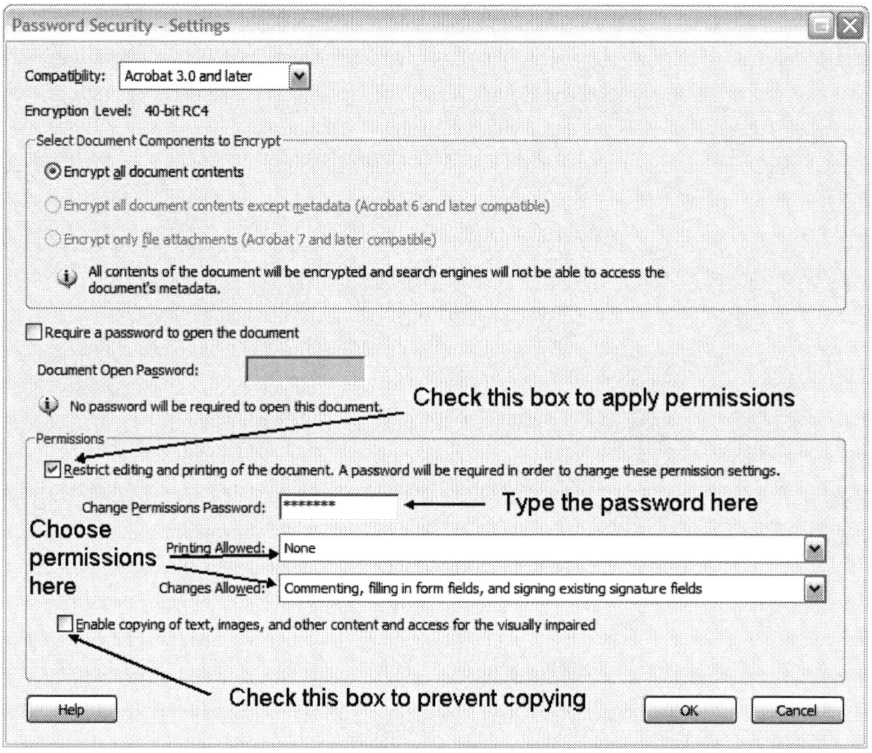

Figure 11.8

Figure 11.9

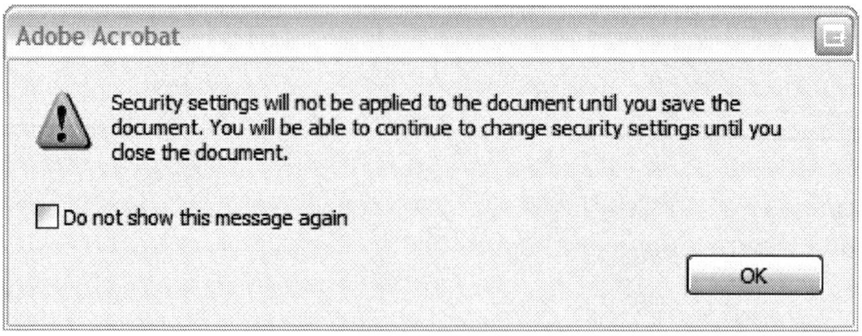

Figure 11.10

§ 11.3 Creating a Security Policy (Document Open)

Security policies streamline the process of securing PDF files. Once a security policy has been created it can be applied to the currently open document with a single click or applied to multiple documents with a batch process (see Chapter 20). To create a security policy that requires a password to open a PDF file, click on the **Secure** icon on the **Tasks** toolbar and select **Manage Security Policies** or:

Menu (Create Security Policy): **Advanced > Security > Manage Security Policies**

Keystroke (Create Security Policy): **Alt+A-C-M** (Figure 11.11)

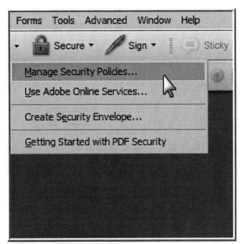

Figure 11.11

◆ The **Managing Security Policies** dialog box will appear (Figure 11.12).

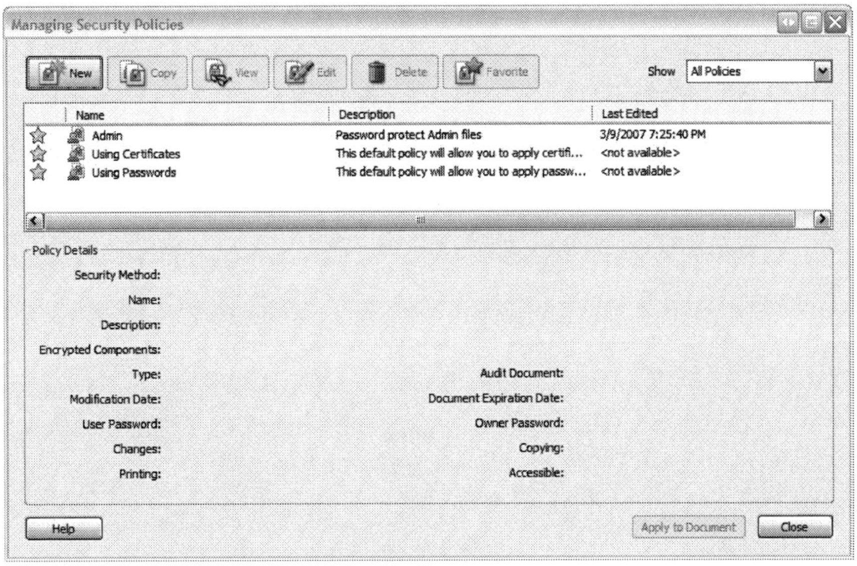

Figure 11.12

◆ Click the **New** button and the **New Security Policy** dialog box appears (Figure 11.13), check the **Use Passwords** radio button.

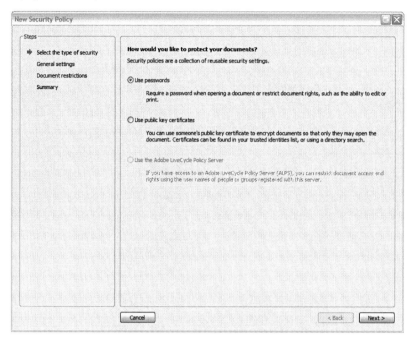

Figure 11.13

◆ Click **Next**, check the **Save these settings as a policy** radio button, give the policy a name and description (the name is required, the description is optional), and check the **Save passwords with the policy** box (Figure 11.14).

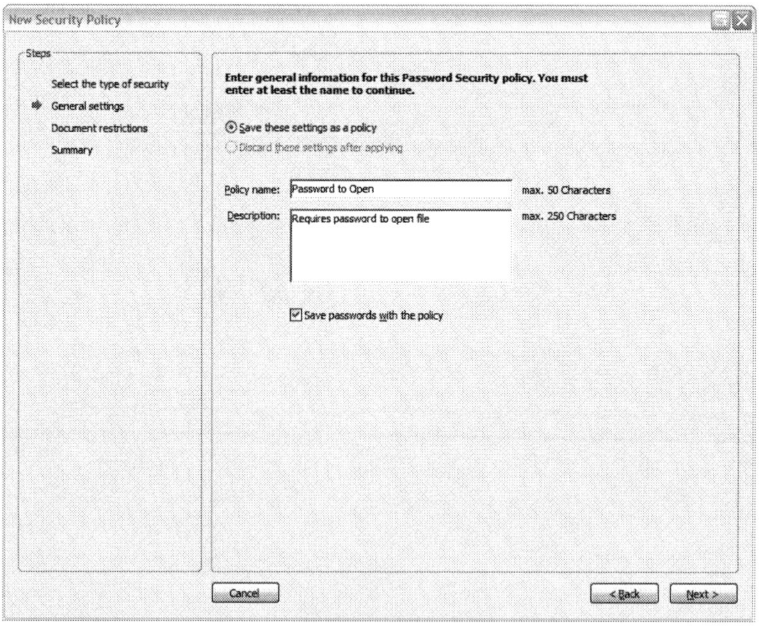

Figure 11.14

◆ Click **Next**, select the desired level of compatibility from the drop down list, leave the **Encrypt all document contents** radio button checked to apply encryption (uncheck the button for no encryption) (Figure 11.15).

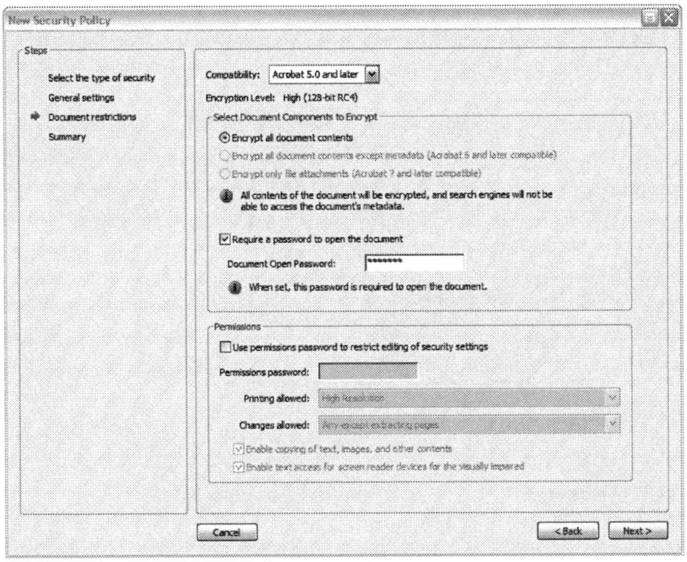

Figure 11.15

◆ Check the box **Require a password to open the document** and enter the password.
◆ Skip the **Permissions** section (don't check the box).
◆ Click **Next**, reenter the password and click **OK**. A summary of the information entered will appear for this security policy, then click **Finish** (Figure 11.16).

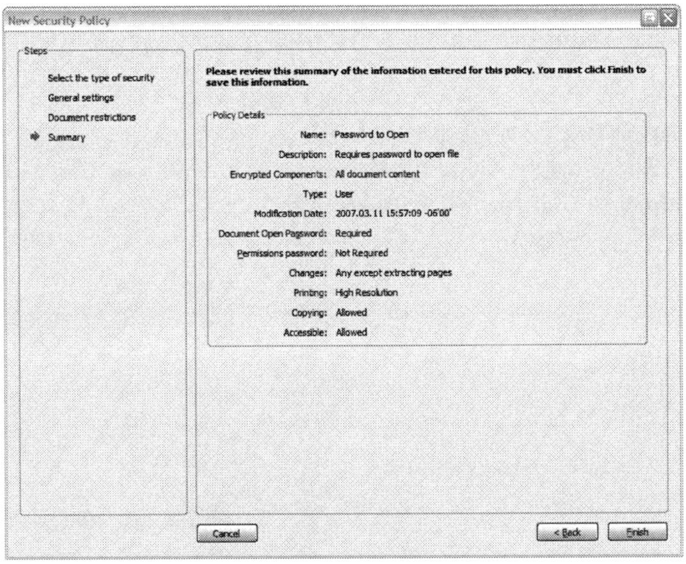

Figure 11.16

After you click **Finish**, you return to the **Manage Security Policies** window. Left-click on the policy you created, to highlight it, then click the **Favorite** button. This last step puts the policy on the drop-down menu you see when you click the **Secure** button on the **Tasks** toolbar (Figure 11.17). To apply this policy to require a password to open a PDF file, click on the **Secure** icon on the **Tasks** toolbar, select the policy (**Password to Open**), or:

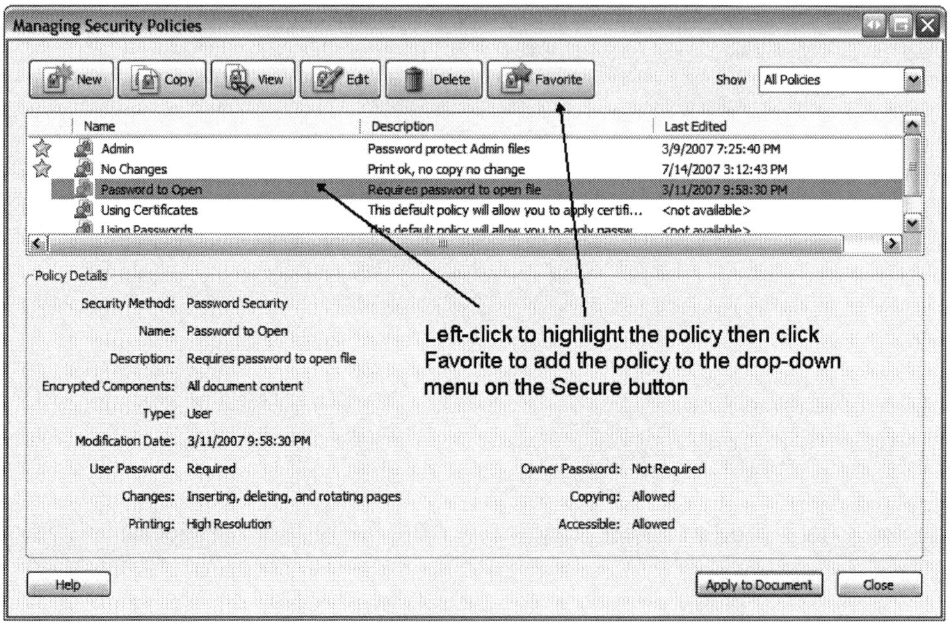

Figure 11.17

Menu (Secure Document): **Advanced > Security (select the policy (Password to Open))**

Keystroke (Secure Document): **Alt+A-C (select the policy (Password to Open))**

If the **Applying New Security Settings** warning dialog appears (Figure 11.18), click **Yes** to apply the security policy. Another warning dialog may appear informing you that the security settings will not be applied until you save the document, click **OK** to proceed.

Figure 11.18

§ 11.4 Creating a Security Policy (Permissions)

To create a security policy that requires a password to change the permissions associated with a PDF file, click on the **Secure** icon on the **Tasks** toolbar and select **Manage Security Policies**:

Menu (Create Security Policy): **Advanced > Security > Manage Security Policies**

Keystroke (Create Security Policy): **Alt+A-C-M**

- ◆ The **Managing Security Policies** dialog box will appear (Figure 11.19).

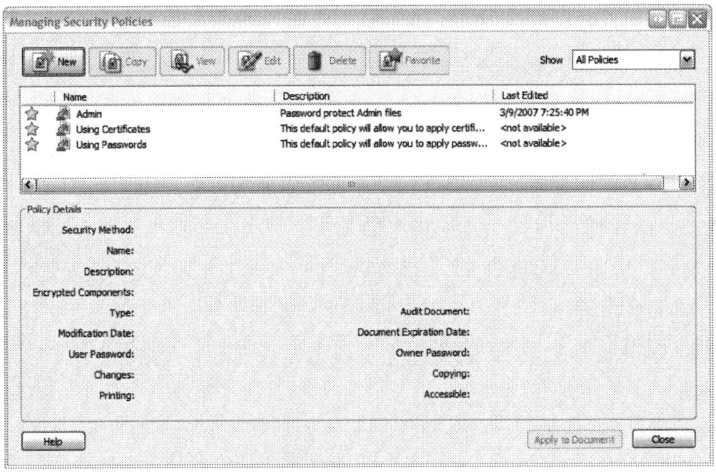

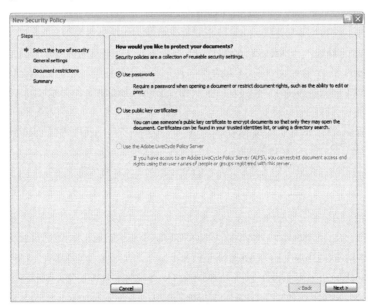

Figure 11.19

- ◆ Click the **New** button and the **New Security Policy** dialog box appears (Figure 11.20), check the **Use passwords** radio button.

Figure 11.20

◆ Click **Next**, check the **Save these settings as a policy** radio button, give the policy a name (call this policy "No Changes") and description (the name is required, the description is optional), and check the **Save passwords with the policy** box (Figure 11.21).

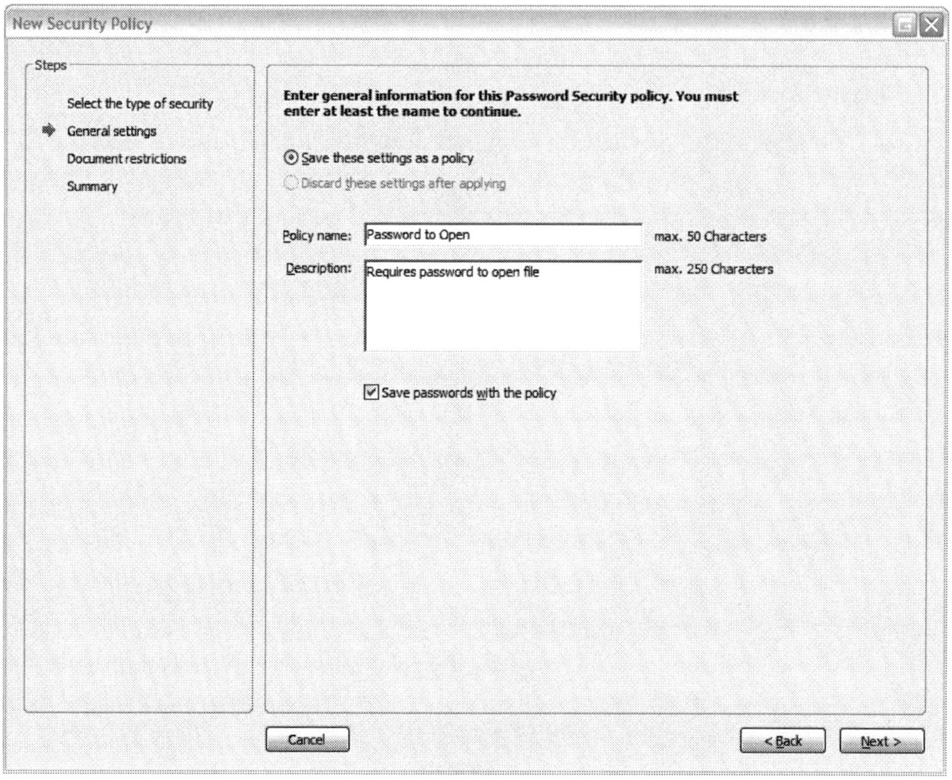

Figure 11.21

◆ Click **Next**, select the desired level of compatibility from the drop down list, leave the **Encrypt all document contents** radio button checked to apply encryption (uncheck the button for no encryption) (Figure 11.22).

◆ Uncheck the box **Require a password to open the document** and enter the password.

◆ Check **User permissions password to restrict editing of security settings** and enter the password.

◆ From the drop-down lists choose the printing and changes allowed, and either check or uncheck the box to **Enable copying of text, images, and other contents.** (In Figure 11.23 selections have been made to allow no printing and no changes, including copying of text, images or other contents.)

◆ Click **Next**, reenter the password and click **OK**. A summary of the information entered will appear for this security policy, then click **Finish**.

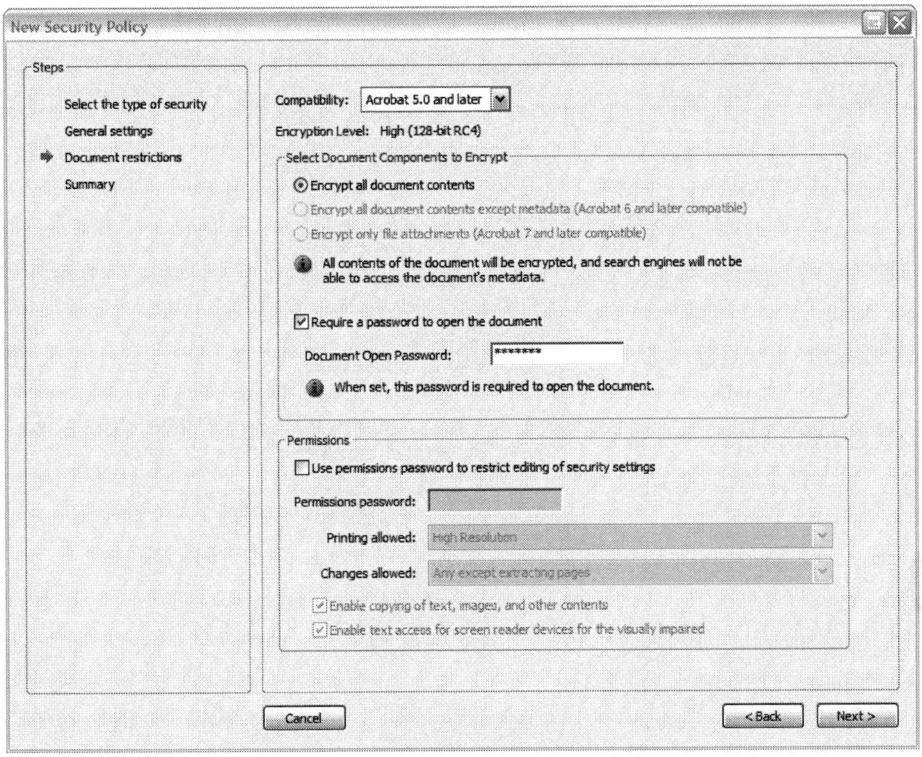

Figure 11.22

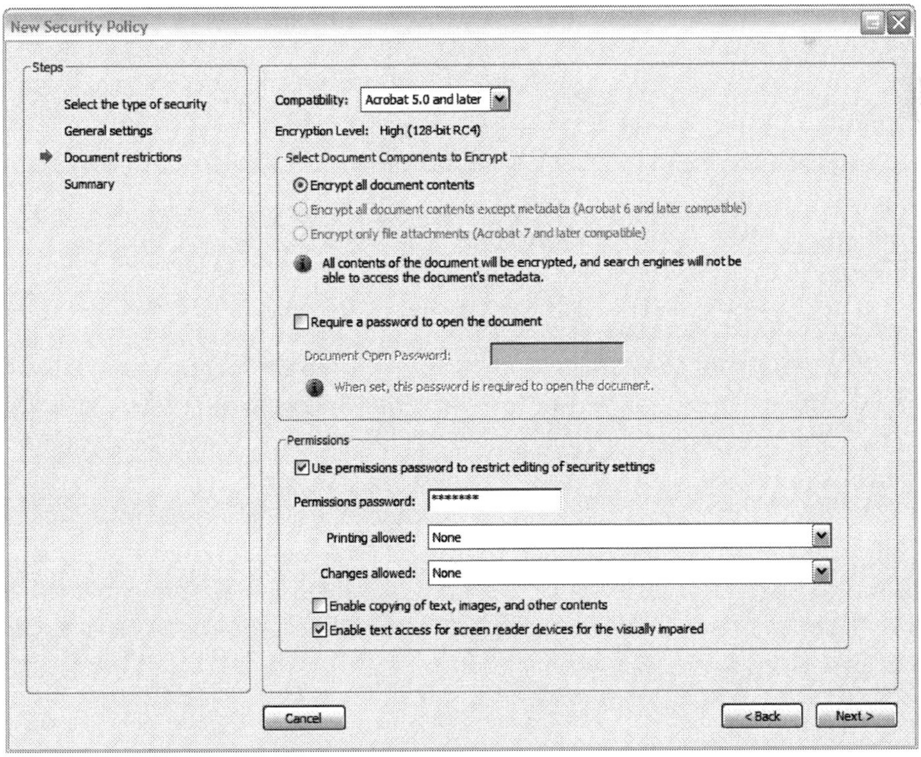

Figure 11.23

After you click **Finish**, you return to the **Manage Security Policies** window. Left-click on the policy you created, to highlight it, then click the **Favorite** button. This last step puts the policy on the drop-down menu you see when you click the **Secure** button on the **Tasks** toolbar (Figure 11.24). To apply this policy to require a password to print, copy or make changes to a PDF file:

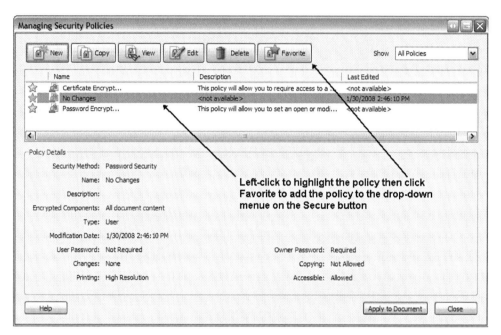

Figure 11.24

Toolbar (Secure Document): Click on the **Secure** icon on the **Tasks** toolbar [select the policy (No Changes)]

Menu (Secure Document): **Advanced > Security (select the policy (No Changes))**

Keystroke (Secure Document): **Alt+A-C (select the policy (No Changes))**

If the **Applying New Security Settings** warning dialog appears, click **Yes** to apply the security policy. Another warning dialog may appear informing you that the security settings will not be applied until you save the document, click **OK** to proceed.

Remember that you can create new, copy, edit or delete security policies to suit your particular needs. A batch process (see Chapter 20) can be created and run to apply a security policy to multiple documents. This can come in handy if you generate financial reports on a monthly basis and want to secure them as a batch rather than one at a time.

§ 11.5 Advanced PDF Security (Certificate)

You can restrict PDF files so that they can only be opened by selected users. To select those users, you must have their digital identification certificates so that their identities can be associated with the document. If you plan to use this feature, it might be worthwhile to create a folder on your local hard disk drive for storing certificates (such as C:\TrustedCertificates). Each person who has rights in the document must send you a certificate so that you can associate his or her identity with a specific document. This might be useful when working with co-counsel to prevent the unauthorized viewing of privileged information. Using Trusted Certificates for document security is akin to using certificates to validate secure digital signatures.

For more detailed information on this topic, see the Complete Acrobat Help document.

Menu (Help): **Help > Complete Acrobat Help**
Keystroke (Help): **Alt+H-H**

The help manual opens as a separate document. On the **Contents** tab, select **Adding Security to PDF Documents**.

Saving Web Pages to PDF 12

With Acrobat installed, you can convert any printable file displayed on your computer to PDF, including Web pages. But Acrobat goes one better by allowing you to create a PDF file from an entire Web site. Whether generated by printing or creating, PDF files derived from Web pages are image-on-text files. Printing a Web page to PDF is a simple function that produces an image-on-text file of the page displayed. Creating a PDF file of a Web site, on the other hand, captures much more information, including links and imbedded media files (audio, video, flash, and so on). When creating a PDF file of a Web site, you decide how many levels to capture (this feature was called Web Capture in prior versions of Acrobat). PDF files created from Web pages can include active links from the pages, depending on the number of levels captured (Get Only *n* Levels). If the linked pages are not included in the PDF, Acrobat prompts the user to open the pages in a browser (in other words, connect to the Internet and open the page in the default browser).

Why would you want to create a multilevel PDF file of a Web site? Consider municipal codes, county regulations, court rules, and the like. Often, these primary source materials are available online and you may want to have them available when no Internet connection exists, or you may want to include them on a CD-ROM to be delivered to a court or client. Indeed, the CD-ROM option can be particularly useful as these files are often quite large. The Federal Rules of Civil Procedure, created with the levels-to-capture set to two, initially produced a 267-page PDF file that was 1.4 megabytes (MB).

Creating a PDF file of a Web site produces a static image of the pages captured. This can be helpful in litigation where expert witnesses may have materials posted on a Web site. You can capture those materials as they exist at a point in time; if the expert later changes the content, you have an exact copy of what was previously posted. The resulting PDF file displays the URL as well as the date and time that the pages were captured (Figure 12.1).

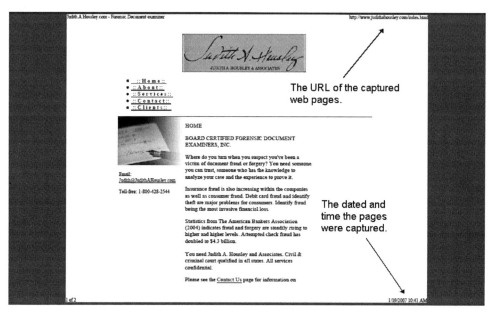

Figure 12.1

§ 12.1 Printing Web Pages to PDF

Printing a Web page to PDF converts the currently visible page to a PDF file. When you place an order online, rather than printing a paper copy of the receipt, print it to PDF and save it in an appropriate location. When you have a page that you want to print, simply tell the browser to print (typically **Ctrl+P**), and select the Adobe PDF printer. The **Adobe PDF Document Properties** dialog box will open (Figure 12.2). On the **Adobe PDF Settings** tab you can make various choices:

- *Default Settings*. Select a preconfigured setting for compression, quality, fonts, etc.
- *Adobe PDF Security*. Select if you want to create a secured PDF file.
- *Adobe PDF Output Folder*. Browse to a specific folder to use as the default location or be prompted when supplying the file name.
- *Adobe PDF Page Size*. Leave this set to **Letter** or choose from a bewildering list of paper sizes (you know what JIS B3 is, right?).

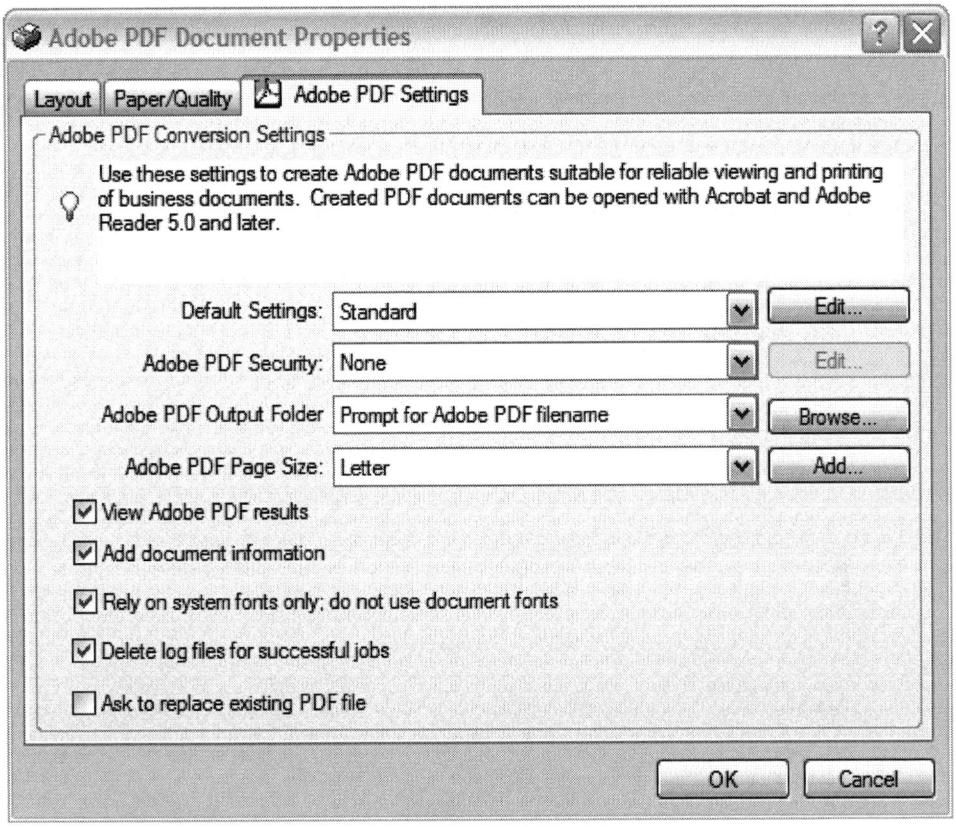

Figure 12.2

- *View Adobe PDF results.* Leaving this box checked causes the page printed to PDF to open in Acrobat.
- *Add document information.* This option supplies information about the page you printed such as the file name, date and time of creation.
- *Rely on system fonts only; do not use document fonts.* Deselect this option to download fonts when creating the PDF file. All your fonts will be available in the PDF file, but it will take longer to create it. Leave this option selected if you are working with Asian-language documents.
- *Delete log files for successful jobs.* Automatically deletes the log files unless the job fails (as if you really cared about that).
- *Ask to replace existing PDF file.* Check this option to receive a warning when you are about to overwrite an existing PDF with a file of the same name.

§ 12.2 Creating a PDF File from a Web Site

Like most tasks in Acrobat, you can create a PDF from Web pages in several ways.

Toolbar (Create PDF from Web Page): Click on the **Create PDF** button on the main toolbar and select **From Web Page** (Figure 12.3)

Menu (Create PDF from Web Page): **File > Create PDF > From Web Page**

Keystroke (Create PDF from Web Page): **Alt+F-F-W**

Keystroke (Create PDF from Web Page): **Ctrl+Shift+O**

If you regularly create PDF files from Web pages consider adding the **Create PDF from Web Page** button to the **File** toolbar. With the button on the toolbar, the Web page to PDF creation process can be initiated with a single click (Figure 12.4). Regardless of the method employed or the version used, the **Create PDF from Web Page** opens dialog box (Figure 12.5).

Now, do the following:

1. Type (or easier, paste) the URL of the Web site.
2. Select the number of levels to capture or select **Get entire site**.
3. Click **Create**.

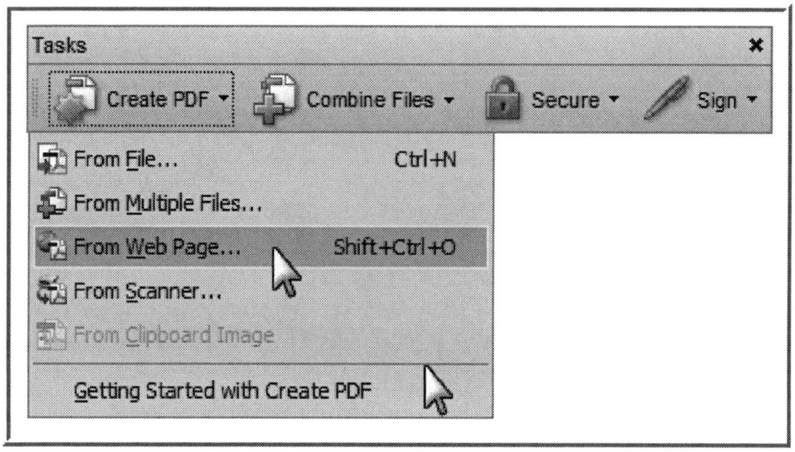

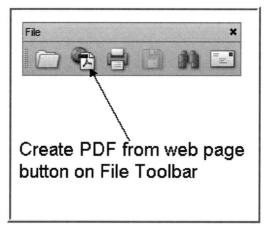

Figure 12.3

Figure 12.4

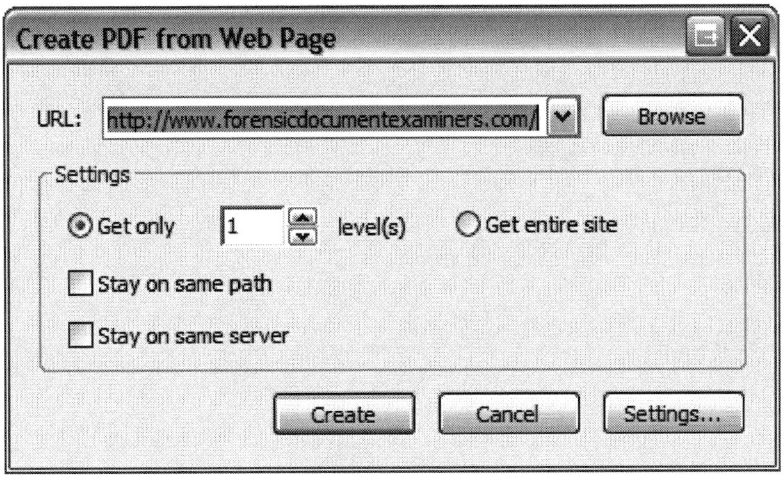

Figure 12.5

Now sit back and wait for the amount of information selected to be downloaded to your computer and converted to PDF format. Depending on the amount of information selected and the speed of your Internet connection, this may take a short time or long time. The Federal Rules (267 pages, 1.4 MB) took approximately fifteen minutes over a 500+ KB connection.

§ 12.3 Web Page Capture Settings

Okay, so that's the basics of creating a PDF from a web site. This is a very powerful feature with many custom settings available that deserve attention. So let's go back to the **Create PDF from Web Page** dialog box (see Figure 12.5), and click on the **Settings** button. The **Web Page Conversion Settings** dialog box opens (Figure 12.6). Notice the two tabs: **General** and **Page Layout**.

§ 12.3.1 General Settings

In the **General** tab of the **Web Page Conversion Settings** dialog box, check **Create bookmarks** to create a tagged bookmark for each converted Web page, using the page title (taken from the HTML title element) as the bookmark name. If the page has no title, the URL is used as the bookmark name.

Check **Create PDF tags** to store a structure in the PDF file that corresponds to the HTML structure of the original Web pages. This can be particularly useful for complex documents that contain structure information (such as a table of contents, headings, and so on). If this option is selected, you can create tagged bookmarks for paragraphs, list elements, table cells, and other items that use HTML elements.

Check **Place headers and footers on new pages** to place a header and footer on every page. The header shows the Web page title; the footer shows

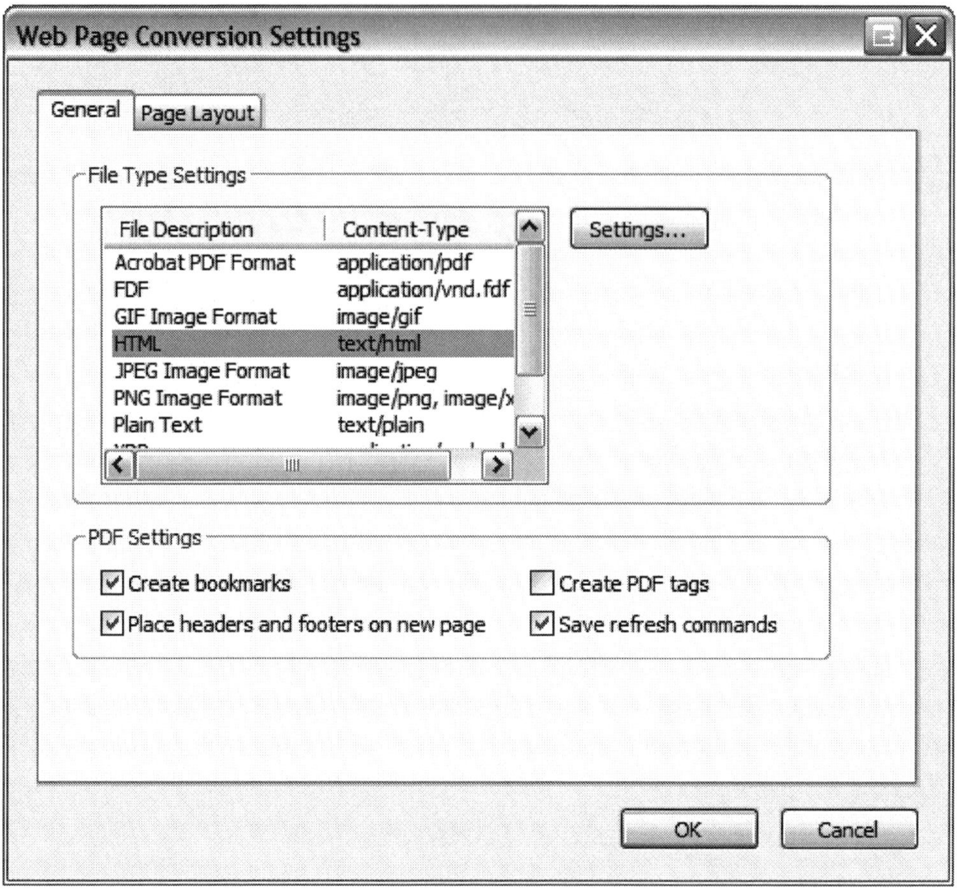

Figure 12.6

the page URL, the page number in the downloaded set, and the date and time of the download. This can be useful for "authenticating" documents for use in litigation.

Check **Save refresh commands** to save a list of all URLs and remember how they were downloaded in the PDF file for the purpose of refreshing (updating) pages. This option must be selected before you can update a PDF-converted Web site.

For **File Type Settings**, select the file type to be downloaded. If you select **HTML** (see more HTML options below) or **Plain Text** as the file type, you can control the font properties and other display characteristics.

§ 12.3.2 Page Layout Settings

In the **Web Page Conversion Settings** dialog box, click the **Page Layout** tab (Figure 12.7), and select a page size or enter a custom page width and height in the boxes below the page size menu. Then specify the page orientation and margins. Select the scaling options:

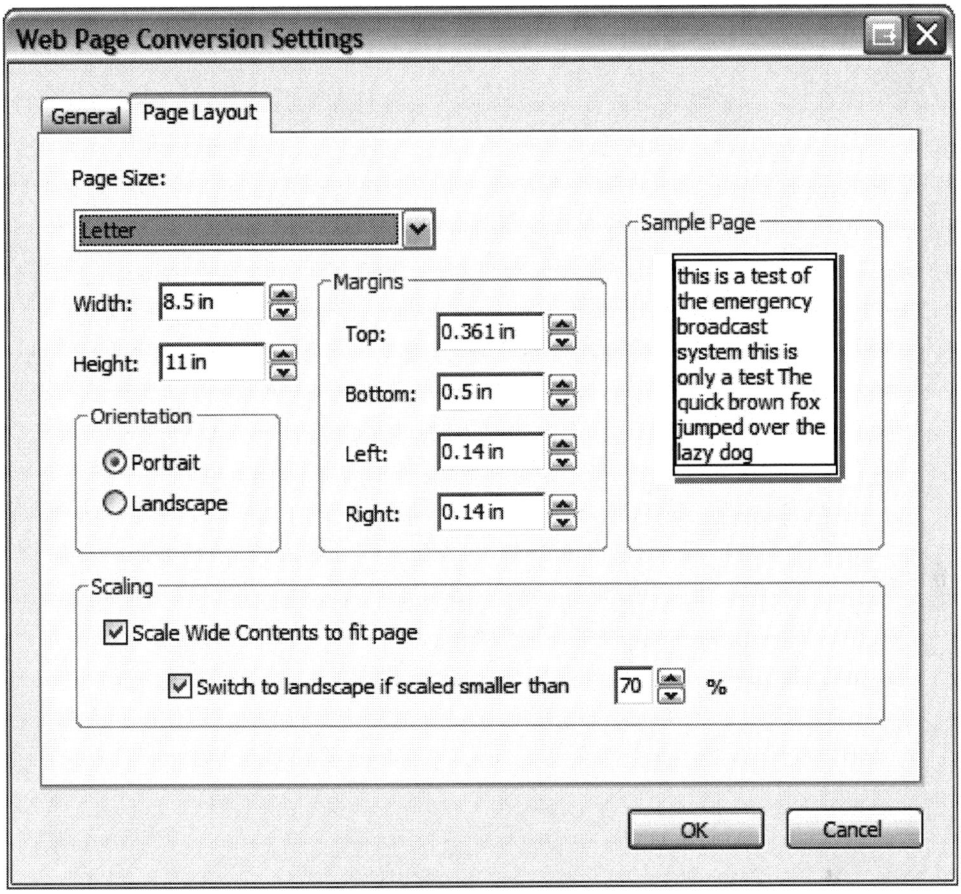

Web Page Conversion Settings

General | Page Layout

Page Size:

Letter

Width: 8.5 in

Height: 11 in

Orientation
- ● Portrait
- ○ Landscape

Margins
- Top: 0.361 in
- Bottom: 0.5 in
- Left: 0.14 in
- Right: 0.14 in

Sample Page

this is a test of the emergency broadcast system this is only a test The quick brown fox jumped over the lazy dog

Scaling
- ☑ Scale Wide Contents to fit page
  - ☑ Switch to landscape if scaled smaller than 70 %

OK | Cancel

Figure 12.7

- *Scale Wide Contents to fit page* rescales a page's contents, if necessary, to fit the width of the page. If you do not select this option, the paper size is adjusted to fit the page's contents as necessary.
- *Switch to landscape if scaled smaller than* changes the orientation of the page from portrait to landscape if the contents of a page are scaled beyond a specified percentage. If the PDF version will be less than 70 percent (the default setting) of the original size, the display switches to landscape. This option is available only if portrait orientation has been selected (if landscape orientation was selected, then all pages are captured in landscape orientation).

§ 12.3.3 Additional HTML Capture Settings

In the **General** tab of the **Web Page Conversion Settings** window, double-click HTML, or select **HTML** and click **Settings**. The **HTML Conversion Settings** window opens (Figure 12.8). In the **General** tab, select from the following options:

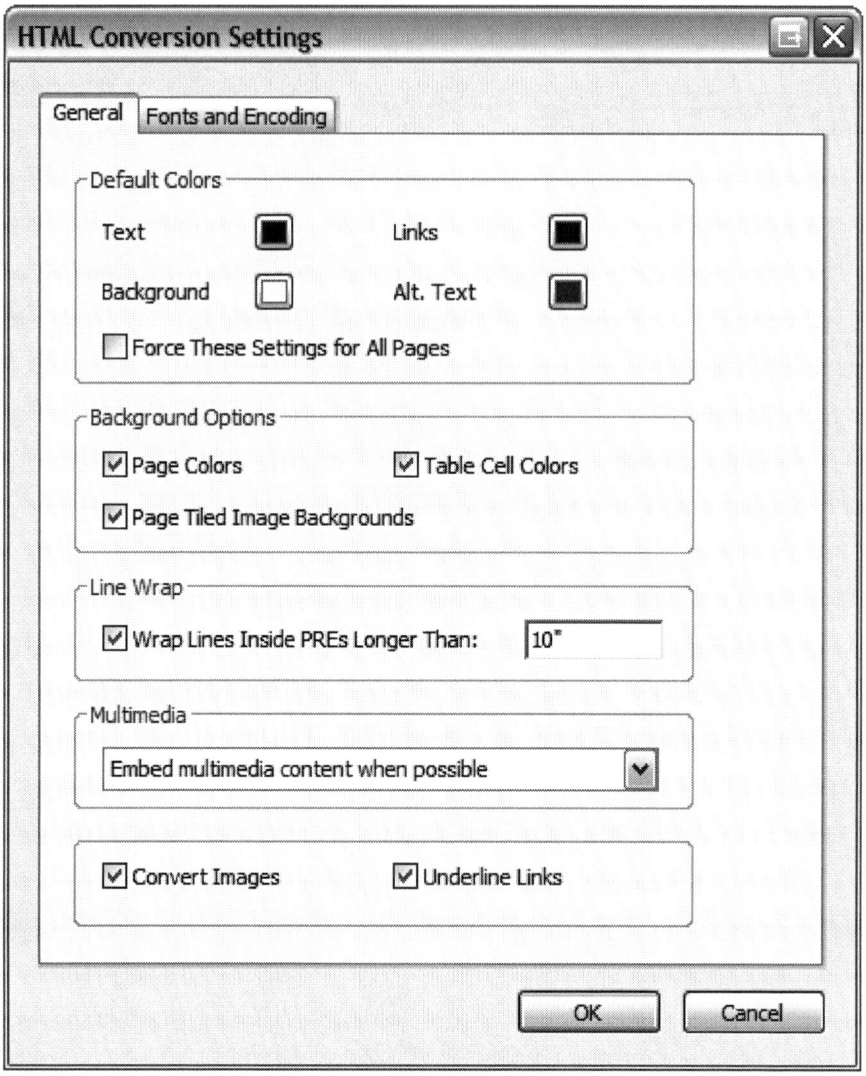

Figure 12.8

◆ *Default Colors* sets the default colors for text, page backgrounds, links, and text that replace an image in a file when the image is unavailable. For each color, click the color button to open a palette, and select the color. To use these colors on all pages, select **Force These Settings for All Pages**. If you do not select this option, your color choices are used only on pages that do not have colors defined.

◆ *Background Options* specify whether to display colors and tiled images in page backgrounds and colors in table cells. If you do not select these options, converted pages may look different than they do in the Web browser, but they may be easier to read if printed.

◆ *Wrap Lines Inside PREs Longer Than* wraps preformatted (HTML) lines of text if they are longer than a specified length. The Web page is scaled so the longest line on the page fits on the screen. Select this setting if an HTML file you're downloading has unreasonably long lines of preformatted text.

◆ *Multimedia* options determine whether to reference multimedia (such as .swf files) by URL, disable multimedia capture, or embed multimedia files when possible.

◆ *Convert Images* includes images in the conversion to PDF. If you do not select this option, an image is indicated by a colored border (and possibly text, if specified by page design).

◆ *Underline Links* underlines textual links on the pages.

The **Fonts and Encoding** tab provides options that are not likely to be needed in the average law office (Figure 12.9).

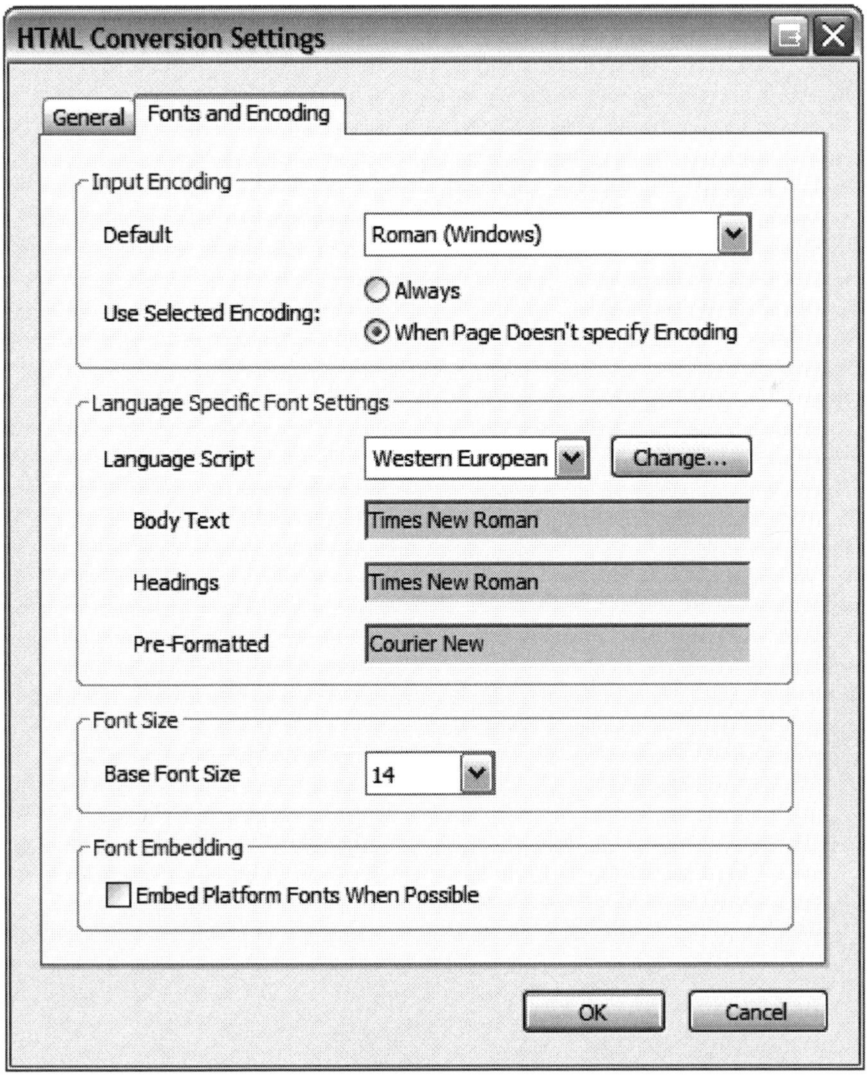

Figure 12.9

Plug-ins

Plug-ins: now here's something that might be difficult or at least intimidating for those who don't regularly dig into their software. But plug-ins are easy enough to understand; they are software modules that add capabilities to Acrobat, allowing you to be more productive. Web browsers have long used plug-ins to add functionality, but we can go back farther than that. Think of the macros that you have written or acquired and then saved in a specific folder so that your word processing application could perform additional tasks (like formatting and printing envelopes). Plug-ins are to Acrobat as macros are to word processing applications. But, you ask, what can plug-ins do that Acrobat can't already? Granted, many plug-ins are intended for document production houses, not law firms. But there are, among the hundreds of available plug-ins, those that fit perfectly in the law office. If you are at all curious about plug-ins, visit the following Web sites:

- ◆ **www.adobe.com/store**: click on the **plug-ins** link, then select **Adobe Acrobat** from the list of applications.
- ◆ **www.planetpdf.com**: click on the link for **PDF Store**.

Plug-ins must be stored in the plug-ins folder in order to load correctly (C:\Program Files\Adobe\Acrobat [version #]\ Acrobat\ Plug-Ins). When you buy or download a free plug-in, look for instructions on how to install it to the proper folder.

There are plug-ins for building better PDF forms, for managing documents and collections of documents, for enhancing links and bookmarks, and just about anything else you can imagine. Plug-ins for Bates numbering and for redacting confidential or privileged information offer features and functions not found in versions prior to Acrobat 8 Professional. Even with Acrobat 8 Professional installed, there may be reasons to use a third-party plug-in for Bates numbering or redaction.

§ 13.1 Bates Numbering

Bates numbering, or Bates stamping, refers to numbering each page of a document with a unique number. Bates numbers allow lawyers to keep track of all documents produced or received during the course of litigation. The numbers increase by one digit on each page. In the past, Bates numbers were applied to paper documents using a hand-stamp machine originally manufactured by the Bates Manufacturing Company. The machines were prone to errors (if, for example, the operator turned two pages instead of one) and were messy to work with (the stamp elements were metal and required regular applications of indelible ink). Asking a staff person to Bates number a stack of documents almost guaranteed receiving a dirty look.

Macros for both Word and WordPerfect generate Bates-number labels. Using a macro to create Bates-number labels allows lawyers to prefix the numbers with an alpha code (resulting in a number such as "DLM000001"). Bates-number labels work best on clear return-address labels because they are small (eighty per page). However, the labels come at a price, and applying one label to each page is, to say the least, labor intensive and creates the opportunity for errors to occur.

PDF files can be Bates numbered with Acrobat 8 Professional (see Chapter 17), or by using a plug-in built for that purpose in earlier versions (you can use the plug-ins discussed below in Acrobat 8). Bates numbering PDF files is fast, clean, and 100% accurate. A thousand pages can be Bates numbered in less than five minutes. No pages are skipped and no one ends up with indelible ink on their hands. The two most popular Bates numbering plug-ins are discussed below. Note: if you use StampPDF or IntelliPDF BATES PRO to apply Bates numbers to image-only PDF files, you may not be able to use the OCR function built into Acrobat (some third-party OCR applications, such as OmniPagePro, will OCR stamped image-only PDF files). Adobe has attempted to resolve this issue by telling the OCR engine to ignore text printed within a certain distance of the edge of the page. To be safe, if you want the ability to search Bates numbered documents, perform OCR with Acrobat before applying the numbers.

§ 13.2 StampPDF (Bates Numbering Plug-in)

The big difference between the Bates numbering built into Acrobat 8 Professional and that provided by StampPDF is permanence. Bates numbers applied with Acrobat 8 Professional can be removed (unless permissions security has been applied to the file); those applied with StampPDF cannot (they are permanent—something to keep in mind when using this plug-in). A lesser difference is the ease of use. StampPDF is quick and easy; Bates numbering with Acrobat 8 Professional is a bit more complicated.

StampPDF by Appligent (**www.appligent.com**) allows users to easily include the date, time, contact information, page numbers, watermarks, disclaimers, or any text in any font in any color. Moreover, one specific feature of StampPDF recommends this plug-in for any lawyer using Acrobat in the context of litigation: Bates numbering. The StampPDF plug-in lets you add *permanent* text to any PDF file by just choosing a menu item within Acrobat—no need to launch a separate application. Text may be added diagonally across a document as watermarks ("Draft" or "Confidential," for example), or as headers or footers. Text stamps may be made in a variety of fonts and text styles, including color. Information stamped into the PDF file becomes part of the document and is present when it is displayed and printed. You can specify text size, font, justification, top or bottom placement, diagonal orientation, and whether text is printed on top of or underneath the existing PDF file contents. Text can be stamped in black, white, any shade of gray, or any RGB color. Formatting choices can be saved in a template file for use with other PDF files to automate the stamping process.

Stamping is done by entering text and formatting choices in a dialog box that appears when you select a **StampPDF** command from the **Acrobat Document** menu.

Menu (StampPDF): **Document > Single Stamp**
(No keyboard command)

The **Stamp Parameters** dialog box opens (Figure 13.1).

§ 13.2.1 Setting the Beginning Bates Number

Bates numbering with StampPDF is fast and efficient. The plug-in allows numbers in the format of six characters (for example, 000001 for page 1). The **Stamp Parameter** dialog includes **Bates Number** in the drop-down list of codes. It lets you begin Bates numbering with the number and page you specify (if you don't specify a beginning number, then the first page is stamped 000001). For example, you can stamp the start page with 000999, the next page

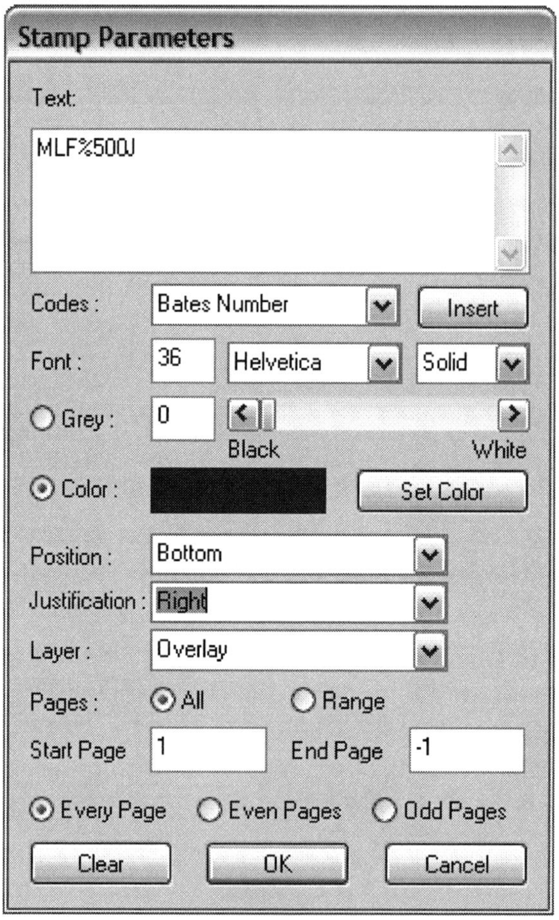

Figure 13.1

with 001000, and so on. You begin Bates numbering with a specific number by including the number in a variable in this format: **%[page number]J**. For example, **%999J** stamps the first page with 000999, the next page with 001000, and so on. To begin Bates numbering with 999 on the first page in the document being stamped:

1. In the stamp file, enter 1 for the **StartPage** parameter.
2. Enter **%999J** for the **Text** parameter.

You should probably make an easy-to-find note on how to set the Bates starting number, as this is likely to be a task performed just infrequently enough to evade memorization.

§ 13.2.2 Adding Prefixes to Bates Numbers

If you have moved from mechanical Bates numbering machines to labels in order to include prefixes in the Bates number (and to keep your hands clean), this feature of StampPDF will be a welcome discovery. Using Stamp-

PDF, you can add a prefix to Bates numbers by including the prefix before the variable, such as **ABA%J**. **ABA%J** stamps the first page with ABA000001, the next page with ABA000002, and so on. To include a prefix in the Bates number, simply insert the desired text in front of the Bates numbering variable (the Bates numbering variable is **%J**). If you want the first page to be ABA000999, then the text in the **StampPDF** dialog box would look like this: **ABA%999J**.

§ 13.3 IntelliPDF BATES (Bates Numbering Plug-in)

IntelliPDF BATES is a plug-in for Acrobat that creates and applies custom Bates numbering to PDF files. It is extremely powerful, but the power comes at the cost of complexity. IntelliPDF BATES can create up to sixteen (thirty-two in the Pro version) stamps per page. Each stamp can consist of up to eight elements (numeric, alphabetical, alphanumeric, roman numerals, and so on) and be up to thirty-two characters long. You control the stamp's creation: the font, size, color, background color, stamp increment, stamp placement, and more. IntelliPDF BATES provides more controls that StampPDF, and as a consequence is slightly more difficult to use. IntelliPDF BATES adds a plug-ins menu to the Acrobat menu bar and places a button on the **Advanced Editing** toolbar. It also installs a user's guide that can be accessed from the Help menu.

> Menu (IntelliPDF BATES Help): **Help > Plug-In Help > IntelliPDF BATES**
> Keystroke (IntelliPDF BATES Help): **Alt+H-U-I**

§ 13.3.1 Using IntelliPDF BATES

To create and apply Bates stamps using the IntelliPDF BATES plug-in:

> Toolbar (IntelliPDF BATES): Click on the **IntelliBATES** button on the **Advanced Editing** toolbar
> Menu (IntelliPDF BATES): **Plug-Ins > IntelliPDF Bates**
> Keystroke (IntelliPDF BATES): **Alt+P-I**

The **IntelliPDF Bates** dialog box appears, which is divided into five major areas: Bates (upper left), Elements (middle left), Bates Preview (upper-lower left), Advanced Options (lower left), and Full Preview (right). The control buttons are in the lower right.

§ 13.3.2 Position, Background, and Pages (Bates Section)

The Bates section of the IntelliPDF Bates dialog box has three tabs for setting the position, background, and pages of each stamp to be applied. Remember, you can apply more than one stamp at a time using IntelliPDF BATES. The

Background tab allows you to select a background color for the stamp and adjust the opacity of the background from 0 to 100 percent (transparent to solid).

§ 13.3.3 Properties and Font (Elements Section)

The **Elements** section of the **IntelliPDF BATES** dialog box has three tabs for setting the properties and font of the current stamp. Properties refers to the type of Bates stamp (numeric, alphabetical, alphanumeric, numeric-alpha, static text, or Roman numerals). Properties in the **Elements** section also lets you control the number of characters in the stamp (length), the beginning value (initial value), and the increment value in terms of how much to increase the stamp and how often (to increase by one every page should be the default).

§ 13.3.4 Preview (Bates Preview Section)

This space gives a general depiction of what the stamp elements look like.

§ 13.3.5 Advanced Options Section

The **Advanced Options** section of the **IntelliPDF BATES** dialog box has six tabs for specifying the creation method (Creation), the number of copies (Copies), whether or not to create bookmarks (Bookmarks), whether to use batch mode, which allows the stamp to be applied serially to a group of PDF files (Batch Mode), whether to scale or shift the content so that it is not covered by the stamp (Scale), and a file lookup window to browse for saved sets of preferences (Preferences). The **Creation** tab lets you choose between applying the stamp to the original document or creating a copy of the original document and stamping the copy. The default setting calls for the stamp to be applied to a copy; a good idea, because once the file has been saved the stamp cannot be removed. The **Copies** tab lets you decide how many copies of the stamped document to generate. The copy has the name of the original with "__Bates" appended at the end. If the **Bookmark** option is checked, the plug-in generates a bookmark for each Bates stamp. This helps you to navigate within the stamped pages. Bates stamp bookmarks appear under the section of the bookmarks area. The **Scale** tab allows you to scale a page content while stamping to prevent stamps from overriding the content of the source document. Use the **Move Content To** option to adjust the position of the scaled page content. Finally, the **Preferences** tab can be used to set up a default path for storing your stamp profiles (presets).

§ 13.3.6 Full Preview Section and Action Buttons

The **Full Preview** section of the **IntelliPDF Bates** dialog box displays the current page of the open PDF file, showing the placement of the stamp or stamps that have been set up. The action buttons at the bottom right of the dialog box are to **Load** a preset stamp profile, **Save** the current profile as a preset, **Stamp** to apply the current stamp or stamps to the open document, and **Cancel** (quit without saving or stamping).

§ 13.4 Redacting Information (Redax Redaction Plug-in)

When you share documents with others electronically, the need to redact sensitive information arises eventually. Whether you are sending PDF files to opposing counsel or the court, you will some day need to redact privileged or confidential information. Courts are adopting policies that require counsel to redact personal and sensitive information from documents filed with the court that will be open to public access.

Acrobat 8 Professional includes a powerful redaction function (see Chapter 18). For those with earlier versions of Acrobat or who may need more complex redaction features there is Redax (also from Appligent). This plug-in for Acrobat is designed to completely remove text and scanned images from PDF files. You can use Redax to edit PDF files that need sensitive or privileged information removed before they are made public or shared with opposing counsel. To use Redax with image-on-text files, you simply open a document in Acrobat, then with the click of a menu command Redax searches the document, tags the words specified in a selected text file, and overlays them with the corresponding exemption codes (text, white space, or black space). Each tagged selection can be resized, moved, or deleted. Click another command and a new document is created, and the redacted text is replaced with the exemption codes and deleted. Save the new, redacted document, and it's ready for public viewing or sharing with opposing counsel. To create a privilege log, Redax automatically generates a text file of the final redactions that can be imported into a spreadsheet for printing or for future analysis and reference.

Redax can also be used on image-only files, but with certain limitations. First, because there is no text in image-only files, Redax cannot search and tag specific terms to be redacted. Likewise, Redax cannot generate a text file for use as a privilege log. When working with image-only files, Redax replaces all pixels in the selected area with black pixels. Because pixels are replaced, rather than overlaid, the redacted information cannot be extracted from the final document.

Display Mode 14

Acrobat contains a great feature called Full Screen Mode. Think of Full Screen Mode as display mode. In display mode, the toolbars, menus, and navigation panes disappear, and the current page of the open PDF file fills the screen. Because computer displays do not have the same height-to-width ratio as most PDF files (typically based on standard paper sizes in portrait orientation), the image has a border that fills the screen.

Documents displayed in portrait orientation show more border than documents displayed in landscape orientation (you didn't need this book for that tip, did you?). The color of the border can be set in the **Preferences** dialog box, select **Full Screen** in the left column, then choose **Background color** in the **Full Screen Appearance** section (Figure 14.1).

You can use this feature for presentations in the office, in court, or anywhere else. Display mode can be used to present exhibits at trial, much like specialized trial-presentation applications. There are limits to display mode, but they can be overcome quickly if you are willing to drop back to the standard view for highlighting and zooming in on portions of a page. The shift from display mode to normal and back again can be done in the blink of an eye using the keyboard commands. The process of shifting between Full Screen view and one of the standard page views may seem clunky at first, but with use will become smooth and second nature.

A quick and easy alternative to Full Screen Mode can be achieved by "hiding" the toolbars. Press the **F8** key to hide and

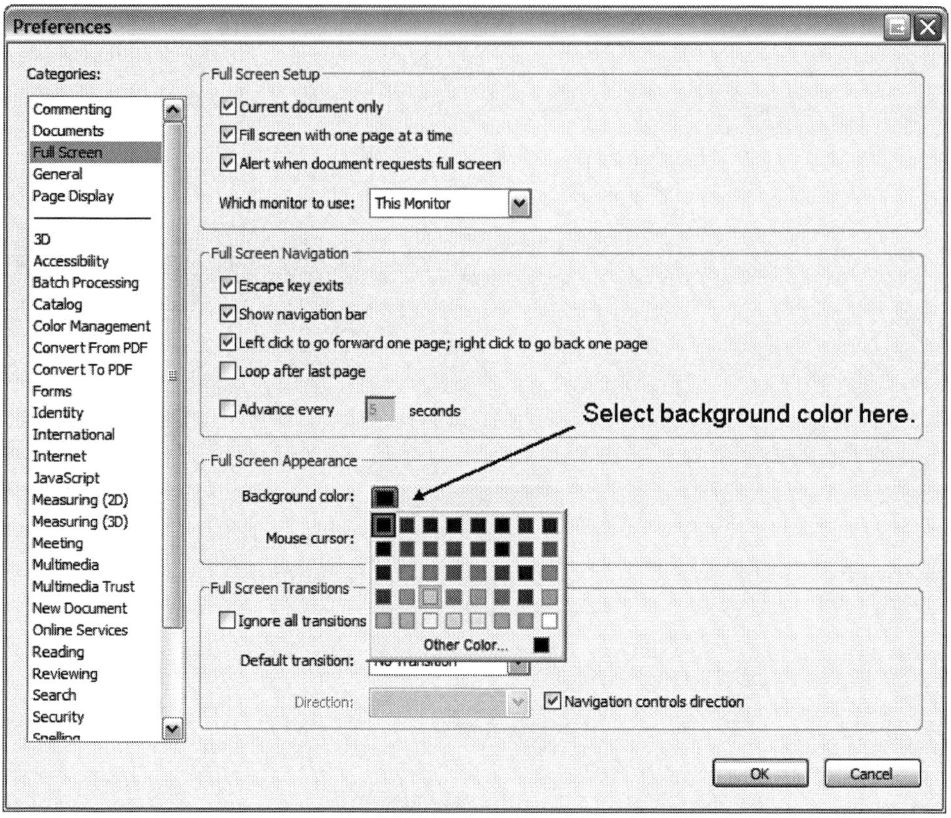

Figure 14.1

unhide the toolbars. The menus, title bar, and navigation icons remain visible on the screen, you simply gain the display real estate taken up by the toolbars (which can be fairly substantial if you display lots of tools). You can gain a bit more screen space by hiding the menu bar with the **F9** key (press **F9** again to restore the menu bar).

Before we go into the details, you might be wondering why you would want to use Acrobat for presentations, rather than Microsoft PowerPoint. The short answer is that if you prepare your presentation in PowerPoint and then print (or publish) it to PDF, anyone with Acrobat Reader can view it. Your audience does not need to have PowerPoint or use the same operating system as you. Your presentation is relatively secure in that you have not sent the viewer the native application file (in PowerPoint format). If your presentation includes full images of pages of original documents, then inserting those full pages into a PDF file works much better than trying to show a full 8 1/2-by-11 page in PowerPoint. Keep in mind that PowerPoint is presentation software, while Acrobat is digital document software. If you need to give a presentation, then PowerPoint might be the better tool. On the other hand, if you need to display and work with digital documents, then Acrobat is the better choice. If you need to give a presentation that includes digital documents, prepare the slides using PowerPoint, print the slide show to PDF, and then insert documents at the desired locations.

Coupling Acrobat's display mode with Adobe Photoshop (or the consumer-grade Photoshop Elements) creates a beefed-up tool. Using Photoshop Elements, you can create a PDF slide show from a mixed collection of PDF image-only or image-on-text documents and photographs. This can be especially useful when combining mixed files into a single PDF for use as a trial exhibit notebook. With Photoshop Elements you can take that huge collection of digital photograph files (JPEG, TIFF, PSD, and so on) that your client, investigator, or expert witness gave you and convert them to a single multipage PDF file. That document can then be enhanced with bookmarks, links, comments, and Bates numbers.

§ 14.1 Using Full Screen View

If you think that Full Screen Mode, or display mode, would be accessed through the **View** menu, you're thinking the right way, and you'll find it there in Acrobat 8. In earlier versions, Full Screen Mode was accessed from the **Window** menu (you'll find it there in Acrobat 8 as well as on the **View** menu).

> Menu (Full Screen View): **View > Full Screen Mode**
> Menu (Full Screen Mode): **Window > Full Screen Mode**
> Keystroke (Full Screen Mode): **Ctrl+L**
> Keystroke (Full Screen Mode): **Alt+W-F**

Once in **Full Screen Mode** there are many ways to navigate from page-to-page. Pick a method that works for you. The two main choices are between using the keyboard or mouse.

- Keyboard Navigation:
  - Move forward one page
    - **Page Down**
    - **Down Arrow**
    - **Right Arrow**
    - **Space Bar**
    - **Enter**

  - Move back one page
    - **Page Up**
    - **Up Arrow** key
    - **Left Arrow** key

Because the **Space Bar** and **Enter** keys advance one page but don't have a "back one page" counterpart, you might not want to rely on them for navigation.

- Mouse (pointer) Navigation:
  Advance one page—**left click**
  Go back one page—**right click**

To use the mouse buttons to navigate as described above you must check the **Left click to go forward one page; right click to go back one page** option in the **Full Screen Navigation** section of the **Full Screen Preferences**. You can scroll both directions with the scroll wheel unless you have the **Hand tool** selected (and it is by default the active tool), and selected **Make Hand tool use mouse-wheel zooming** in **Preferences (General)**. In addition to using the mouse (pointer) buttons, you can use the mouse to navigate via a "navigation bar" if you activate that option in **Preferences**. To activate the **Full Screen Mode** navigation bar:

Menu (Activate Full Screen Mode navigation bar): **Edit > Preferences > Select Full Screen** in the left column and check the box **Show navigation bar** in the **Full Screen Navigation** section

Keystroke (Activate Full Screen Mode navigation bar): **Ctrl+K**, Select **Full Screen** in the left column and check the box **Show navigation bar** in the **Full Screen Navigation** section

Keystroke (Activate Full Screen Mode navigation bar): **Alt+E-N**, Select **Full Screen** in the left column and check the box **Show navigation bar** in the **Full Screen Navigation** section (Figure 14.2)

The navigation bar shows up in Full Screen Mode as a pair of directional symbols (< and >) and a page icon with a curved arrow (Figure 14.3). Clicking the latter exits Full Screen Mode. The navigation bar disappears after about three seconds. Simply mouse-over the lower left area of the screen to make it reappear.

To advance to a specific page while in Full Screen view:

Keystroke (Go To Page): **Shift+Ctrl+N** the **Go To Page** dialog box appears; simply key in the desired page number and press **Enter** or click **OK** (Figure 14.4).

Using the **Go To Page _n_** function allows you to jump from one exhibit (image) to another in a nonlinear manner so long as you have a list of the page numbers on which each exhibit (image) begins. You jump to the first page of the exhibit then use the Page Down, Arrow Down, Right Arrow keys or left click to advance one page at a time (bookmarks are not visible in Full Screen Mode).

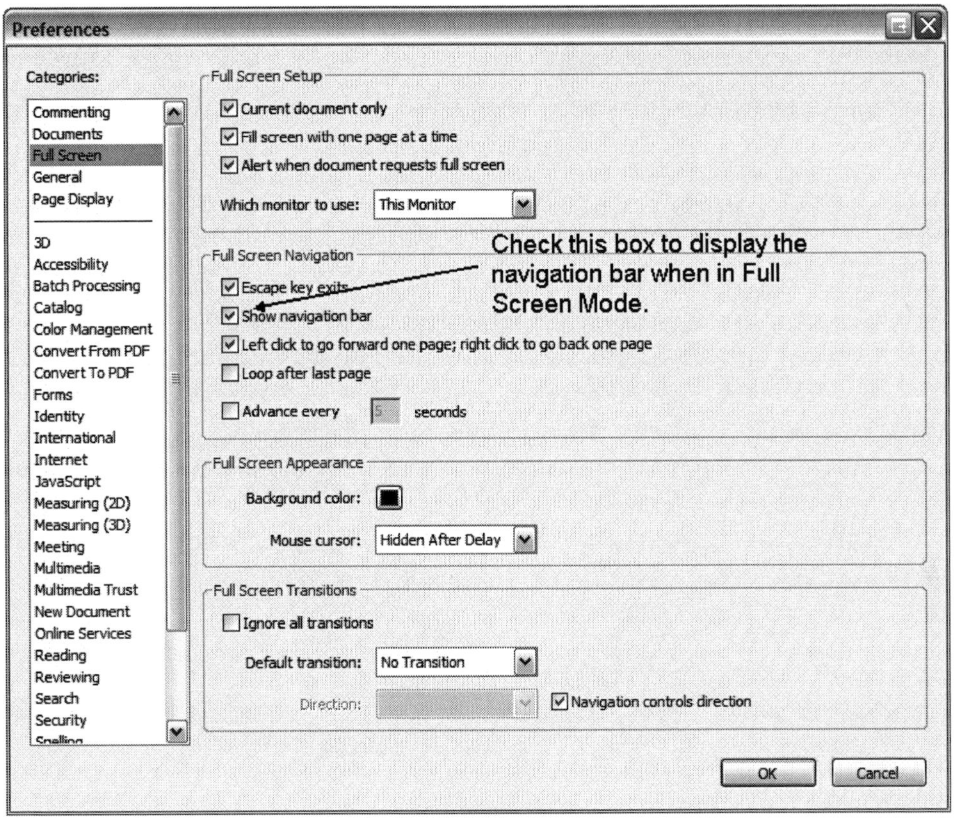

Preferences

Categories:

Commenting
Documents
Full Screen
General
Page Display

3D
Accessibility
Batch Processing
Catalog
Color Management
Convert From PDF
Convert To PDF
Forms
Identity
International
Internet
JavaScript
Measuring (2D)
Measuring (3D)
Meeting
Multimedia
Multimedia Trust
New Document
Online Services
Reading
Reviewing
Search
Security
Spelling

Full Screen Setup

☑ Current document only
☑ Fill screen with one page at a time
☑ Alert when document requests full screen

Which monitor to use: This Monitor ▾

Full Screen Navigation

Check this box to display the navigation bar when in Full Screen Mode.

☑ Escape key exits
☑ Show navigation bar
☑ Left click to go forward one page; right click to go back one page
☐ Loop after last page
☐ Advance every ⬚5⬚ seconds

Full Screen Appearance

Background color: ⬛
Mouse cursor: Hidden After Delay ▾

Full Screen Transitions

☐ Ignore all transitions
Default transition: No Transition ▾
Direction: ⬚ ☑ Navigation controls direction

OK   Cancel

Figure 14.2

Figure 14.3

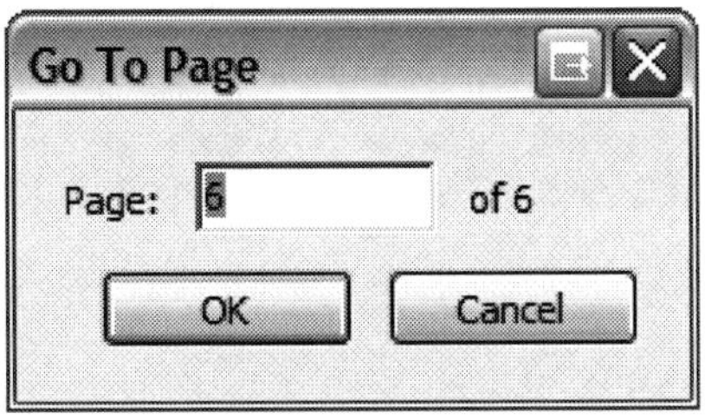

Go To Page

Page: ⬚6⬚ of 6

OK   Cancel

Figure 14.4

To leave Full Screen view (display mode) and return to the normal view, simply press the **Esc** (Escape) key:

Keystroke (Return to Normal View): **Esc**

§ 14.2 PDF Exhibit Notebook

Using Acrobat to create a trial exhibit notebook and then using Full Screen view to display those exhibits at trial is easy and very effective. Here are the basic instructions (you might find a quicker and better way to do this):

First, assuming that all of your exhibits exist as PDF files, mark each for use at trial. Most courts have rules (or at least preferences) for how exhibits are marked. For example, all plaintiff's exhibits are numbered while the defendant's exhibits are lettered.

Next, create an exhibit log (you should probably do this for the other side's exhibits as well). The log can be as simple as the following table (Table 14.1):

Exhibit	Page #	Description	Offered (Yes/No)	Stipulated (Yes/No)	Admitted (Yes/No)
1	2	Letter dated . . .			
2	5	Invoice dated . . .			

Table 14.1

Next, use a word processing application to create a one-page document that says something like (Figure 14.5):

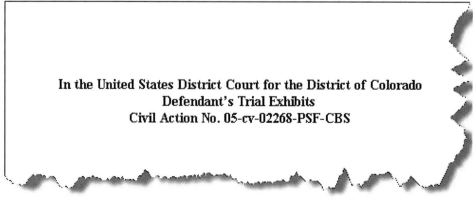

In the United States District Court for the District of Colorado
Defendant's Trial Exhibits
Civil Action No. 05-cv-02268-PSF-CBS

Figure 14.5

Print this page to PDF and use it as the first page of your exhibit notebook. It also serves as a place to park your presentation so that the judge and jury aren't left to stare at an exhibit (unless you want them to).

Once you have created your cover page and have your exhibits marked for identification, combine all the pages into a single PDF file (name it something like AllTrialExhibits.pdf). Start with the cover page and insert the exhibits one at a time. As you insert exhibits, do two things: (1) put the beginning page number in the log on the row for that exhibit, and (2) create a bookmark at the beginning of each exhibit (use names like "1 Smith-Jones Contract" and "2 Smith to Jones Deed"). Putting the page number on the exhibit log and adding bookmarks to your exhibit notebook PDF file assumes that you have exhibits of more than one page. If all your exhibits are only one page, then you could probably get by with renumbering the pages; you would need to renumber the pages to account for the cover page (using virtual page numbering; see Chapter 6). You can then jump to any point in the document by page number. During trial you can navigate between exhibits in normal view using the **Bookmarks** pane or by using the **Go To Page** function (using the exhibit log to determine the first page of the desired exhibit). As a bonus, use the log to keep track of what exhibits were admitted by stipulation, offered and admitted, or offered and denied. The judge, courtroom clerk, and opposing counsel will appreciate receiving copies of the exhibit logs. If you copy all your exhibits to CD-ROM to give copies to the court and opposing counsel, they can use the log to go to a specific page in the exhibit notebook.

To use the Acrobat exhibit notebook during trial, display the cover page and bookmarks. When you want a witness to talk about a particular exhibit, click on the bookmark for that exhibit, lay an appropriate foundation, move to admit, and then use the exhibit. For example:

> **Counsel**: I call your attention to the screen where I am displaying what has been marked for identification as Exhibit 16; are you familiar with subject of the photograph?
>
> **Witness**: Yes.
>
> **Counsel**: Explain the basis of your familiarity with the subject of the photograph.
>
> **Witness**: It's a picture that I took of the scene of the accident.
>
> **Counsel**: Is the photograph a good, fair, accurate, or true representation of the accident scene?
>
> **Witness**: Yes.
>
> **Counsel**: Your Honor, I move for the admission of Exhibit 16.

In a jury trial you may need to use a paper copy of the exhibit to lay the foundation with the witness. Once the exhibit has been admitted, click on the bookmark or go to the page number for that exhibit so that the jury can see it while the witness testifies. If you "park" the display on the cover page in Full Screen view, press **Ctrl+Shift+N**, enter the beginning page number of the desired exhibit, and then press **Enter** or click **OK**.

If you display the exhibit in Full Screen view (**Ctrl+L**), you can still zoom in or out without returning to normal view. However, zooming (magnifying) in display mode only works on the center of the current document; if you need to zoom in on something beyond the center (say information in the upper right-hand corner), you'll need to go back to the normal view and use the dynamic zoom tool.

To zoom in (magnify) while in display mode:

Menu: None
Keystroke (Zoom In Full Screen View): **Ctrl++** (**Control** and "+") to zoom in; **Ctrl+-** (**Control** and "-") to zoom out.
Keystroke (Zoom In Full Screen View): **Ctrl+M**, then select or type the desired magnification. Note: Zoom in Full Screen Mode focuses on the top left of the page; after you zoom in you can then "pan" the page use the up-down-left-right arrow key to bring the desired area to the center of the display.

Experiment in your office with ways to organize and display exhibits using Acrobat. As you develop a system that you are comfortable with, practice it. Practice in your office using Acrobat to review exhibits before depositions or trial. Practice using Acrobat to present exhibits during depositions. In a short time, you will become comfortable using Acrobat to organize and present exhibits. When that happens, there will be no more shuffling of paper in the courtroom.

§ 14.3 Full Screen View Preferences

You can set default preferences for how Full Screen view looks and acts. To access the Preferences dialog box:

Menu (Full Screen Preferences): **Edit > Preferences**
Keystroke (Full Screen Preferences): **Ctrl+K**

When the **Preferences** dialog box appears, select **Full Screen** in the window on the left (Figure 14.6). The dialog box now has two parts: **Full Screen Navigation** and **Full Screen Appearance**. In the **Navigation** section, you can set Acrobat to advance one page at a time, at a set interval, whenever documents are displayed in Full Screen view. Leaving the **Advance every __ seconds** box unchecked requires you to manually advance the pages. If you want Acrobat to continually advance through the pages, check the **Loop after last**

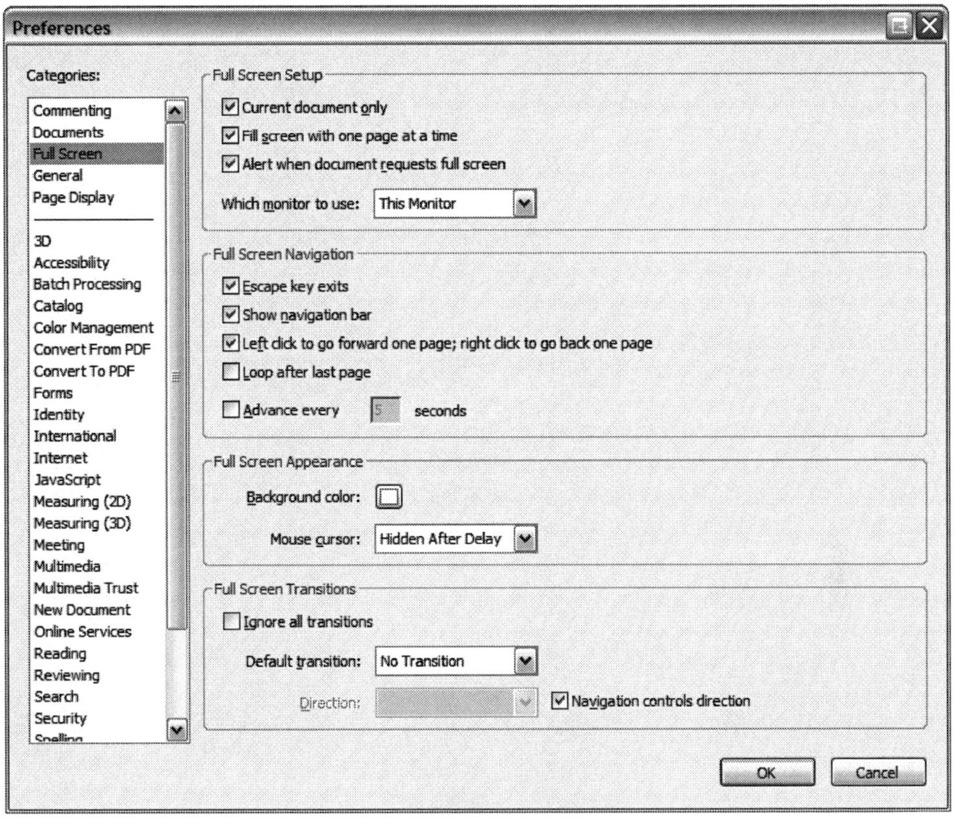

Figure 14.6

page box. When the **Escape key exits** box is unchecked, the only way to exit Full Screen view is to close the document with the keyboard command **Ctrl+F4**.

The bottom section of the **Full Screen Preferences** dialog box controls the default appearance whenever documents are displayed in Full Screen view. You can select from a number of transition types (how one page replaces another); or whether the pointer (Mouse cursor) is always hidden, always visible, or hidden after a delay. Finally, you can set the background color (border color) to any shade that your computer can display (some computers can display more colors than others).

Electronic Briefs 15

This chapter brings together some of the material from other chapters in a practical explanation of how to use Acrobat to create electronic briefs. While an electronic brief is used as the example here, do not limit your thinking to just briefs. Consider complex communications to clients with multiple enclosures, detailed in-house research memos, or contracts with cross-referenced sections, appendices, and exhibits.

§ 15.1 Why Acrobat for Electronic Briefs?

Most appellate court rules do not presently provide for the filing of electronic briefs. However, many courts have expressed an interest in receiving electronic briefs and are in the process of developing internal and public rules. This chapter describes in detail how to create complex digital or electronic documents.

Many courts and government agencies have adopted PDF as the standard file format. Accordingly, the process detailed here relies on Acrobat for assembling the electronic brief. Acrobat also provides a means to convert paper documents to electronic copies that can be attached or linked to the brief. It would be hard to imagine a law firm today not using a computer and word processing application to generate a brief for filing with the court. Because almost all documents generated in the typical law firm are created electronically, the process described here begins at the point when the brief has been completed and would be printed on paper and signed.

§ 15.2 Printing a Markup Copy

Before printing the final word processing file to PDF, print it on paper. The responsible lawyer should review the paper version and mark all references that are linked to source materials (cases, statutes, transcripts, the record on appeal, and so on). Consider also whether the links should appear in a color other than black. Indicating links by way of a different font color helps the reader know where links exist. The tasks of creating the links, changing the color of the text, and assembling the electronic brief can all be delegated to a staff person who works from the printed version with highlighted references.

§ 15.3 Printing to PDF

To print the final brief word processing file to PDF, use a **print** command within the native application that allows for printer selection (WordPerfect: **File > Print**, or **Ctrl+P**, or **F5**; Word: File > **Print**, or **Ctrl+P**), and then choose a printer driver that prints to PDF (see also Section 4.1). When Acrobat has been installed on a computer, the installation routine adds a new virtual printer, Adobe PDF. With this virtual printer, any file on the computer that can be printed to a hardware printer can be printed to PDF. Certain image-file types, such as JPEG, TIFF, and BMP, can be printed to PDF by dragging and dropping the file icon (for example, from Windows Explorer) onto the empty Acrobat document window.

§ 15.4 Scanning to PDF

To use Acrobat to create a PDF file by scanning (see also Section 4.2), from the **File** menu select **Create PDF > From Scanner**, or use keystrokes **Alt+F-F-S**. Acrobat now asks for a file name before the physical scanning process begins; select an appropriate folder and assign a file name. At this point in the process, check the settings for paper size, resolution, and whether the documents will pass through a feeder. Once the document has finished scanning, you have the option to add more pages to the scanner and pages to the PDF file being created. When Done has been selected, the scanned image appears in the document window.

Scan documents at a resolution of **300 dots per inch** (dpi). That resolution produces near-photocopy quality when printed. In order to minimize size of scanned image files, select scanner output settings for **black and white** (sometimes listed as **text** or **line drawing**). Select **color** or **gray scale** output settings only when necessary (these settings produce substantially larger files). If the documents to be scanned contain drawings, handwritten notes, or the like (content not susceptible to OCR), provide a description by way of the **Document Properties** window.

Menu (Document Properties): **File > Properties**
Keystroke (Document Properties): **Alt+F-R**
Keystroke (Document Properties): **Crtl+D** (Figure 15.1)

The **Document Properties** window opens. On the **Description** tab, supply appropriate information (title, author, subject and keywords). The information included in the Document Properties description is included in any index generated and provides a means to locate the document using the Acrobat or Windows Explorer search function.

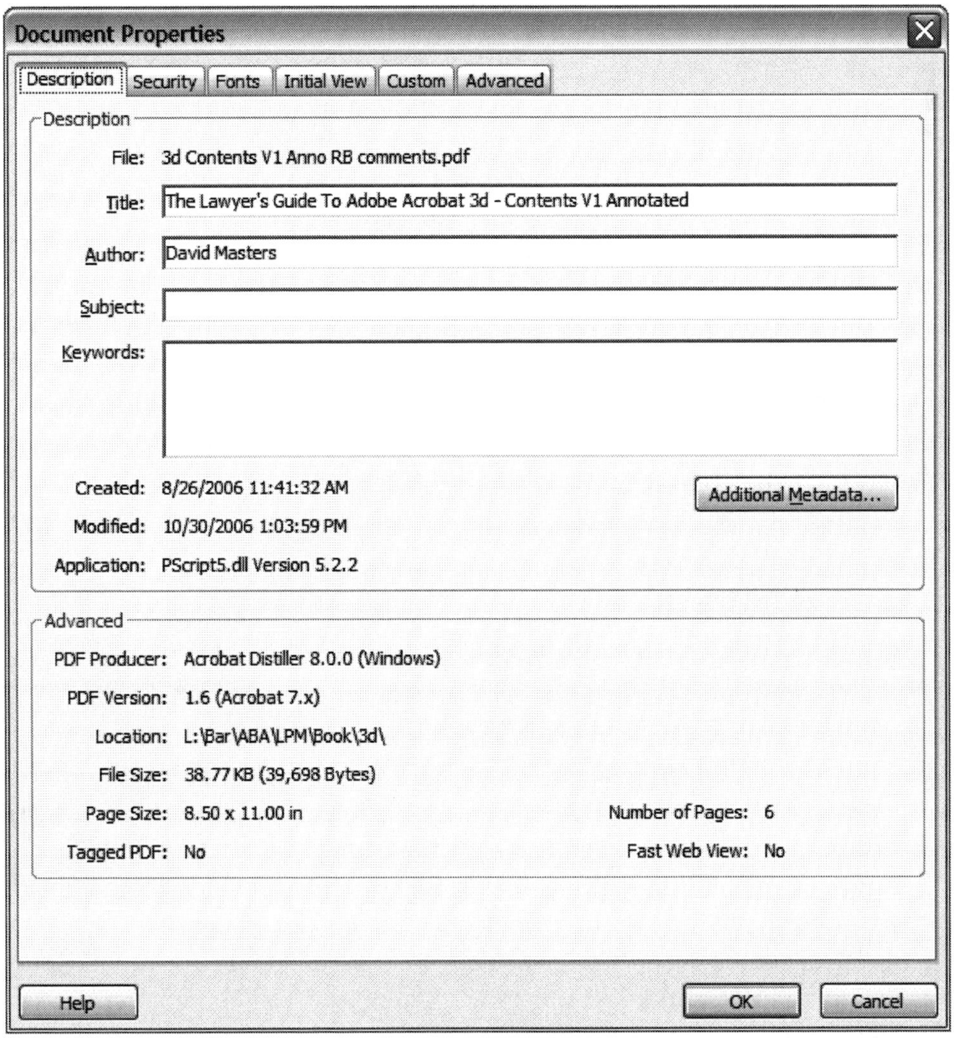

Figure 15.1

§ 15.5 Creating and Organizing the Source Materials

When possible, source materials (such as cases, statutes, and trial transcripts) should be printed to PDF from an existing digital source. For example, case law retrieved from an online source or CD-ROM can be printed directly to PDF. Use short logical names for these materials, such as a short form of their citation (such as "Whinnery 895P2d537"). Observing this naming convention results in the cases arranging themselves in alphabetical order, making them easier to locate when building the links. Avoid using periods, commas, and other punctuation marks when naming these files. Whenever possible, obtain digital copies of transcripts. Using a transcript management application such as RealLegal Binder, Summation, LiveNote, or TextMap, print the transcript to PDF. Alternatively, open the transcript file in a word processing application, adjust the formatting as necessary (often a frustrating process), and then print the file to PDF.

Some source materials to be linked to the brief are not available in digital format. For example, copies of contracts, answers to interrogatories, or affidavits may only be available in paper form. These documents should be scanned and, if they are good copies or originals contain mostly text, then these images should be converted to text by OCR. By performing OCR on these documents they become searchable, and links can be made to pinpoint locations. OCR can be performed from within Acrobat by selecting **OCR Text Recognition** from the Document menu (**Document > OCR Text Recognition**, or by using keystrokes: **Alt+D-C**). Some third-party OCR applications convert PDF image files, retaining an exact copy of the original while creating a text file behind the image. Keep in mind that OCR does not produce perfect results; the primary purpose is to provide a text background that can be searched for quick reference.

§ 15.6 Planning and Organization

Decide whether the reference materials will be attached to the original document (by inserting pages), or maintained as separate document files. Short works, such as motions, lend themselves to inclusion of all reference materials; longer, more complex documents, such as appellate briefs, should link to external documents. No precise guideline can be stated for when to do one or the other, nor have the courts promulgated rules addressing this issue. The detailed procedures described below address both all-in-one documents (simple electronic briefs) and documents with links to external reference materials (complex electronic briefs).

If producing a complex electronic brief, the linking process must be performed on the local hard disk drive. In other words, the final PDF version of the brief and all source materials must exist on the local C drive. This step must be observed—building the complex electronic brief on a network drive results in nonfunctional links when the final product is transferred to CD.

§ 15.6.1 Organization of Complex Electronic Briefs

To begin this process, create a folder for the project, such as CD Smith Brief (using this convention, rather than Smith Brief CD, places all the CD projects in the same area of the hard disk drive when viewed through Windows Explorer). Within the project folder, create subfolders for briefs and source materials, for example:

> Briefs (C:\CD Smith Brief\Brief)
> > Authorities (C:\CD Smith Brief\Authorities)
> > > Cases (C:\CD Smith Brief\Authorities\Cases)
> > > Statutes (C:\CD Smith Brief\Authorities\Statutes)
> > > Regulations (C:\CD Smith Brief\Authorities\Regulations)
> > > CourtRules (C:\CD Smith Brief\Authorities\CourtRules)
> > Transcripts (C:\ CD Smith Brief\Transcripts)
> > Record (C:\ CD Smith Brief\Record)

A set of empty folders can be created and saved for repeated use. This provides a standard taxonomy for all electronic brief disks generated in the future (Figure 15.2).

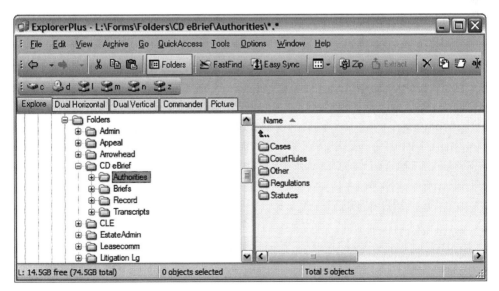

Figure 15.2

A staff person can retrieve cases and statutes from online or CD-ROM sources, print them to PDF, and save them to the appropriate folders. Scan the record to PDF (this way the images of the record on the final CD have the numbering supplied by the trial court appellate clerk). After scanning the record, run the file through an OCR application such as OmniPagePro or the OCR feature in Acrobat.

Menu (OCR): **Document > OCR Text Recognition**
Keystroke (OCR): **Alt+D-C**

If the trial court provides an electronic record, then this step is not necessary.

§ 15.6.2 Organization of Simple Electronic Briefs

The simple electronic brief process may be done at any work station with Adobe Acrobat. Because the brief file and source files are combined into a single PDF file, the final product may exist on a network drive and need not be copied to the local drive. The CD may be recorded from a network source but may work better when the source file exists on the local hard disk drive of the CD-R machine.

When the brief has reached its final form (ready to be printed, and the linked references are color-changed if desired), print it to PDF. Using Acrobat, open the document and bookmark the major divisions (including the first page) by going to the desired location and pressing **Ctrl-B**. After creating the bookmarks, go to the end of the document (**Ctrl+Shift+Page Down** or **Ctrl+End**), and insert the first item to be linked. To insert this document:

Menu (Insert Pages): **Document > Insert Pages**
Keystroke (Insert Pages): **Ctrl+Shift+I**

Find the file representing the pages to be inserted, highlight and double-click it, and click **OK**. After Acrobat inserts these pages, the display remains at the former last page of the document; advance one page (to the first page of the document that was just inserted), and insert a bookmark identifying the document. After these pages have been inserted, go to the end of the document (now the last page of the most recently inserted file), and repeat the process until all source materials have been incorporated into the brief.

When adding documents to the original, group them by type (for example, put all the cases in first, then the transcripts, then the affidavits, then the other exhibits); within each grouping insert the documents in the order of appearance in the pleading.

Think of this as taking photocopies of the cases cited and grouping them together in the order of appearance, then taking a group of transcripts, putting them in order, and attaching them to the growing document. Creating the links to documents that have been inserted into the original document is discussed later.

§ 15.7 Creating the Links

Links are the heart and soul of electronic briefs. Links make electronic briefs interactive and truly powerful. When a citation to a case, statute, or other authority appears in your brief, it can be linked to the cited material so that with a click of the mouse the reader sees the authority you have cited. While the next two sections describe the process for creating links, you may wish to review Section 6.2 for a more detailed discussion on creating links.

Using Acrobat, the responsible lawyer or a staff person opens the brief and begins building the links. Find the first reference in the brief to be linked to a source.

§ 15.7.1 Using Right-Click to Create Links

The easiest way to create links in a PDF image-on-text file is by right-clicking. With the **Select** tool active (Figure 15.3), drag to select the text of the citation (full case name, reference to record, reference to exhibit, and so on). Next, right-click on the selected text and choose **Create Link** (Figure 15.4). The **Cre-**

Figure 15.3

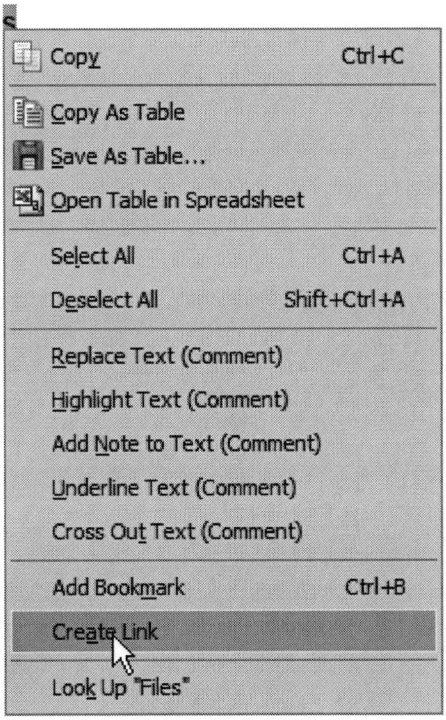

Copy	Ctrl+C
Copy As Table	
Save As Table...	
Open Table in Spreadsheet	
Select All	Ctrl+A
Deselect All	Shift+Ctrl+A
Replace Text (Comment)	
Highlight Text (Comment)	
Add Note to Text (Comment)	
Underline Text (Comment)	
Cross Out Text (Comment)	
Add Bookmark	Ctrl+B
Create Link	
Look Up "Files"	

Figure 15.4

ate **Link** dialog box appears (Figure 15.5). The **Create Link** dialog box in allows you to set the appearance of the link: select **Invisible Rectangle** from the drop down menu. Next, select **Go to Page View** or **Open a file**, browse to the desired destination and click **Set Link**. Assuming that you selected **Invisible Rectangle**, then, after the link has been created click on the **Link** tool (it looks like the links of chain and appears only on the **Advanced Editing** toolbar), the link you created will be highlighted, right-click on the link and select **Use Current Appearance as New Default**. Continue through the brief, setting links. Selecting **Open a file** in the **Create Link** window displays a dialog box permitting location and selection of the destination file.

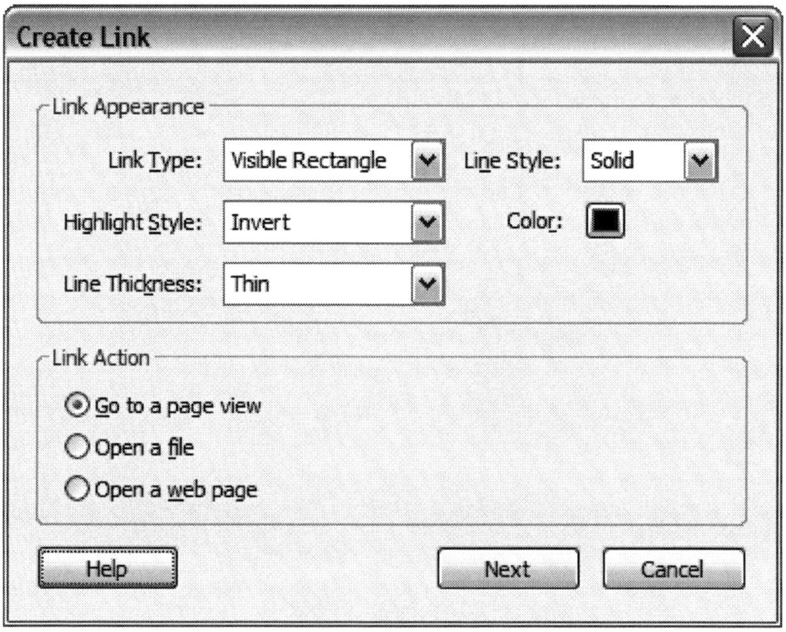

Figure 15.5

§ 15.7.2 Using the Link Tool

Click on the **Link** tool; it looks like the links of chain and appears only on the **Advanced Editing** toolbar (see also Section 6.2) (Figure 15.6). To display the Advanced Editing toolbar, from the **View** menu select **Toolbars > Advanced**

Figure 15.6

Editing. Next, drag a box around the citation (full case name, reference to record, reference to exhibit, and so on), choose **Go to Page View** or **Open a file**, then set the link destination. The **Create Link** dialog box in allows you to set the appearance of the link. Assuming that you select **Invisible Rectangle**, then, after the link has been created select **Use Current Appearance as New Default**. Continue through the brief, setting links. Selecting **Open a file** in the **Create Link** window displays a dialog box permitting location and selection of the destination file.

To make a link go to a specific page in the destination file, open the destination file and navigate to the desired page. Drag to create the link box. When the **Create Link** dialog box appears select **Go to Page View**, then switch to the destination file (**Alt+Tab** or click on the destination file in the Task Bar) and click **Set Link**.

In the simple electronic brief, where all source materials are inserted into the original document, the linking process can be made easier by creating bookmarks to the destinations before beginning the linking process. Go to the first item to be linked, select the **Link** tool, drag a box around the citation or reference, and choose **Go to Page View**. Click on the bookmark for the desired destination then click **Set Link**. Once the link has been established, the dialog box closes. Continue working through the document building links. After all links have been made, a test CD should be given to another staff person, so he or she can walk through the brief, confirming that all links work properly.

§ 15.7.3 Stylistic Considerations

Each brief should include a table of contents with links to the various sections. The table of authorities should link to the first page of source materials. Within the brief, specific citations should be pinpointed whenever appropriate.

§ 15.8 Copying the Finished Product to CD

Creating a CD containing one or more briefs and cited materials requires that the linking process be performed on the local hard disk drive. In other words, the final PDF version of the brief and all source materials must exist on the local C drive (not a network drive). This step must be observed—building the complex electronic brief on a network drive results in nonfunctional links when the final product is transferred to CD. If the folder structure described in Section 15.6.1 has been followed, then the contents page, the "About this CD" file, the files and folders created by cataloging or indexing the materials, and the auto-run feature are in the root folder C:\CD Smith Brief.

§ 15.8.1 Creating and Including a Contents Page

A contents page may be included as a convenience to the court and to others who read the briefs. The contents page is a simple document, prepared with a word processing application and then printed to PDF, listing the primary objects on the disk; each item in the list is linked to the appropriate destination. A sample contents page can be found at the end of this chapter.

The contents page, if included, is opened by the auto-run application. In this way, a user places the CD-ROM in a drive and the contents page automatically opens. Then from the contents page the reader can navigate to the desired brief or record volume by clicking on links.

§ 15.8.2 Creating and Including an "About this CD" File

Include an "About this CD" file on the CD-ROM to aid users. A sample file appears at the end of the chapter. This page provides a place where the user can find a description of the organization and structure of the CD. It also provides a place to describe any errata or special features of the briefs and record compiled on the CD.

§ 15.8.3 Indexing the CD Contents

You can use the Acrobat Catalog feature (Figure 15.7) to create a full-text index of PDF files or document collections. Creating a full-text index can speed up

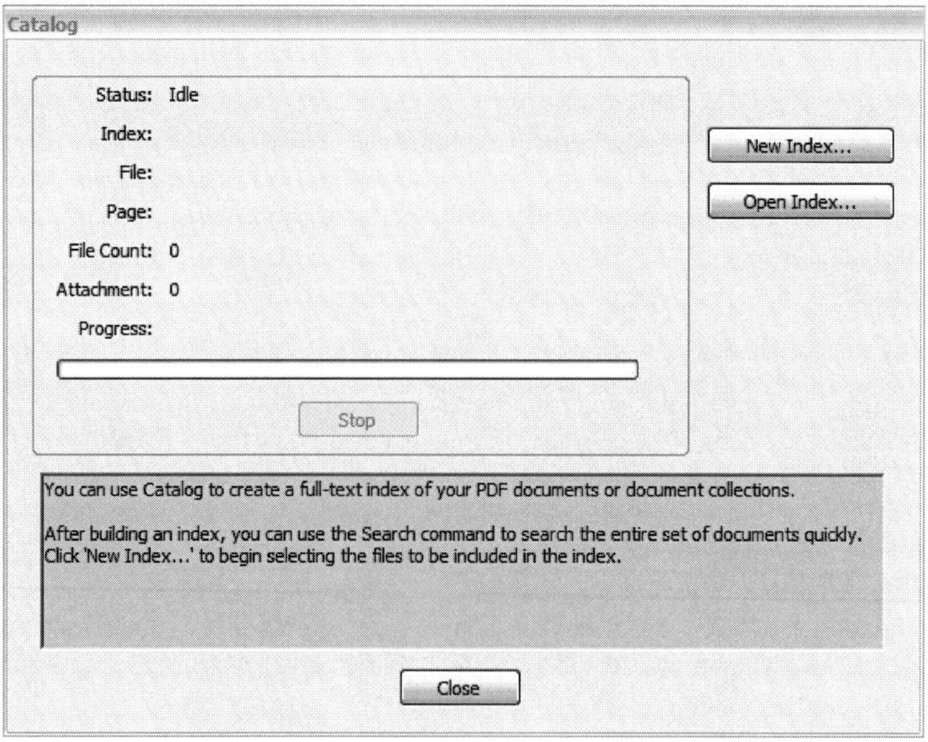

Figure 15.7

the search process. This can be helpful if large PDF file collections of appellate documents need to be searched repeatedly. Note that information contained in comments and document descriptions related to image-only PDF files are included in the index and found using the **Search** function. To create an index:

Menu (Catalog): **Advanced > Document Processing > Full Text Index with Catalog**, then select **New Index**

Keystroke (Catalog): **Alt+A-D-T**, then select **New Index** (Figure 15.8)

The **New Index Definition** dialog box opens. Type a name for the index, provide a description (if desired), select the folders (directories) that contain

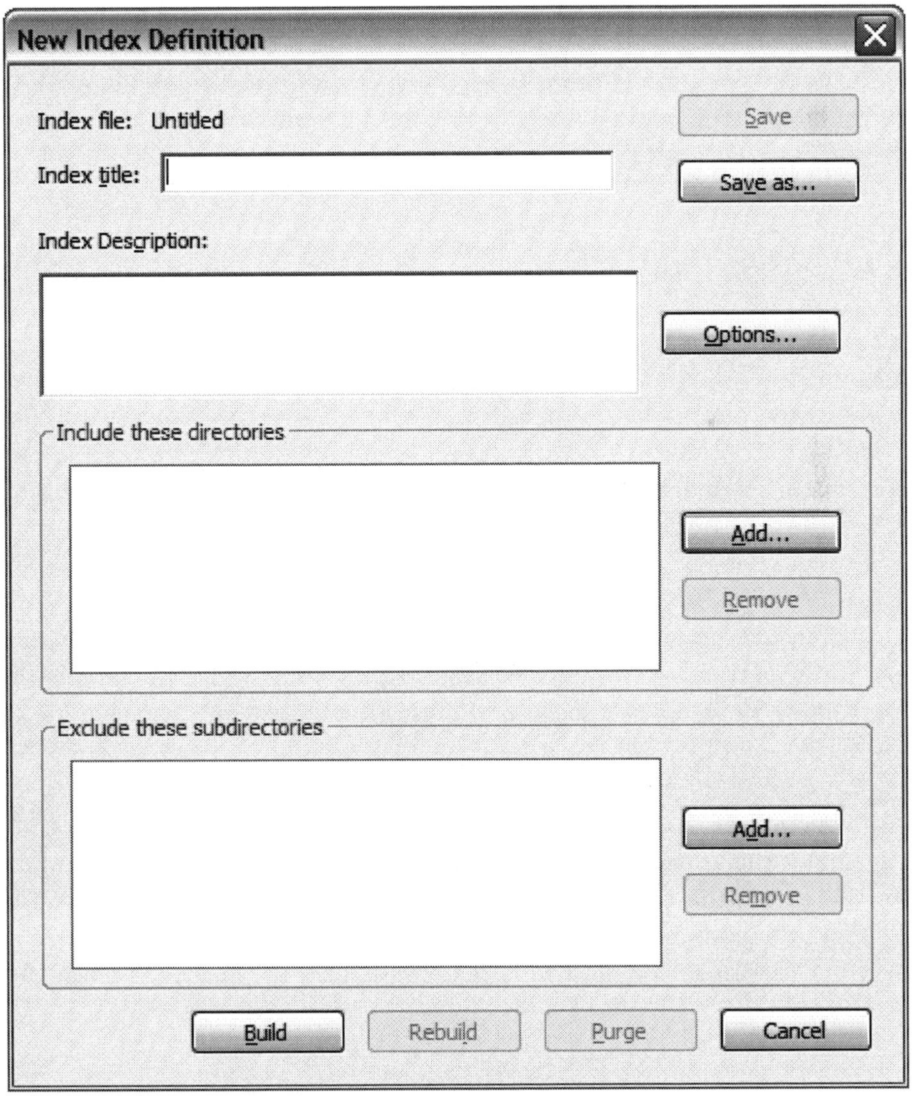

Figure 15.8

the PDF files to be included in the index (you can also select subdirectories to be excluded), and click **Build**. When you build a new index, the results are a new .pdx file and a new folder (named Index) that contains one or more .idx files. The .pdx file, which is small, makes the information in the .idx files available to the search function. The .idx files contain the index entries that a user finds in the index, so their file sizes—individually or collectively—can be large. All of these files must be available to users who want to search the index.

§ 15.8.4 Adding an Auto-run Feature

The auto-run feature does what the name implies: when a CD-ROM is inserted into the computer, it causes an application (Reader or Acrobat) to open a specified file. For electronic briefs you need only a rudimentary auto-run application to instruct the computer to open a specific file, typically the contents page file described above in Section 15.8.1. To find an application that creates the auto-run feature, Google "autorun" and browse through the results until you find what you need.

§ 15.9 Service and Filing

At present, few appellate courts have developed rules for service and filing of electronic briefs. If your court has established rules, by all means follow them; otherwise, two alternatives are described below. While either meets the needs of the court, it would be most desirable to end up with all briefs, cases, and record materials linked on a single disk. Both alternatives require cooperation and coordination among counsel for the parties.

§ 15.9.1 Alternative 1

In this alternative, the appellant files the opening brief on disk. The disk contains the brief, the record, and all legal authorities cited. The brief is constructed with links to the record and authorities. Next, the appellee files an answer brief on CD-ROM. The appellee's disk contains a copy of everything from the appellant's opening-brief disk, as well as the answer brief and any additional authorities cited. If contents pages were used, a new one is generated. Finally, the appellant files and serves the reply brief. This disk contains everything from the opening-brief disk and the answer-brief disk along with the reply brief and any additional authorities cited. Again, if contents pages are used, a new one is created with links to the primary materials on the final disk.

§ 15.9.2 Alternative 2

In this alternative a single disk, containing all briefs, the record, and legal authorities, is filed at some point after all the paper filings have been submitted to the court. This alternative has the hallmark of simplicity, eliminates the task of creating electronic versions of briefs contemporaneously with the paper versions, and allows either or both parties to participate in creating the final product.

Sample Contents Page

CD CONTENTS

[Click Here for Information about this CD]

Appellant's Opening Brief

Appellee's Joint Answer Brief

Appellant's Reply Brief

Record

      Volume I

      Volume II

      Volume III

      Volume IV

      Volume V

      Volume VI

      Volume VII

Cases

Statutes

Court Rules

Miscellaneous

Sample "About this CD" File

ABOUT THIS CD

<u>Rationale</u>. This CD was prepared by _____, as a convenience to the court and counsel. If your computer has a CD-ROM drive and Adobe Acrobat or Acrobat Reader, you need only insert the CD; it should auto-run and open to a CD Contents page. If it does not auto-run, use Windows Explorer, Acrobat, or the Reader program to open the file "001 Contents."

<u>Errata</u>. While preparing the digital versions of these briefs we noticed several typographical errors in _____. We did not correct the errors but did make the links to incorrectly cited cases and statutes go to the appropriate documents.

<u>File Format</u>. All files on this CD are in Adobe Portable Document Format (PDF). There are image-only PDFs and image-on-text files. Image-only PDFs are just that; images only, just digital photocopies of paper documents. Image-on-text files have an exact image of the hard copy with text behind the image. Image-on-text files are created by printing to PDF or by running a PDF image-only file through an optical character recognition (OCR) application. On this CD, the first nine pages of Appellant's opening brief were scanned and then OCR'd; the remainder of the opening brief was obtained from Appellant's counsel in PDF format. The Appellant's Appendix was scanned; no OCR was performed on the Appendix; thus, the Appendix consists of PDF image-only files. The Appellant's reply brief was scanned and OCR'd. The Appellee's answer brief was printed to PDF, as were all of the cases and selected statutes.

<u>Links</u>. The Table of Contents in each brief has been linked to the appropriate section in the body of the brief. Additionally, references to the record and citations to case law have been linked to their respective sources. Note: the links are not color coded. Move the pointer over a citation to the record or case law, when the "hand" changes to a hand with a "pointing finger," click and referenced material is displayed. To return to the main document use the Return to Previous View button. If you drill down very far into the documents, it may be easiest simply to reopen the main contents file, rather than clicking the Return to Previous View button numerous times.

<u>File Structure</u>. The CD has been set to auto-run and open to the CD Contents page. All of the cases cited by the parties are collected in a folder named Cases. There are no links from the CD Contents page to the individual cases (there are links from the Table of Authorities to each case). Each volume of the Appellant's Appendix has been included in a folder named ApltApndx. Statutes cited by Appellee have been reproduced and linked. Court rules cited by the parties have not been reproduced and linked.

Acrobat in the Paper-Free Office **16**

This chapter brings together material from other parts of the book in a practical explanation of how to use Acrobat as the foundation for a paper-free office. Because Acrobat allows us to handle digital documents in ways similar to how we work with paper documents, it can provide the foundation for a paper-free office.

§ 16.1 Why Go Paper Free with Acrobat?

Consider for a moment what it would be like to be able to find documents at your desk without rummaging through file cabinets or boxes. Think of all the paper you put in files because someday you might need it, only to never see it again. Consider the unpleasant process of closing those files and moving them to storage. Recall the times you've gone to storage to retrieve a single piece of paper. Now, consider keeping all those documents in electronic format, readily available if needed, and then closing files by dragging them from an active work directory to an archive directory.

Paper takes up space, weighs a lot, becomes misplaced or even lost, and is just plain cumbersome to work with. Your client brings you three banker boxes of documents. You spend hours sifting and organizing the documents into folders, which are in turn organized in various Redwelds. You spend hours rummaging through the folders and Redwelds knowing that one document can be found in there—somewhere. On the day of trial you pull out the trusted dolly and load up your boxes and Redwelds and head to the courthouse; or maybe it's the day of closing and you head to the closing conference with your boxes of documents. The Redwelds are splitting at the seams; they begin to fray and tear. Then opposing counsel makes mention of that one special document. You race through the boxes, Redwelds, and folders. Your fingers tear through the pages. There is better and easier way. Switch to electronic files—digital copies, paper free or paperless—call it what you will. Electronic files can be organized, stored, moved from place-to-place, and retrieved far more efficiently than printed to paper documents.

Acrobat provides good image acquisition capabilities and the ability to perform optical character recognition (OCR) on the images while retaining an exact image of the scanned pages. PDF files can be shared with just about anyone who has a computer, including clients, other lawyers, and the courts. Federal and state courts that have activated systems for the electronic filing of documents have settled on PDF as the standard. If the courts are using PDF, then it should be a good standard for use in the office.

In addition to using Acrobat for creating PDF files by acquiring images with a scanner or printing image-on-text PDF files from native applications, you can use Acrobat to make the PDF files truly useful. As you know from the earlier chapters, you can add bookmarks and sticky notes to image-only files. You know that if the files have a text background, you can highlight (pick your color—any color), underline, and strike through. PDF files with background text can be searched; image-only files cannot be searched but information contained in the **Document Properties** or in attached notes is included in indexes of document collections.

§ 16.2 Law Office Information Systems

Lawyers and law firms process information. We receive information from clients and other sources, we add information gained from research and experience, and we deliver information. The information that lawyers deliver takes many forms. It may be a pleading, an oral presentation to a court, an opinion letter, or an agreement; but in the end, lawyers process and deliver information.

Most of the information that comes into the law office arrives in the form of documents. For that matter, most of the information output from law offices—work product—goes out as some form of document. Taking a very simple and abstract view of the typical law office, there are three primary systems involved in processing documents:

◆ A document generation system
◆ A document copying or replication system
◆ A document retention or filing system

The document generation system includes more than computers and printers; it includes fax machines, couriers, and the daily mail. The outside sources generate as many documents as the internal systems—documents that contain information that lawyers need to analyze, store, and retrieve. When documents come into the law office, the information system looks something like Figure 16.1.

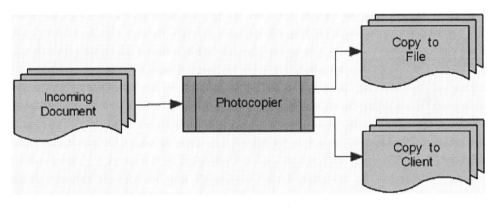

Figure 16.1

When the law firm generates a document for delivery to a third party, the information system looks like Figure 16.2.

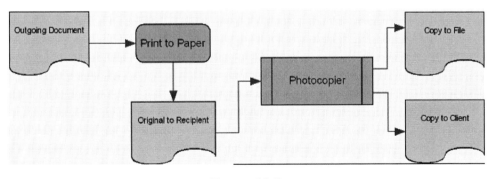

Figure 16.2

In addition to the basic incoming and outgoing document scenarios, consider the special case of litigation documents. When a collection of documents comes in during litigation, whether from the client or an opposing party, it is typically preserved as a clean set, which is then photocopied and Bates numbered. Each of these sets of printed to paper copies (the clean set and the numbered set) are stored in folders, notebooks, and boxes. The Bates numbered set is then copied to create a working set. You now have three sets of the same documents: (1) a clean set; (2) a numbered set; and (3) a work set. With this in mind, later in the chapter, we create electronic folders for the clean set (DocClean), the Bates numbered set (DocsNumbered), and the work set (DocsWork). Sets for distribution to other parties can be shared electronically or printed to paper as the need arises. When dealing with litigation documents, the typical law office information system looks something like this Figure 16.3.

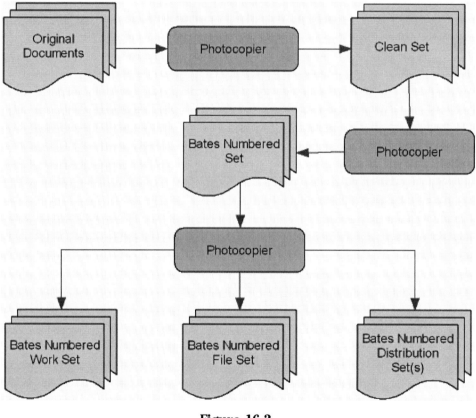

Figure 16.3

§ 16.3 Basic Document Management

In the preceding illustrations, documents (whether incoming or outgoing) pass through the copying or replication system. In the typical office, a photocopier acts as the copying or replication system. In the paper-free office, a scanner replaces the photocopier. Incoming documents pass through the scanner, rather than a photocopier, producing digital copies that are stored electronically. Outgoing documents, rather than being scanned or photocopied, are retained in their original digital format and printed (converted) to the same format as scanned documents. Digital copies can be replicated at will, quickly and easily.

When documents come into the paper-free law office, the information processing system changes only slightly from the photocopier paper-based system. It looks like Figure 16.4.

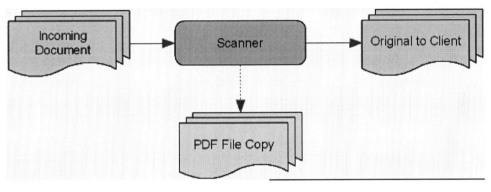

Figure 16.4

At the other end of the process, when the law firm generates outgoing documents, the information processing system looks like Figure 16.5.

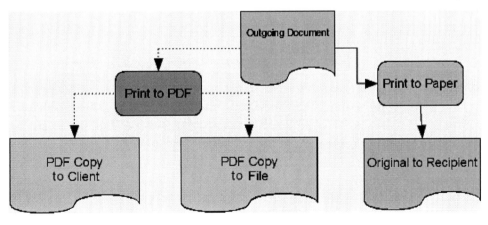

Figure 16.5

To move to a paper-free office using Acrobat, you need follow only a few simple rules:

◆ *Rule Number One:* When a paper document that you want to retain a copy of comes into the office, it goes through the scanner. A simple rule with few exceptions. With Acrobat you convert paper to PDF (see Section 4.2).

◆ *Rule Number Two:* All items of outgoing work product are printed (converted) to PDF. Printing to PDF can be as simple as clicking a button on a toolbar that invokes the Adobe PDF print driver; you then select the folder where the PDF version of the document is stored (see Section 4.1). Printing to PDF differs from printing to a physical printer in that no toner or paper is used; otherwise, the final product (file copy) looks just like what would come out of a physical printer. In some cases, pleadings are filed electronically with the court, copies are served on the other parties by the filing service (either electronically or by mail), and a copy of the pleading is sent to the client as an attachment to an e-mail message. Looking at the process in this scenario, the work product never exists in paper form. Adherence to Rules Number One and Two generates a lot of PDF files and the need for the next rule.

◆ *Rule Number Three:* Store digital images of all incoming paper and outgoing work product in logical folders. Logical folders can mean different things to different people. The client-level folder structure could be arranged numerically if clients are assigned numbers. In that case, folders could be arranged numerically by matter. With any numerically based system you need an index to guide to the correct folder. With the client-level folder structure based on client names, rather than numbers, user need only know the client name to then find the appropriate matter.

§ 16.4 The Digital Filing System

What system do you use right now, today, to find a given piece of paper? Perhaps it sounds something like this: Every client matter has a file, and somewhere you have an index of all those files (so if you want to find the Smith file and can't remember where in the filing system it resides, you go to the index, find the file identifier (such as a file number) and then locate the file. Now you know the document you want is in the Smith file—great—but what if the Smith file contains five thousand or ten thousand pages? At this point, the paper filing system starts to break down. How many subfolders are you willing to create, and how do you keep track of them? Unless you have an absolutely huge number of files, or a moderate number of really big files, then the paper filing system can be replicated, refined, and expanded in the digital world.

Whatever system you use, in whatever form, it constitutes a database— a collection of data organized for search and retrieval. Numerically, alphabetically, alphanumerically arranged folders are but a collection of data organized for search and retrieval. At the other extreme, a major task of computer operating systems (e.g., Windows, the Mac OS, Linnux, etc.) is to organize the 0's and 1's on the storage media (hard disk drive) so that all stored information can be rapidly searched and retrieved. Think of a library with a collection of 100,000 books. Before computers, we used card catalogs to organize the data housed in the library so that it could be searched and retrieved. The lists and indexes needed to organize, search, and retrieve information from paper document collections are the flat-file database kin of library card catalogs. When was the last time you used the physical card catalog at the library?

§ 16.4.1 The Logical Folder System

It may help to think of the digital filing system in terms of a physical filing system. The digital file room consists of electronic filing cabinets filled with folders that contain everything found in traditional paper files. Think of a shared hard disk drive as the file room. The cabinets within the room are large divisions on the disk; within those cabinet-size divisions are folders for each client matter. Most client matter folders are further divided into subfolders to aid in organization.

As high-tech as scanning and printing to PDF may sound, the storage and organizational system can adhere to an old-fashioned filing cabinet metaphor. The physical filing cabinets exist, probably in a room referred to as the "file room." The digital filing cabinets exist in virtual space (on a computer hard disk drive shared over a local area network). Just as the typical law office may have a physical filing cabinet for administrative files (insurance, banking, taxes, etc.), another for the collection of forms, and one or more to store client files—the paper-free office has similar "virtual" filing cabinets. The digital filing cabinets have names: Admin; Forms; Client; Personal; Etc. Notice that these virtual filing cabinets are named by the kind of information they contain. That's the first step in organizing information so that it can be searched and retrieved (the definition of a database). You would not look in the Admin filing cabinet for a client file, now would you? Each computer on the network links to the filing cabinets by mapping one or more network drives, such as X:\Client. Now each desktop has access to the filing cabinet "Client" that contains all client files. Within the "Client" filing cabinet are folders, one for each client, such as X:\Client\Smith. We have added another dimension to our data base; first we go to the correct filing cabinet (the one that contains the client files) and then we look for a folder that bears the sought after client name. If a client has several matters, then that client folder has a subfolder for each distinct matter, such as X:\Client\Smith\Corporation and X:\Client\Smith\Wills. We just added another layer to our database; another set of criteria by which we can search for and retrieve the information stored in our office. Within each client matter folder are folders for various types of documents, such as correspondence, pleadings, expense receipts, research, privilege, and so on. Now the granularity of the database goes from course to fine. For an example of what this looks like, see Figure 16.6.

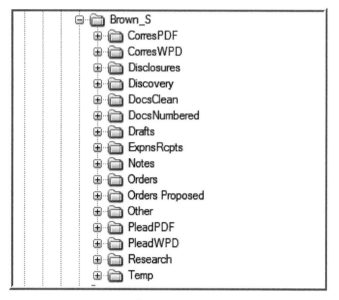

Figure 16.6

A simple system for electronic filing can be implemented and standardized by creating a set of predefined subfolders for client matters. A standard set of folders can be created for litigation, transactional, or other types of matters. The matter subfolders sort information by categories that *you* assign. If information fits two categories, you can put it in two places. For example, you might have a folder for pleadings where you put all pleadings associated with a matter, including discovery requests and responses. But then you might also find it convenient to have a separate folder to make it easier to find discovery requests and responses. Or, you might create a folder named "Orders" and put copies of (you guessed it) court orders that can also be found in the pleadings folder.

Screen shots of the folder system are helpful, but perhaps you can't see the detail. Here's a sample pre-defined folder structure for small litigation matters.

- ◆ CorresPDF [all correspondence in PDF]
- ◆ CorresWPD [all outgoing correspondence in native WordPerfect format]
- ◆ DocsClean
- ◆ DocsNumbered
- ◆ DocsWork
- ◆ ExpenseReceipts

- ◆ Orders
- ◆ OrdersProposed
- ◆ Other
- ◆ PleadPDF [all pleadings in PDF]
- ◆ PleadWPD [all pleadings in native WordPerfect format]
- ◆ Research
- ◆ Temp [a good place to hold native format files received from clients or opposing counsel before conversion to PDF]

In Figure 16.7, the main folder bears the name "Litigation Sm," meaning that this folder contains the file structure for new (small) litigation matters. The subfolders in the Litigation Sm folder are empty; when opening a new litigation file, simply highlight the **Litigation** folder, then select all (**Ctrl+A**), copy, and then paste this file structure onto the folder created for the new matter. Now, every litigation file has the same structure, at least to start with. As you can see, this file structure provides more detail than what you have been using in the paper world, and of course you can add all the subfolders you want and then simply drag and drop the contents from one folder to another. File reorganization can't be much easier.

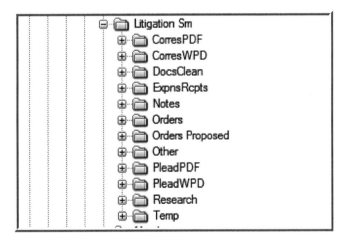

Figure 16.7

§ 16.4.2 The Dual-Folder System

In order to maintain a digital file that looks like a paper file, consider using dual folders for correspondence and pleadings. One folder contains the native application files (Word, WordPerfect, Excel, and so on), and the other has the PDF versions. For example, correspondence files created with WordPerfect are stored in a subfolder named "CorresWPD." All correspondence files in PDF format are stored in a subfolder called "CorresPDF" (Figure 16.8). A similar dual-folder system exists for pleadings (Figure 16.9).

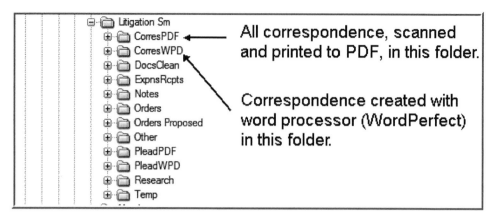

Figure 16.8

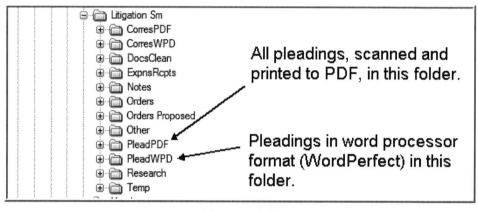

Figure 16.9

There are two reasons for maintaining dual folders. First, keeping the original work product in its native format allows for easy reuse. Second, the PDF folder acts like the old paper file; it contains all of the incoming and outgoing correspondence or pleadings, as the case may be. The files within the folders are named following a simple convention; see Section 16.4.3 below.

§ 16.4.3 File-Naming Conventions

The logical folder system described above goes a long way toward organizing most document collections so that information can be searched for easily and found quickly. But, to make sense of the documents within the folders, file-naming conventions should be adopted and strictly adhered to. The files within the folders are named following simple conventions; the first part of the name always contains the date of the document in reverse year-month-day order, followed by a few descriptive terms, such as X:\Client\Smith\PleadPDF\070327 Complaint. By inserting the date at the beginning of the file name, all documents in a given folder are sorted in year-month-day order (Figure 16.10). If the

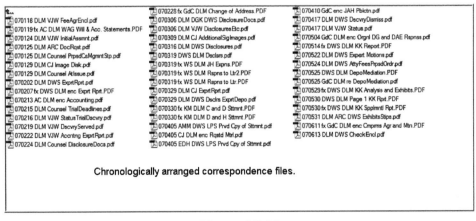

070303 FA CivilCoverSheet.pdf
070303 FA Complaint.pdf
070322 KP MotionToDismiss.pdf
070327 KP Answer CrossClaim.pdf
070416 FA Rspns Mtn ToDsmss.pdf
070419 FA Reply To Counterclaim.pdf
070427 FA 1st AmndCmplnt.pdf
070427 FA MtnToAmendCmplnt.pdf
070430 KP MtnToDsmss Reply.pdf
070510 KP Answer CrossClaim.pdf
070605 FA Summons to SRB.pdf
070605 SRB AcceptService.pdf

070605 SRB EntryOfAppearance.pdf
070607 SRB AnswrCrssclm.pdf
070608 FA RtrnSrvc DPorter.pdf
070608 KP Answr1stAmndCmplnt.pdf
070615 FA Rply To KP CC.pdf
070618 DP Answer 1stAmdComp and CC.pdf
070618 KP AmndCrxClm.pdf
070618 KP MtnAmnd CrxClm.pdf
070619 FA MtnCmpAnswer.pdf
070619 FA Rply MtnCmpAnswer.pdf
070619 FA Rply To DP CC.pdf
070619 KP DP RspnsMtnCmpAnswr.pdf
070625 KP DP Disclosures.pdf

070625 SRB Answer.pdf
070626 KP DP R16 ConfCert.pdf
070628 SRB Rply MtnAmndXClaim.pdf
070629 FA RspnsMtnAmndAnswrs.pdf
070629 KP DP MtnAmndAnswrs.pdf
070629 KP DP RplyMtnAmndAnswr.pdf
070702 KP DP 2AmndAnswr.pdf
070702 KP DP 2ndMtnAmndAnswrs.pdf
070703 FA Rspns2ndMtnAmndAnswrs.pdf
070703 KP DP MtnSttsCnfmc.pdf
070706 FA RspnMtnStsCnf.pdf
070706 KP DP RplyMtnAmndAnswers.pdf
070706 SRB RspnMtnStsCnf.pdf

Using the date (yymmdd) as the first part of the file name arranges documents in chronological order.

Figure 16.10

file being named (saved and filed) is an item of correspondence, consider using the date (in reverse order), followed by the initials of the author, followed by the initials of the recipient, followed by a short description (such as X:\Client\Smith\Corres\070531 DLM MDH AmendedPrivLog). By using this convention for correspondence, you can quickly find letters by looking at the date, author, and recipient portion of the file name (Figure 16.11).

070118 DLM VJW FeeAgrEncl.pdf
070119fx AC DLM WAG Will & Acc. Statements.PDF
070124 DLM VJW InitialAssmnt.pdf
070125 DLM ARC DocRqst.pdf
070125 DLM Counsel PrpsdCaMgmntStp.pdf
070129 DLM CJ Image Disk.pdf
070129 DLM Counsel AtIssue.pdf
070202 DLM DWS ExprtRprt.pdf
070207fx DWS DLM enc Exprt Rprt.PDF
070213 AC DLM enc Accounting.pdf
070215 DLM Counsel TrialDeadlines.pdf
070216 DLM VJW StatusTrialDscvry.pdf
070219 DLM VJW DscvryServed.pdf
070222 DLM VJW Accrtng ExprtRprt.pdf
070224 DLM Counsel DisclosureDocs.pdf

070228 fx GdC DLM Change of Address.PDF
070306 DLM DGK DWS DisclosureDocs.pdf
070306 DLM VJW DisclosuresEtc.pdf
070309 DLM CJ AdditionalSigImages.pdf
070316 DLM DWS Disclosures.pdf
070319 DWS DLM Declars.pdf
070319 fx WS DLM JH Expns.PDF
070319 fx WS DLM Rspns to Ltr2.PDF
070319 fx WS DLM Rspns to Ltr.PDF
070329 DLM CJ ExprtRprt.pdf
070329 DLM DWS Dsclrs ExprtDepo.pdf
070330 fx KM DLM C and D Sttmnt.PDF
070330 fx KM DLM D and H Sttmnt.PDF
070405 AMM DWS LPS Prvd Cpy of Sttmnt.pdf
070405 CJ DLM enc Rqstd Mtrl.pdf
070405 EDH DWS LPS Prvd Cpy of Sttmnt.pdf

070410 GdC enc JAH Pblctn.pdf
070417 DLM DWS DscvryDismiss.pdf
070417 DLM VJW Status.pdf
070504 GdC DLM enc Orgnl DG and DAE Rspnss.pdf
070514 fx DWS DLM KK Report.PDF
070522 DLM DWS Expert Motions.pdf
070524 DLM DWS AttyFeesPrpsdOrdr.pdf
070525 DWS DLM DepoMediation.PDF
070525 GdC DLM re DepoMediation.pdf
070529 fx DWS DLM KK Analysis and Exhibits.PDF
070530 DWS DLM Page 1 KK Rprt.PDF
070530 fx DWS DLM KK Spplmntl Rpt.PDF
070531 DLM ARC DWS ExhibitsStips.pdf
070611 fx GdC DLM enc Cmprms Agr and Mtn.PDF
070613 DLM DWS CheckEncl.pdf

Chronologically arranged correspondence files.

Figure 16.11

§ 16.4.4 The System in Action

Implementation of Rule Number One (when a paper document that you want to retain a copy of comes into the office, it goes through the scanner) can be accomplished quite easily. The mail (correspondence, pleadings, bills, and so on) goes to an assistant who scans each piece, stores the image to the appropriate client or administrative folder, and then distributes the paper to the proper recipient within the office (lawyer, paralegal, bookkeeper) for action.

It is no more difficult to scan a document and properly name the PDF file than it is to make a photocopy and put it in the correct physical folder; indeed, it may be easier. When a letter arrives from opposing counsel, it goes through the scanner, and then goes to the proper recipient within the office. A letter is written to the client that discusses the enclosure that typically begins, "Enclosed for your review and records please find an item of correspondence that we received from opposing counsel. We have retained a copy in our records." Following this procedure, paper comes in, goes through the scanner, then goes out to the client. In some cases, with the right client, you simply send an electronic mail message and attach a digital copy; the original letter then goes to the recycle bin or shredder.

Following a few simple rules, any office can switch from paper to digital filing: (1) scan all incoming documents to PDF, (2) print all outgoing work product to PDF, (3) create a virtual filing cabinet with folders for each client matter, (4) segregate document types within the client matter folders into appropriate subfolders, and (5) use dates or a numbering system when naming files so that they display in chronological order.

§ 16.4.5 Document Management Alternatives

If the document management system described above does not sound robust enough for your office, consider an industrial-strength solution. It will, of course, be some type of database that permits you to organize the information in your office so that it can be searched and retrieved. However, if all you want is a system that indexes all of your files so that you can run a computer search to find the Smith lease, or locate that motion to compel a psychiatric examination, you already have it—it's called Windows Explorer. You can use Windows Explorer to find files containing specific words (Acrobat document summaries and text box comments are included in the information searched by Explorer). If you need more than Windows Explorer can deliver, then consider Worldox or iManage. They provide industrial-strength file management (at a price, of course—not just in dollars, but in training and in following a regimented system of coding files). In the middle, between Windows Explorer and industrial-strength, are case-management programs (or groupware) like Amicus Attorney, Time Matters, and Abacus. These programs have document management capabilities, some more than others. Try implementing a good logical in-house electronic file system like that described above; if you can't find your documents with that system (aided by Windows Explorer when the going gets rough), then look at document management system applications like Worldox and iManage. Remember, when you create a large collection of PDF image-on-text files, you can index the collection, which then allows you to search the entire collection.

§ 16.5 Digital Document Storage Requirements

As a general rule, when scanned at 300 dpi, a single scanned page (letter size) requires storage space of approximately 50 KB. This is an average and assumes the image was acquired and stored as black and white or line drawing, not color or gray scale. A single drawer in a filing cabinet holds approximately ten thousand pages. To store the same ten thousand pages electronically requires 500 megabytes (MB) of storage space. A single compact disc (CD-ROM, CD-R, or CD-RW) holds 700 MB, or the equivalent of 1.4 file cabinet drawers. An entire four-drawer filing cabinet (forty thousand pages) then requires only 2 gigabytes (GB). A single-layer DVD holds 4.3 GB, or the equivalent of two four-drawer filing cabinets; a double-layer DVD holds 8.7GB, or the equivalent of four four-drawer filing cabinets. A 100 GB hard disk drives currently sell for less than $100; that's the capacity of fifty four-drawer filing cabinets. If you think in terms of boxes, instead of filing cabinets, one box holds approximately 2,500 pages. Those same 2,500 pages require only 125 MB of digital storage space. Five boxes of documents fit on a single CD-ROM with room to spare. Even if the space required for a single page, scanned at 300 dpi, was doubled to 100 KB, ten thousand pages (one full file cabinet drawer or four boxes) requires only 1 GB of electronic storage capacity.

The available space for digital document storage continues to grow while prices continue to drop. Contrast that with the fixed physical space for storing paper files and the continual increasing costs of such storage. Document collections should be stored on a network drive, either an internal hard disk drive. When planning or acquiring storage devices, consider the speed at which documents can be retrieved. Fast hard disk drives (7,200 RPM or 10,000 RPM) are much preferred. If stored documents are available across a network, fast Ethernet (100 MB/second) provides good performance. Standard Ethernet (10 MB/second) and 801.11(b) wireless (11 MB/second) do not provide sufficient bandwidth if you create large scanned documents (documents in excess of a thousand pages). 801.11(g) wireless (54 MB/second) works okay; the upcoming (still in draft format, but products are available) 801.11(n) wireless will provide the equivalent (100 MB/second) of wired Fast Ethernet.

The discussion of storage space requirements to this point has addressed only scanned documents. Documents printed to PDF require much less storage space. For example, a six-page word processing document 30 KB in size grew to 70 KB when printed to PDF, but would have been 300 KB if scanned.

Bates Numbering **17**

Acrobat 8 does "Bates numbering." But, what is Bates numbering and why would a lawyer need it? Let's start with the "Bates" part. Bates is a registered trademark of General Binding Corporation. Like Kleenex™ or Xerox™. Bates numbering refers generically to applying sequential numbers or alphanumerical markings to documents so that each page may be uniquely identified. The "Bates" in Bates numbering, refers to the handheld stamping machines that are (or were) used to apply sequential numbers or alphanumerical markings that were made by the Bates Numbering Machine Company.

Bates numbering or stamping is used in the legal and business fields to sequentially number images or documents as they are processed, for example, marking documents during the discovery phase or in preparation for trial, or identifying business receipts. Manual Bates stamping used a self-inking stamp that increased a sequential number each time it was pressed down on a document. The usual process used in legal firms is as follows: 1) Get a bunch of documents from the client, a witness, or the other side; 2) Make a clean copy of the documents; 3) Bates stamp the documents; and 4) Make copies of the Bates-stamped documents as needed (e.g., for production to other parties to the litigation).

As you might expect, the use of mechanical stamping machines to mark documents has gone the way of the buggy-whip. An intermediate replacement for the mechanical stamp was the use of a macro, in a word processing application (e.g., WordPerfect™ or Microsoft Word™), to create sequentially numbered labels (typically using small, clear, return-address labels because they come 80 per sheet). The labels were then painstakingly applied, one page at a time, to the collected documents.

With the advent of scanners, litigation documents today are typically scanned to an image file format, most frequently PDF. Once paper pages have been converted to digital pages, the application of Bates numbers can be accomplished more efficiently and without errors. Prior to Acrobat 8, Bates numbering of PDF files was accomplished through the use of a "plug-in." See Chapter 13. A "plug-in being a small bit of software that plugs into and works within a larger application. In this case, the plug-in worked within Acrobat to provide Bates numbering functionality.

The Bates numbering in Acrobat 8 is a function of **Header and Footers** but is found on the **Advanced** menu, by selecting **Document Processing**, then **Bates Numbering**.

Menu (Bates Numbering): **Advanced > Document Processing > Bates Numbering > Add or Remove**

Keyboard (Bates Numbering): **Alt+A-D-A**

Once **Add** has been selected a dialog box allows selection of one or more files, including all open files (Figure 17.1). If multiple files are selected, they should be arranged in the desired order before moving on so that the Bates

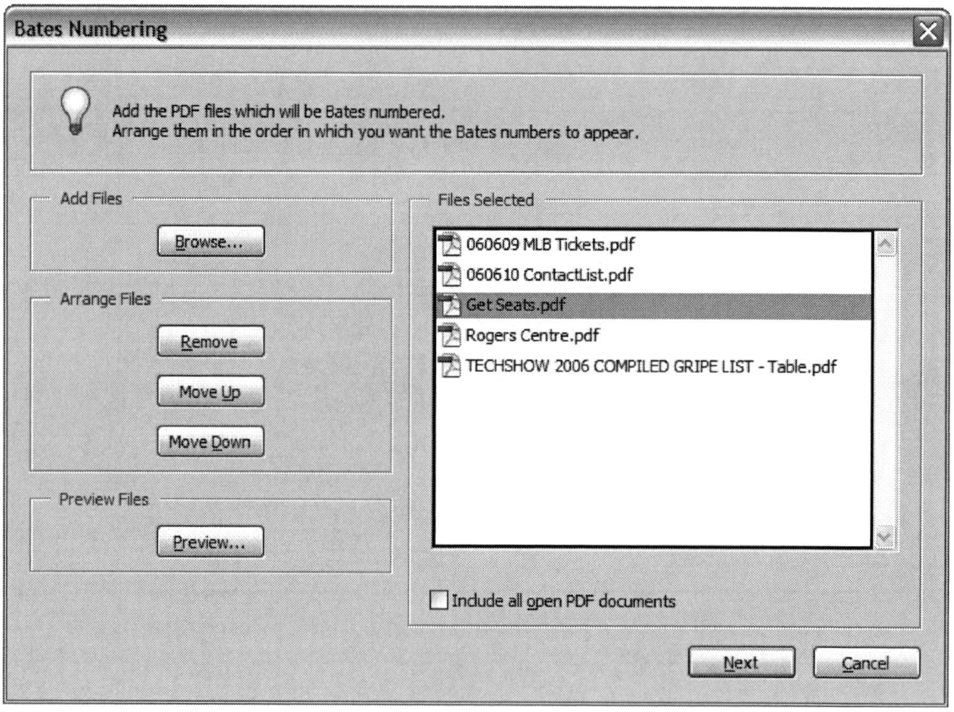

Figure 17.1

numbers are applied in desired order. After the file or files have been selected, click **Next** and an **Add Header and Footer** dialog box appears (Figure 17.2). Here you select the location: left, center or right; and header (top of page) or footer (bottom of page). At this point, before inserting the Bates Number code into the desired location box, make your choice for the font, size and color for the Bates numbers. Using a color other than black makes the numbers stand out when reviewed on screen or if the documents are printed in color (if printed with a black-and-white printer, the color will translate to black). Click in the desired location box (Left Header, Center Header, Right Header; Left Footer, Center Footer, Right Footer) then click on the **Insert Bates Number** button. When you click on the **Insert Bates Number** button, a small dialog box

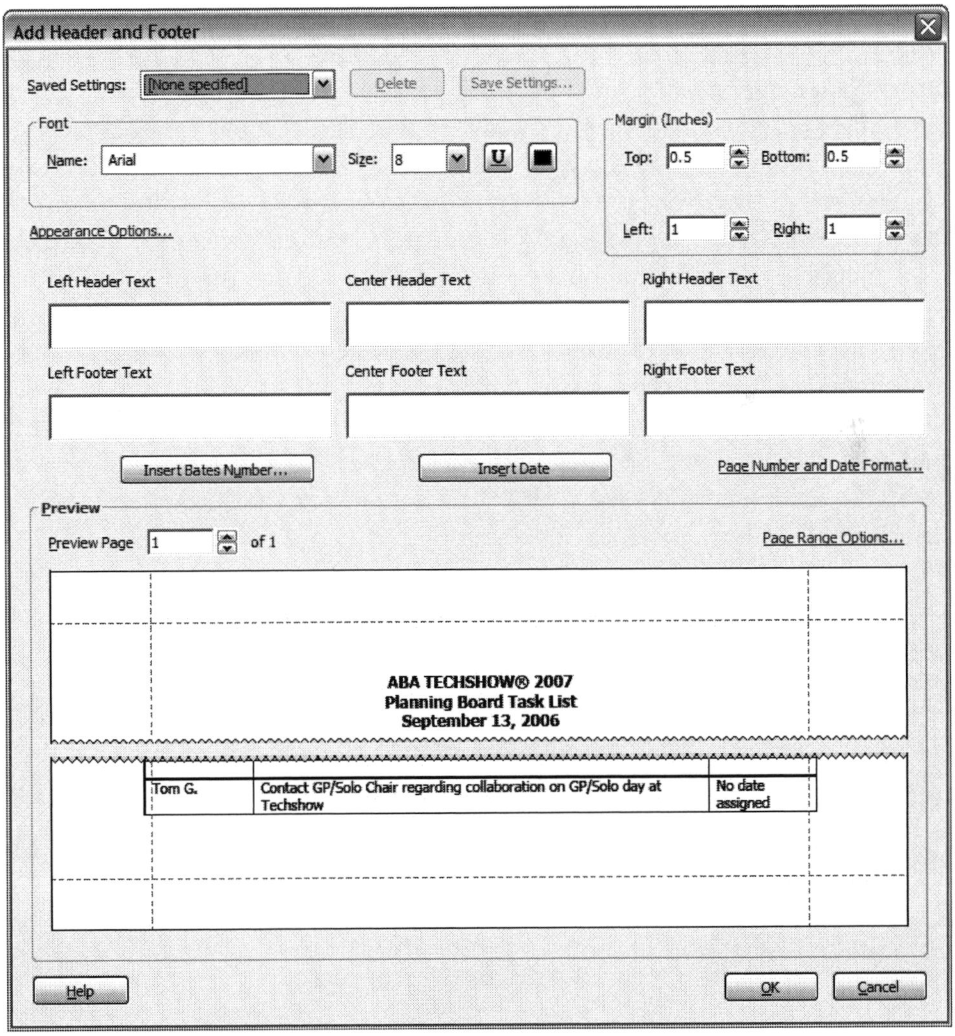

Figure 17.2

opens, offering Bates numbering options (Figure 17.3). Here, select the number of digits, the starting number, and specify any prefix and, or, suffix. When the options have been selected press **OK**. The information (code) for the selected Bates numbering options appears in the location field on the **Add Header and Footer** dialog box with a preview of the first page. Clicking **OK** produces a message box informing you that Bates numbering has been successfully applied to the selected PDF files.

If you have been using Bates numbers before moving to digital files, you know the reasoning and importance that underlies this practice. If you are new to Bates numbering, understanding why this represents a best practice will lead to considerations of how you number documents. In the context of litigation, the Federal Rules of Civil Procedure and most corresponding state court rules require the disclosure of all documents that a party may use to support its claims or defenses. Conversely stated, documents that are not disclosed cannot be used to support claims or defenses. In addition to disclosures, documents are produced or received through Rule 34 requests for production. Beyond disclosures and discovery, documents may also be produced or obtained pursuant to subpoenas. Whether documents are produced or obtained through disclosure, discovery or subpoena, it becomes important to have a record of precisely who produced what to whom. When the documents bear unique sequential numbers or alphanumerical markings, questions about whether they were or were not produced can be avoided. For example, when 1,000 pages are Bates numbered and produced there can be no dispute about whether a particular page or set of pages was included. When an opposing party produces or discloses documents that are not Bates numbered, consider marking them and then serving a request that the party admit that the Bates numbered copies are all of the documents that they produced or disclosed.

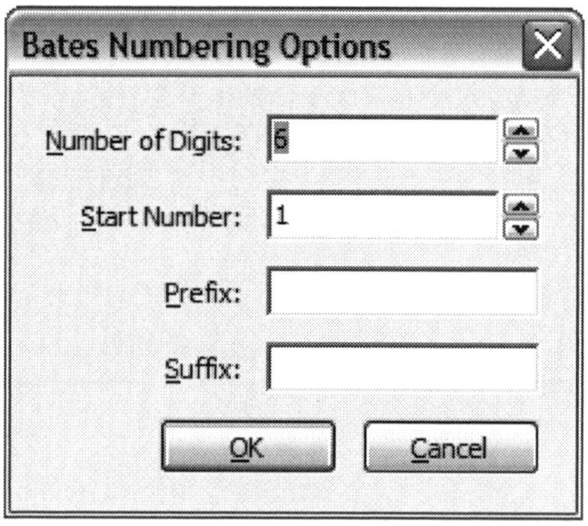

Figure 17.3

As you know or might imagine, litigation documents can come from a wide variety of sources. Given the potential for a wide variety of sources, you should take time to consider the importance of the alpha-portion of the Bates number. Documents produced by a party can be alpha-labeled with letters that identify the party. Likewise, those from non-party witnesses and experts can be alpha-marked to correspond the source.

When you start using Acrobat to apply Bates numbers to digital documents, the hassles and errors associated with mechanical stamps and labels are avoided. No pages are skipped, no number used twice. You will have better control over the documents associated with any litigated matter. Better document control means better information management, and managing information is what litigation is all about.

Redaction

When documents must be produced but contain information that cannot or should not be made public or seen by the opposing party, that information must be redacted. Personal identifiers in "protected health information," bank account, credit card, and Social Security numbers, financial information and the like all must be protected from disclosure in various circumstances. Horror stories abound and embarrassing examples of unsuccessful efforts to redact sensitive information in electronic files can readily be found through Internet searches. We can assume that you do not wish to add to those stories and examples.

With paper documents, sensitive information was redacted with overlay tapes, or more commonly by using a felt-tip marker. When the documents to be produced are PDF files, sensitive information can be removed using the **Redaction** tool in Acrobat 8 Professional. Prior to Acrobat 8, redaction within PDF files required the use of a plug-in. Most commonly used was Redax (**www.appelligent.com**). The Redaction function in Acrobat 8 permits the marking and removal of both text and any portion of image-only PDF files. When working with image-on-text files, words, phrases, or any string of characters can be searched for and automatically marked for redaction. The Acrobat redaction function does not "cover up" text or image areas, it replaces the marked areas pixel-for-pixel with what you define for the redaction fill. The replaced areas cannot be recovered from the PDF file. In that sense, a redacted PDF is very secure. Keep in mind that the redacted information might be recoverable from the computer that was used to apply the redaction by a highly skilled forensic expert.

The redaction process, generally speaking, involves two steps: 1) information within a document is "marked" for redaction; and, 2) the redaction is applied. In Acrobat 8 Professional, the redaction process can be initiated in several ways. One method involves selecting the Advanced menu and choosing Redaction.

Menu (Redaction): **Advanced > Redaction**
Keystroke (Redaction): **Alt+A-O**

The preferred method would be to display the **Redaction** toolbar. (Figure 18.1)

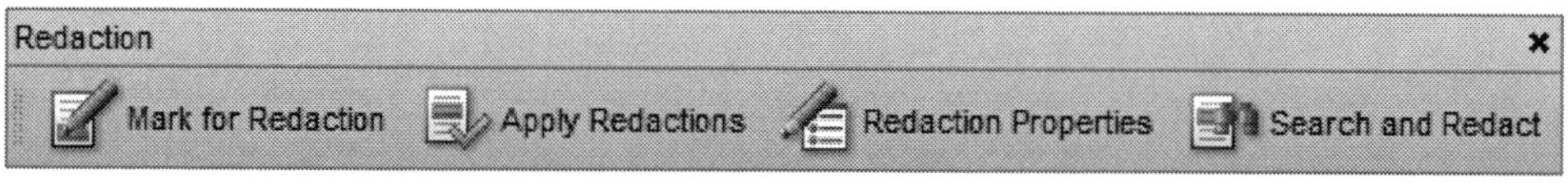

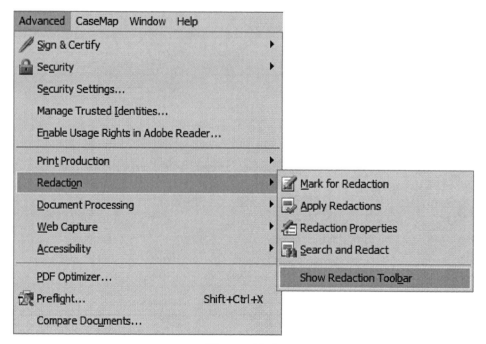

Figure 18.1

This can be done by selecting the **Advanced** menu, then **Redaction**, and highlighting **Show Redaction Tool Bar** (Figure 18.2)

Figure 18.2

Menu (Display Redaction Toolbar): **Advanced > Redaction > Show Redaction Toolbar**

Keystroke (Display Redaction Toolbar): **Alt+A-O-B**

The Redaction toolbar can also be displayed from the **View** menu by selecting **Toolbars** and **Redaction**.

Menu (Display Redaction Toolbar): **View > Toolbars > Redaction**

Keystroke (Display Redaction Toolbar): **Alt+V-T-O**

§ 18.1 Manual Mark for Redaction

To manually mark areas of a PDF file for redaction, click on the **Mark for Redaction** tool on the **Redaction** toolbar or from the **Advanced** menu, after selecting **Redaction**. Notice that the Redaction tool is "smart." It appears as a cross-hair when over an image-only area, and looks something like a book (an icon meant to represent text) when over a text area. With the **Redaction** tool active, move through the PDF file selecting text or areas of the image to mark them for redaction. To select text, place the redaction tool at the beginning of the text to be marked, left-click and hold down the left mouse button while dragging the tool across the text to be marked. If the area to be marked is image-only, place the **Redaction** tool cross-hair up and to the left of the area to be selected, then hold down the left mouse button and drag down and to the right. Alternatively, you can place the cross-hair down and to the right of the area to be marked, hold down the left mouse button and drag up and to the left.

§ 18.2 Search and Mark for Redaction

When working with image-on-text PDF files, words, numbers and phrases can be searched for, found, and marked for redaction. Search and mark for redaction will NOT work on image-only PDF files. Keep in mind that image-on-text files created by OCR may (will) contain some recognition errors, which means that searches may hit false results or more likely, miss intended targets. To search and mark for redaction, click on the **Search and Redact** button on the **Redaction** toolbar and a **Search** box appears (Figure 18.3). Notice that you can search within the current PDF file or all PDF files within a specified folder. By default, the search window displays the MyDocuments folder.

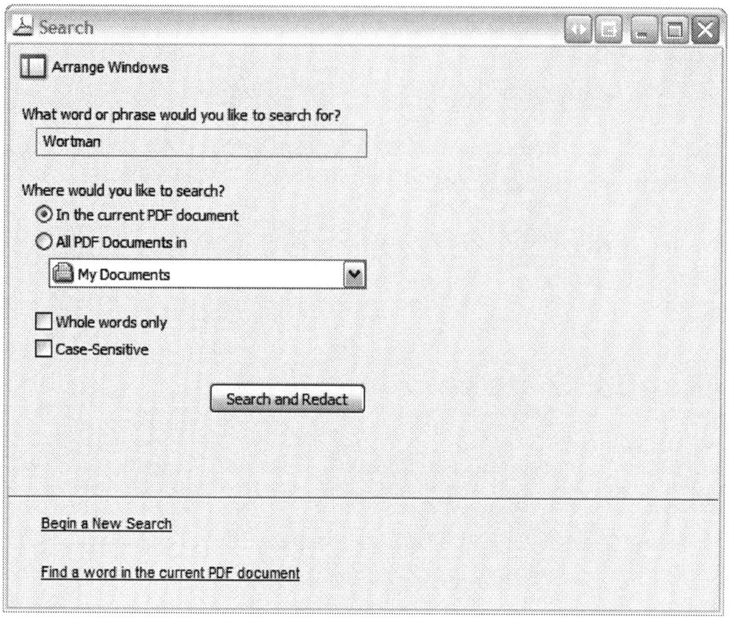

Figure 18.3

The drop-down menu allows you to select local or network drives or, at the bottom of the list you can select **Browse for Location** (Figure 18.4). Select-

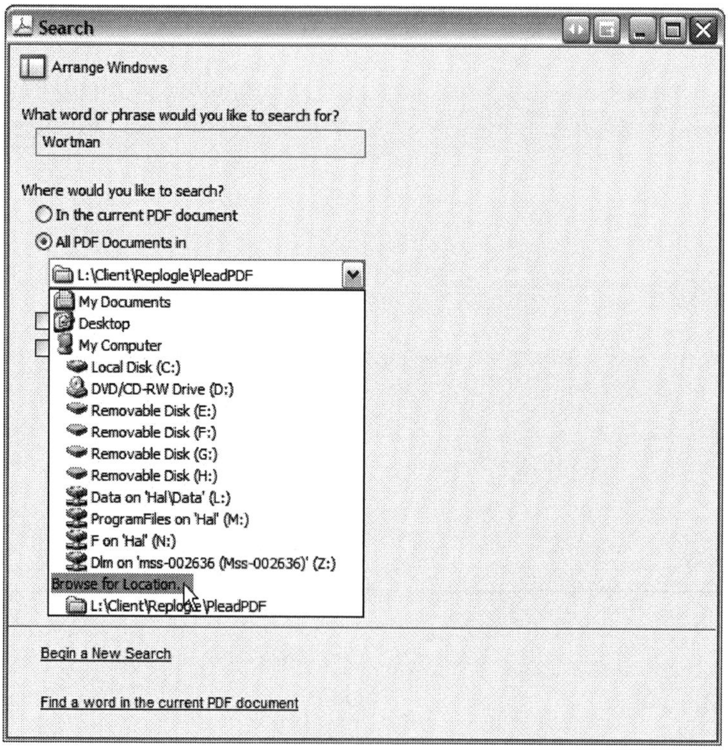

Figure 18.4

ing **Browse for Location** produces a **Browse for Folder** window (Figure 18.5) from which you can navigate to and select an appropriate folder containing the PDF files to be searched and marked for redaction.

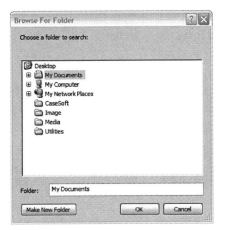

Figure 18.5

After selecting whether to search the currently open file or PDF files contained in a specific folder, type the word or phrase that you want to search for then click the **Search and Redact** button. When the search finishes the results will be displayed in the search window (Figure 18.6). Figure 18.6 shows the re-

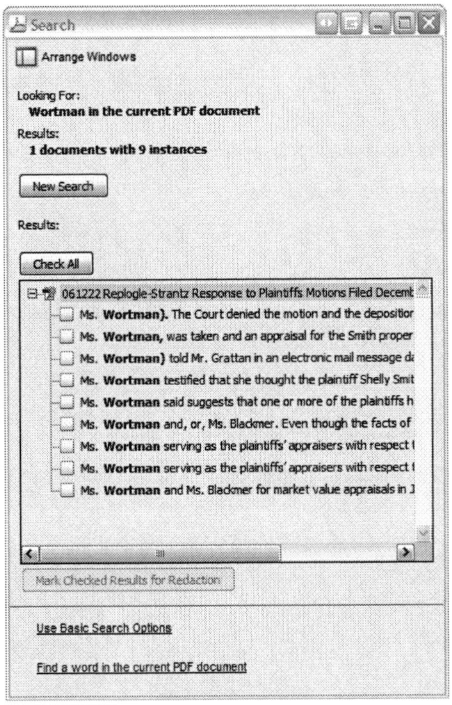

Figure 18.6

sults of the search for "wortman" within the current PDF file. At this point, Acrobat has found the search term in the current file or all of the PDF files in the specified folder, but nothing has been marked for redaction. To mark all of the found word or phrase results, click the **Check All** button (or, you can manually check each box in the search results list) (Figure 18.7). Note that once you **Check All**, the button changes to **Uncheck All**.

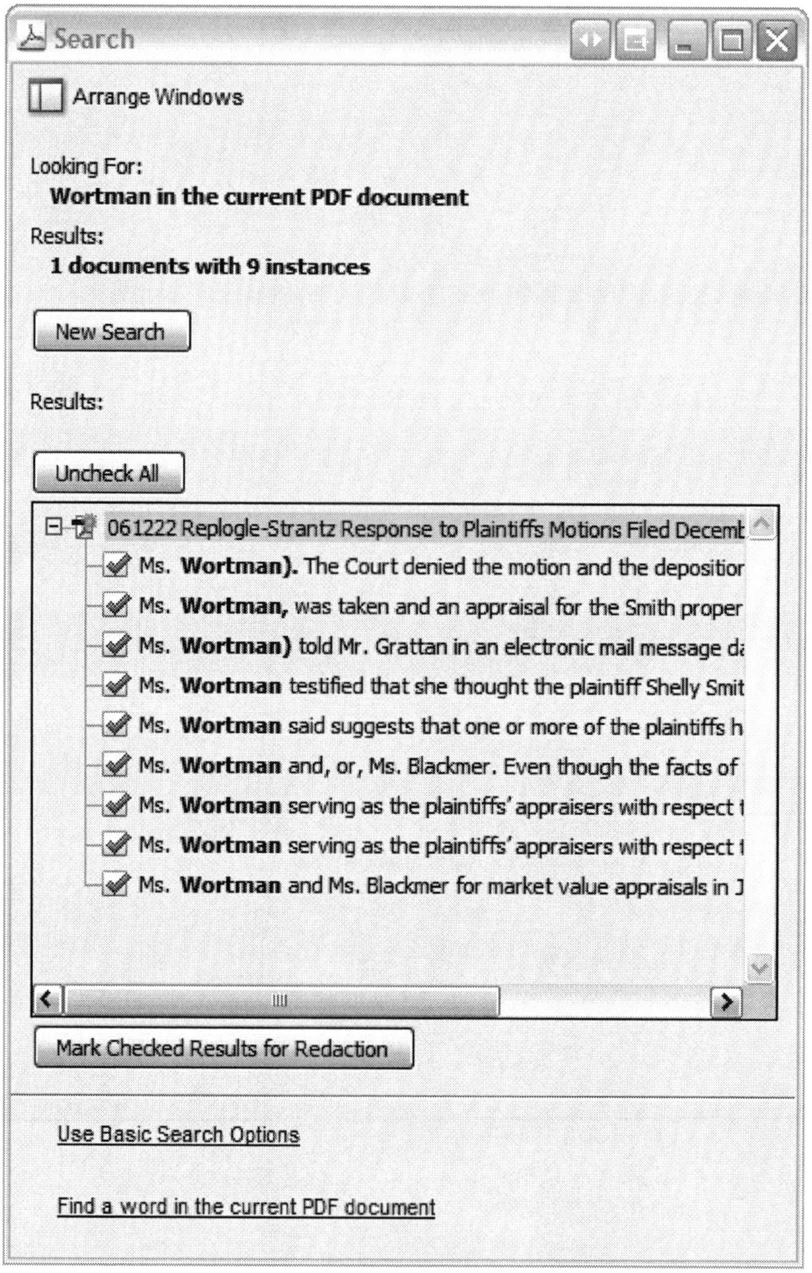

Figure 18.7

After you have checked some or all of the search results the **Marked Checked Results for Redaction** button becomes active; click that button to mark for redaction the selected results. All checked instances of the search results will be marked for redaction. If you look at the currently open file, or one of the files in the specified folder, you will see that the selected search results have been marked for redaction (Figure 18.8). Up to this point you have only marked items for redaction; redaction has not been applied.

us your best appraisal for that.
Charged with that, Ms. Wortman and her supervisor,
Ms. Blackmer, conducted a cost basis appraisal as well as a
market value appraisal and averaged the two.
THE COURT: Did someone tell Ms. Wortman that I
wanted a cost basis appraisal?
MR. GRATTAN: Not -- that is what she testified to.
I believe that is in complete error. And I believe that
Ms. Wortman's deposition in general is awfully confused.
THE COURT: So yo

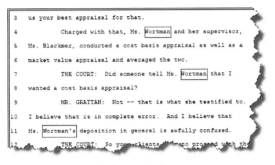

Figure 18.8

§ 18.3 Redaction Properties

Before applying redaction you may want to visit the **Redaction Tool Properties** (Figure 18.9). Acrobat allows you to select the redacted area fill color and

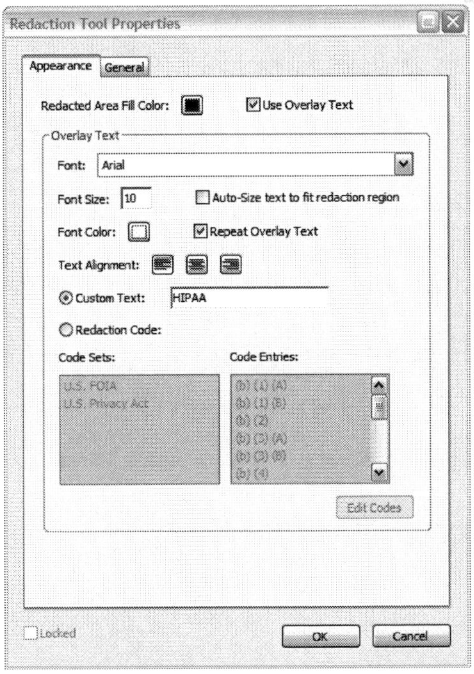

Figure 18.9

add a text overlay. If you check the **Use Overlay Text** box then you have the option to specify text properties (font, size, color, alignment, etc.). There are also code sets that can be applied that specify sections of the federal Freedom of Information Act or the federal Privacy Act. In Figure 18.9 black has been selected for the Redacted Area Fill Color, **Use Overlay Text** has been checked (white Arial 10 point specified), and custom text "**HIPAA**" has been entered.

§ 18.4 Applying Redaction

After all areas within a document have been marked for redaction the document can be saved and closed. This is not a required step but may be appropriate if, say, one person marks the file for redaction while another approves and applies the redaction. For example, a paralegal may review and mark files for redaction, save them, then pass the files along to an attorney in the office who will approve and apply the redactions. If you save the PDF file before applying redaction a text box will appear warning that the document contains redaction marks that have not yet been applied (Figure 18.10).

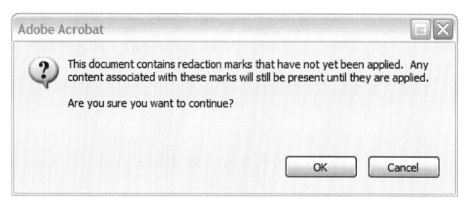

Figure 18.10

To apply the redactions click on the **Apply Redactions** button on the **Redaction** toolbar or from the **Advanced** menu select **Redaction** then **Apply Redactions**.

Menu (Apply Redaction): **Advanced > Redaction > Apply Redactions**
Keystroke (Apply Redaction): **Alt+A-O-A**

At this point a very important, but far from foolproof, message appears (Figure 18.11). After redaction marks have been applied and the file saved, **THE REDACTED INFORMATION CANNOT BE RETRIEVED!** The warning message suggests that you will be prompted at the next save to use a new file name but the prompt does not warn you that failure to do so will result in the total and final loss of all redacted information. If you quickly hit **Ctrl+S** and click **Yes** to permit overwriting the existing file, whether you intended to or not, you will have irrevocably removed all redacted information. **USE WITH CAUTION.** A good practice would be to create copies of files to be redacted and save them with a new name or in a different folder before beginning the redaction process.

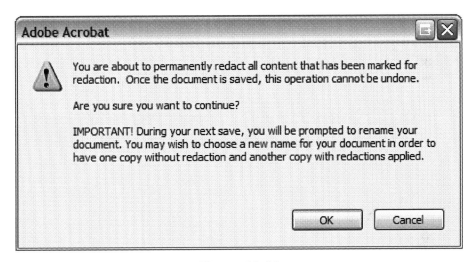

Figure 18.11

When you are sure that you are ready to apply redaction click **OK** in the warning and the specified redaction will be applied to all marked areas or search terms, and information removed from the file or files. When redaction has been applied a text box appears telling you that redactions have been successfully applied and asking whether you want to examine the document for additional information; clicking **Yes** examines the document, clicking **No** proceeds with application of the redaction (the **Examine Document** function is discussed in detail in Chapter 21) (Figure 18.12). Remember, after redaction has been applied and the file saved **THE REDACTED INFORMATION CANNOT BE RETRIEVED!**

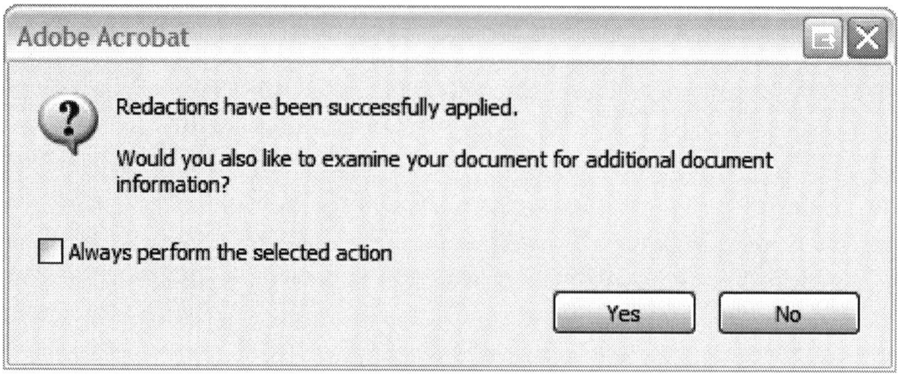
Adobe Acrobat
Redactions have been successfully applied.
Would you also like to examine your document for additional document information?
Always perform the selected action
Yes
No

Figure 18.12

Acrobat PDF Forms 19

With Acrobat Professional you can create forms. Although creating forms might be one of the more difficult Acrobat functions, it's easier than ever. Learning to create and work with forms can be invaluable to a law firm. Consider the benefits of forms for use with both clients and staff—client intake forms, checklists, new employee forms.

"Forms" created with word processing applications, such as Microsoft Word or Corel WordPerfect, are actually documents that use lines and shapes to create the look of a form. When recipients fill in the blanks, the "form" begins to shift, as lines move around and formatting changes. You can take a form like this, convert it to PDF, and the resulting file is still not a fillable form, although it can be filled out when printed or with the Acrobat **Typewriter** tool. With Acrobat Professional, forms can be taken a step further to create actual, fillable documents.

§ 19.1 Creating Forms

Forms are created with Acrobat, as you might expect, from the **Forms** menu (Figure 19.1). Selecting **Create New Form** from the menu starts the Form Wizard (Figure 19.2). At this point you make the choice to create a form from a template, an existing electronic file (word processing or spreadsheet file), by importing data from a spreadsheet, or by scanning a paper form.

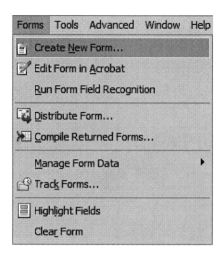

Figure 19.1

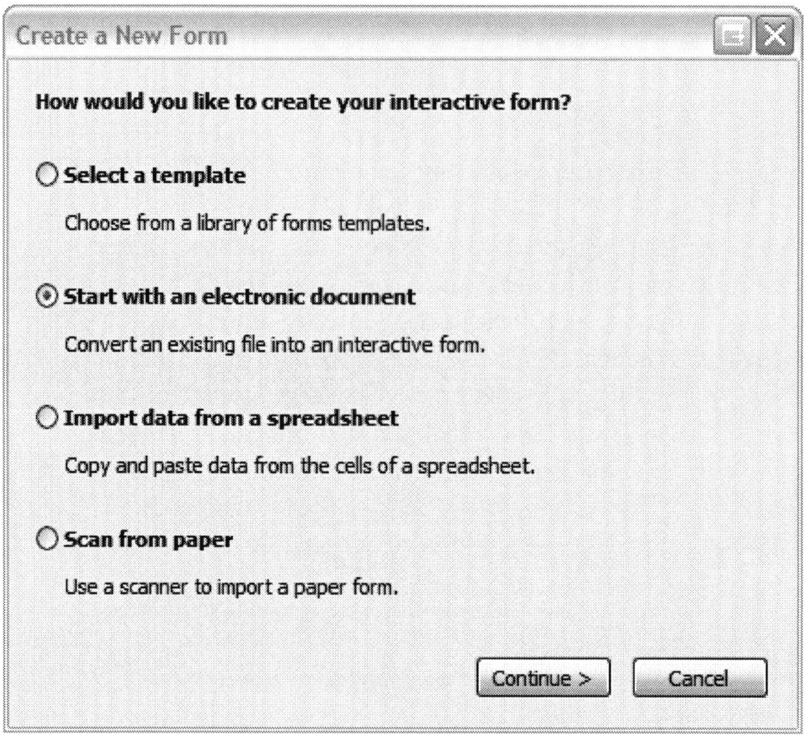

Figure 19.2

§ 19.2 Creating a Form from an Existing File

To create a form from an existing file select **Start with an electronic document** on the **Create a New Form** window, then click **Continue** (this, of course, assumes that you have an existing "form" to work from). An information box appears, read it if you will, then click **Continue** and the **Form Wizard** window appears (Figure 19.3). The number of steps indicated, 1 of 4 or 1 of 5, will depend on whether you choose **Import a file from file system** or **Use the current document**. If you choose to import a file, browse to find it, click **Next**, and it will appear in a new Acrobat window. Clicking the **Next** button takes you to the next step in the process. If you chose to work with the current document you will already be at this step (Figure 19.4). Here you decide whether to have Acrobat look for form fields (**Run Auto Field Detection**) or place the form fields manually (**Place Fields by Hand**). Try running auto detection; if no fields are found you can go back (click the **Previous** button) and select **Place Fields by Hand**.

When you click **Finish**, Adobe Live Cycle Designer will start to permit form editing (Figure 19.5). The **Designer** application opens with the **New Form Assistant** dialog box, where you can choose to add return email and print buttons in the form (Figure 19.6). After you make choices the new form appears in the Designer work area (Figure 19.7).

At this point you have left Acrobat and are working with the form in Adobe Live Cycle Designer. This application has very helpful How To instructions that will guide you through the finer points of editing your forms. Below the How To instructions are libraries of form fields (favorites, standard, custom and barcodes). Simply click and drag form elements from the library into

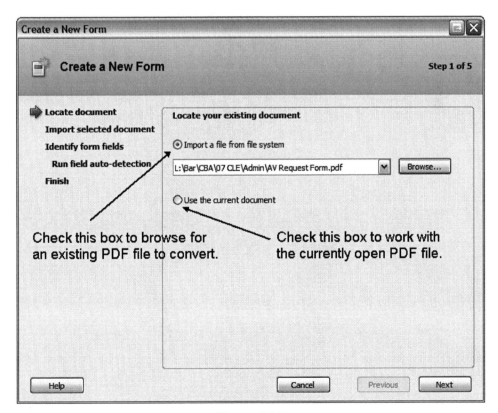

Figure 19.3

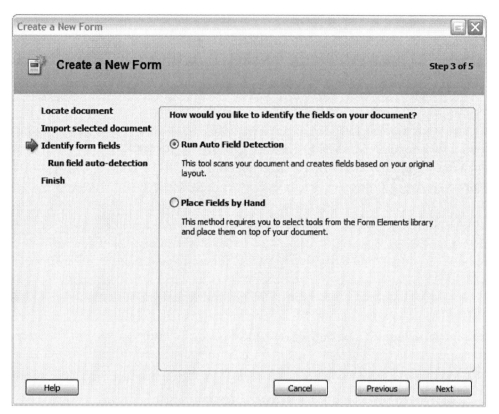

Figure 19.4

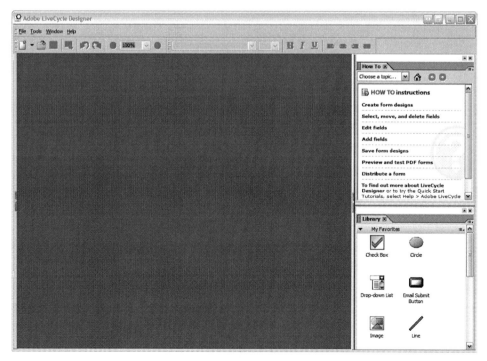

Figure 19.5

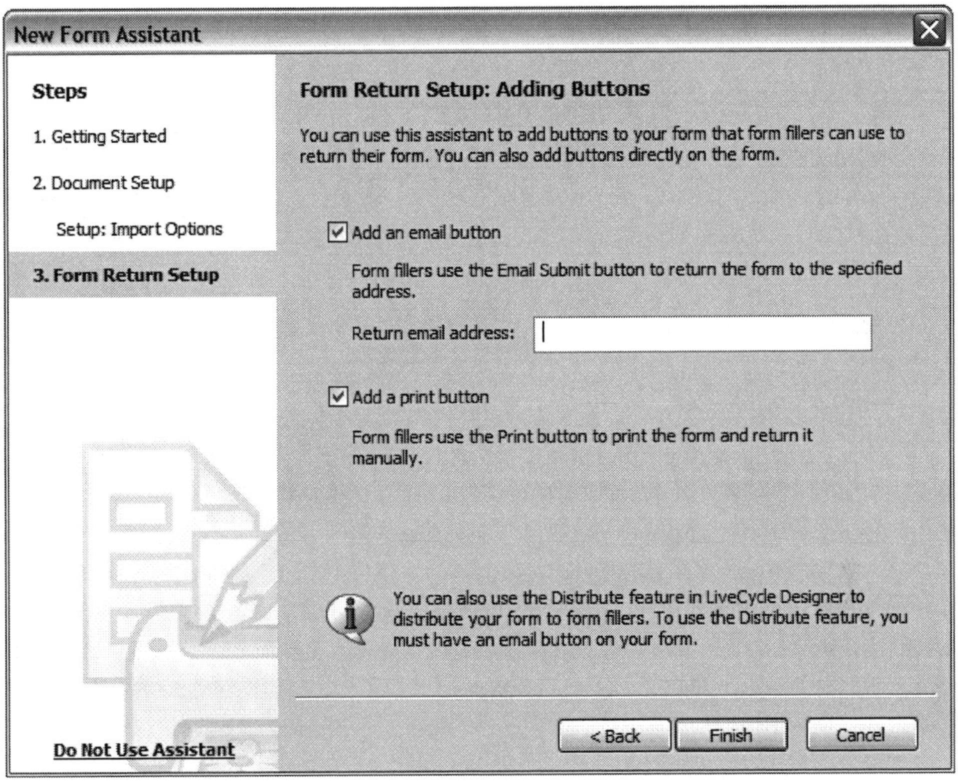

New Form Assistant   ✕

Steps

1. Getting Started

2. Document Setup

   Setup: Import Options

3. Form Return Setup

Form Return Setup: Adding Buttons

You can use this assistant to add buttons to your form that form fillers can use to return their form. You can also add buttons directly on the form.

☑ Add an email button

   Form fillers use the Email Submit button to return the form to the specified address.

   Return email address: [   ]

☑ Add a print button

   Form fillers use the Print button to print the form and return it manually.

ⓘ You can also use the Distribute feature in LiveCycle Designer to distribute your form to form fillers. To use the Distribute feature, you must have an email button on your form.

Do Not Use Assistant

[< Back]   [Finish]   [Cancel]

Figure 19.6

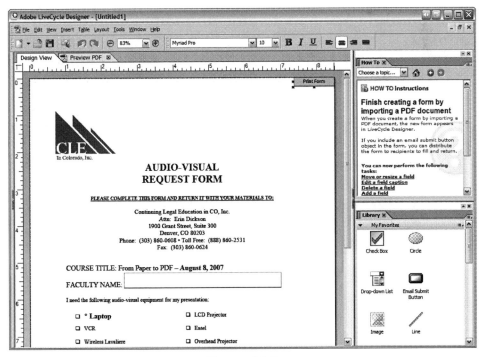

Figure 19.7

the work area and place them where you want them. Note that you can click on the **Preview PDF** tab at any time to see what the finished form will look like.

With Acrobat Professional, forms can be enabled to let users of Acrobat Reader save the form with the information intact. In the past, users of the Reader could fill out a form and send the data back, but the form itself would not allow the data to be saved in the Reader. Now, by enabling this functionality, users of the free Reader can save form data. To enable a PDF form so that users of the free Reader can save form data:

Menu (Enable Reader Usage): **Advanced > Enable Usage Rights in Adobe Reader**

Keystroke (Enable Reader Usage): **Alt+A-N**

When you click the **Save Now** button in the **Enable Usage Rights in Adobe Reader** window (Figure 19.8), Adobe Reader users will be able to save form data, add comments, sign in existing signature fields. Beware the "note" in this window: once Reader is enabled certain editing functions will be restricted.

Using the **Distribute** and **Collect** options on the **Forms** menus, you can send the form to recipients, and then receive the form back via electronic mail. By clicking on the returned document in the electronic mail, Acrobat merges the data from each returned form, showing not only the filled form, but also parsing the data so that it can be viewed separately from the form. The data collected can then be exported to a .CSV file to read and manipulate with Microsoft Excel or another spreadsheet program. The collection and mining of data from PDF forms goes way beyond the scope of this book. So good luck, and be careful out there!

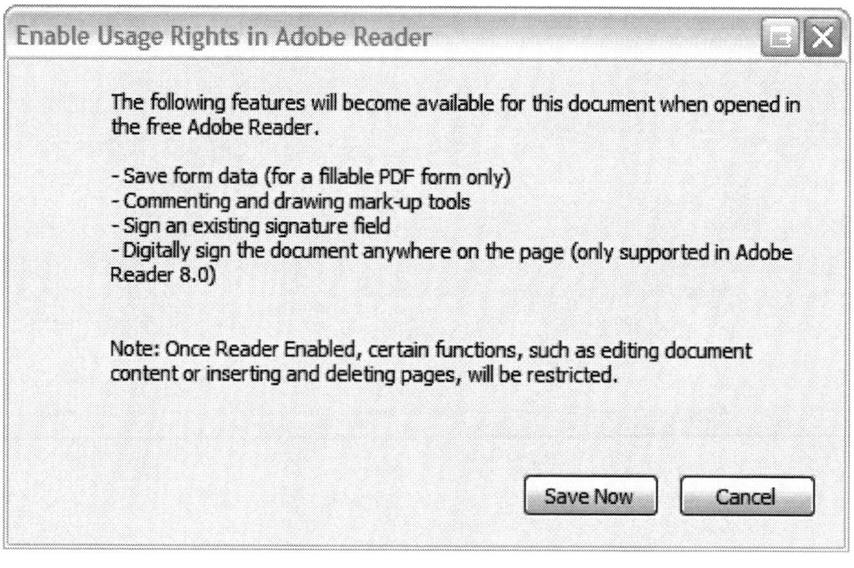

Enable Usage Rights in Adobe Reader

The following features will become available for this document when opened in the free Adobe Reader.

- Save form data (for a fillable PDF form only)
- Commenting and drawing mark-up tools
- Sign an existing signature field
- Digitally sign the document anywhere on the page (only supported in Adobe Reader 8.0)

Note: Once Reader Enabled, certain functions, such as editing document content or inserting and deleting pages, will be restricted.

Save Now   Cancel

Figure 19.8

Batch Processing 20

As the chapter title implies, with Acrobat 8 Professional you can perform certain tasks on a group or batch of PDF files. Acrobat Professional ships with a number of predefined "batch processes" or sequences, for example Batch OCR, Print All, and Save All as RTF. You can also create and save your own custom batch-processing sequences. If you need to apply one or more routine sets of commands to PDF files, you can save time and keystrokes by using an automated batch sequence—a defined series of commands with specific settings and in a specific order that you apply in a single step. You can apply a sequence to a single document, to several documents, or to an entire collection of documents.

The utility of batch processing is realized when you need to perform certain tasks on large collections of PDF files. Batch processes are limited to "certain tasks." You cannot write batch sequences for all Acrobat functions. That said, think of a large set of PDF files that you might want to run a batch process on. Okay, if you can't think of any, here's an idea. All of the financial reports from your back-office application (accounting, time and billing) are printed to PDF. You would rather not have these files available to all employees in your office, but at the same time you want them readily available to you and one or two key employees or principals. The next section describes the process to create a batch process to secure those files. In the following section (20.2), walks through the steps of running the batch process on selected files.

§ 20.1 Creating a Batch Sequence

To create a batch sequence:

Menu (Batch Processing): **Advanced > Document Processing > Batch Processing**

Keystroke (Batch Processing): **Alt+A-D-B**

The **Batch Sequences** window appears (Figure 20.1). Click the **New Sequence** button, the **Name Sequence** box appears (Figure 20.2). Type a name for the sequence in the box; click **OK**. The **Edit Batch Sequence-Apply Security** window appears (Figure 20.3). When you click on the **Select Commands** button the **Edit Sequence** window appears, where you select the tasks that can be incorporated into a batch sequence (Figure 20.4). Remember, it's not

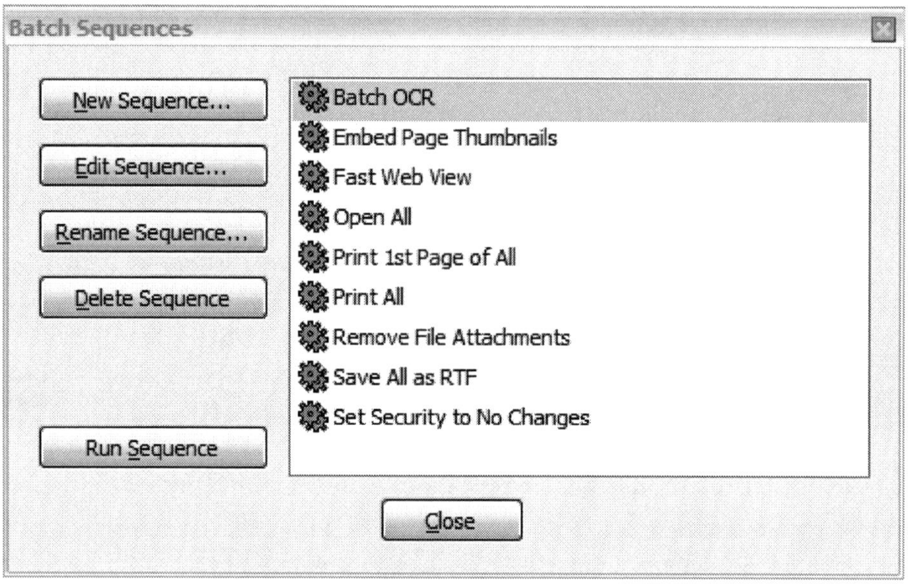

Figure 20.1

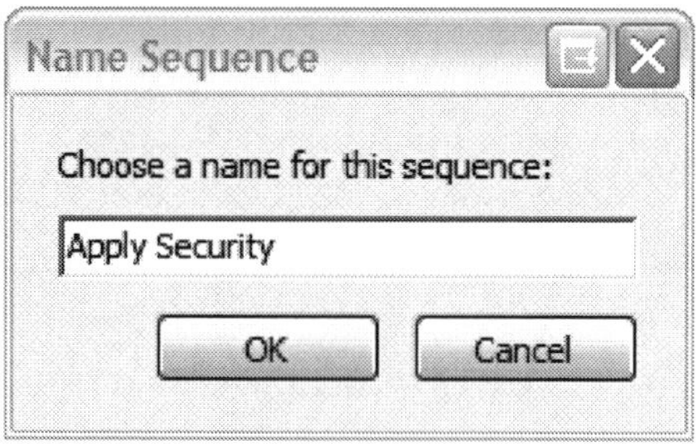

Figure 20.2

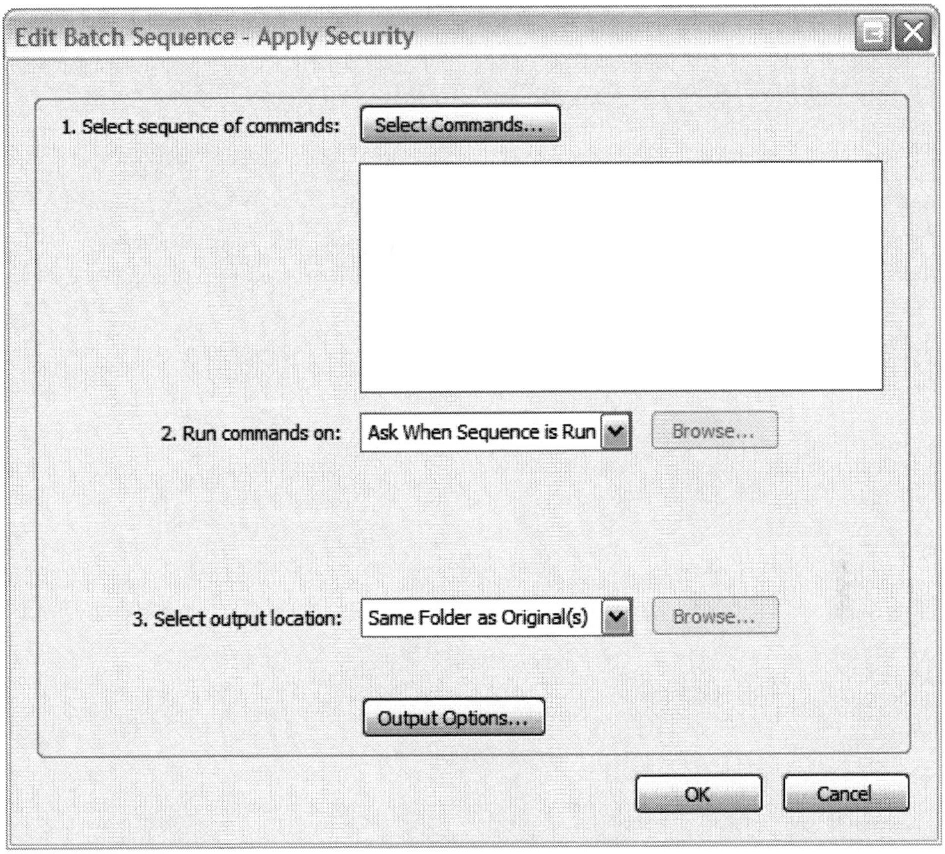

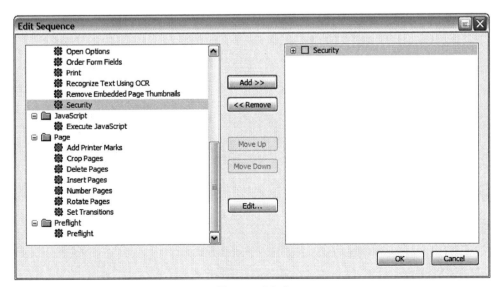

Figure 20.3

Figure 20.4

all tasks that can be run with batch processes. The list of tasks in the **Edit Sequence** window are the only choices (unless you do your own programming). For this example, select **Security**, move it to the right window with the **Add>>** button, then click the **Edit** button. A **Document Security** box appears with the default "None" selected (Figure 20.5). Use the drop-down menu to select **Password Security**. Now the **Password Security—Settings** window appears. Check the **Require a password to open the document** box, then type the desired password in the **Document Open Password** box (Figure 20.6). Confirm

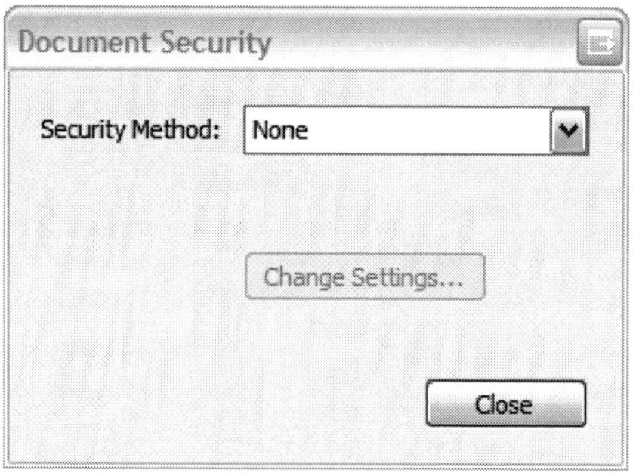

Figure 20.5

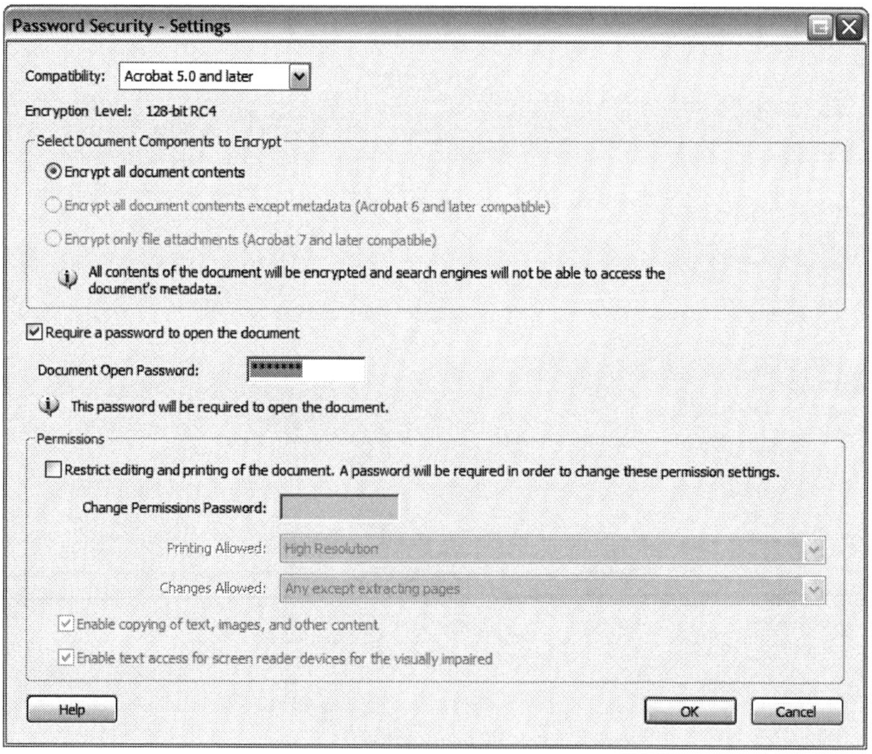

Figure 20.6

the password in the next box and you are returned to the **Document Security** window (Figure 20.7); click the **Close** button then click **OK**. You are now back at the **Edit Batch Sequence-Apply Security** window where you specify what files the sequence will be run on and where the modified files will be saved.

From the **Run commands on** drop-down menu, select whether the sequence will be performed on: (1) files specified when the sequence is run; (2) selected files or selected folders; or (3) the files open in Acrobat (Figure 20.8).

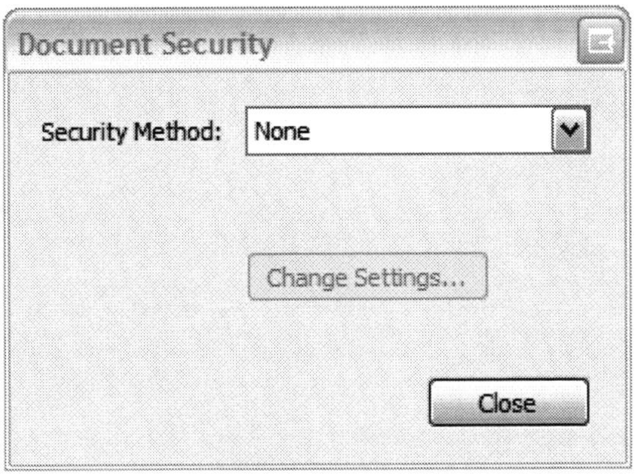

Figure 20.7

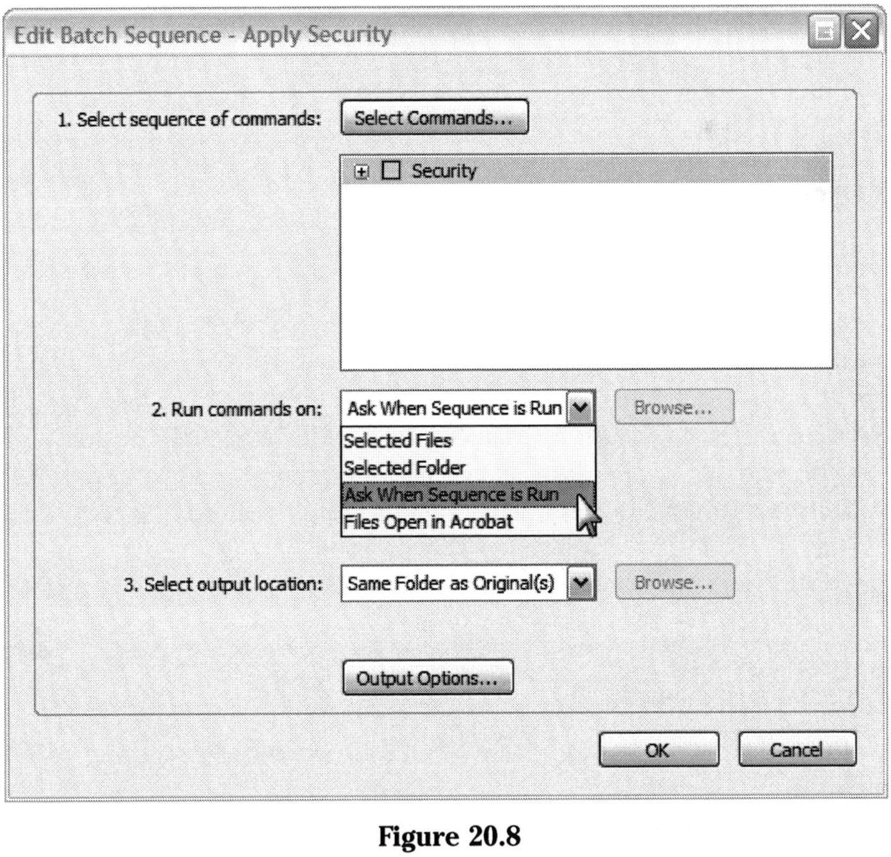

Figure 20.8

From the **Select output location** drop-down menu, select where the processed files will be saved (same as originals, a specific folder, a folder specified when the sequence runs, or not saved at all). (See Figure 20.9.)

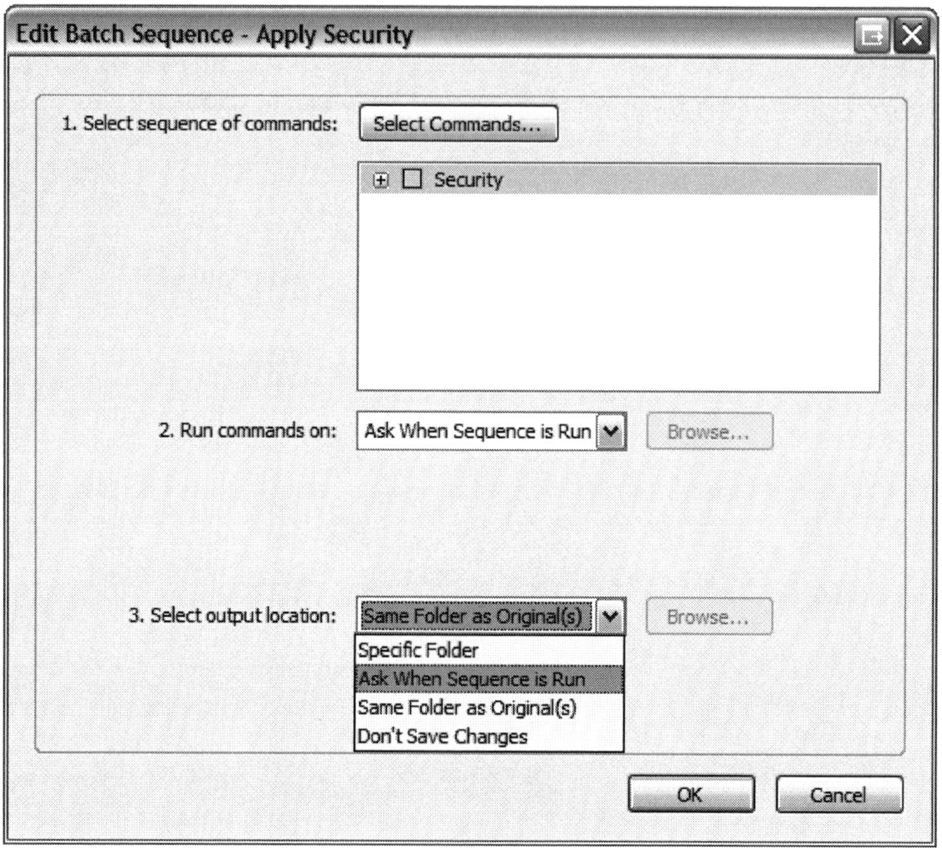

Figure 20.9

Finally, click the **Output Options** button to specify how the processed files will be named, what format they will be in, and whether the original files will be overwritten (Figure 20.10). When **Output Options** have been specified click **OK** to return to the **Edit Batch Sequence-Apply Security** window, click **OK** again to return to the starting point (Batch Sequences window), which now lists the newly created sequence named "Apply Security" (Figure 20.11).

§ 20.2 Running a Batch Sequence

To run a batch sequence:

Menu (Batch Processing): **Advanced > Document Processing > Batch Processing**

Keystroke (Batch Processing): **Alt+A-D-B**

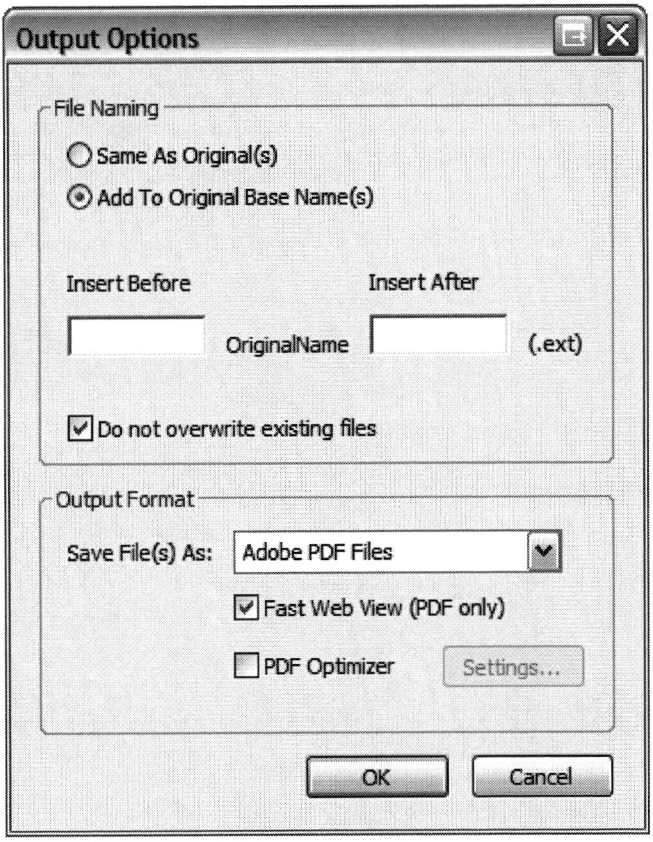

Figure 20.10

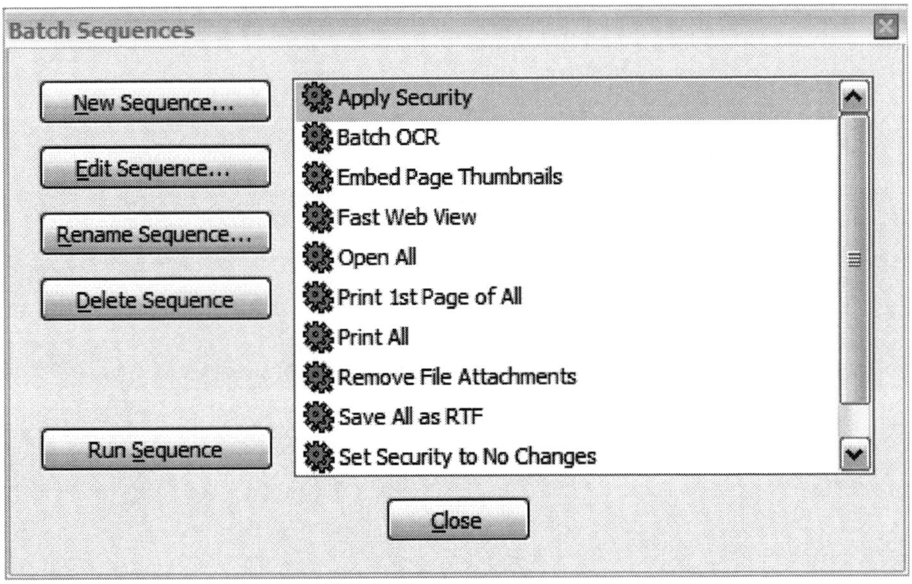

Figure 20.11

The **Batch Sequences** window appears (Figure 20.12). Select a batch process (sequence) to run and click the **Run Sequence** button. What happens next depends on the sequence you selected to run. Depending on the commands included in the selected sequence, the options to be specified will vary. For this example we run the **Apply Security** sequence created in the previous section. The first window that appears is the **Run Sequence Confirmation-Apply Security** window (Figure 20.13).

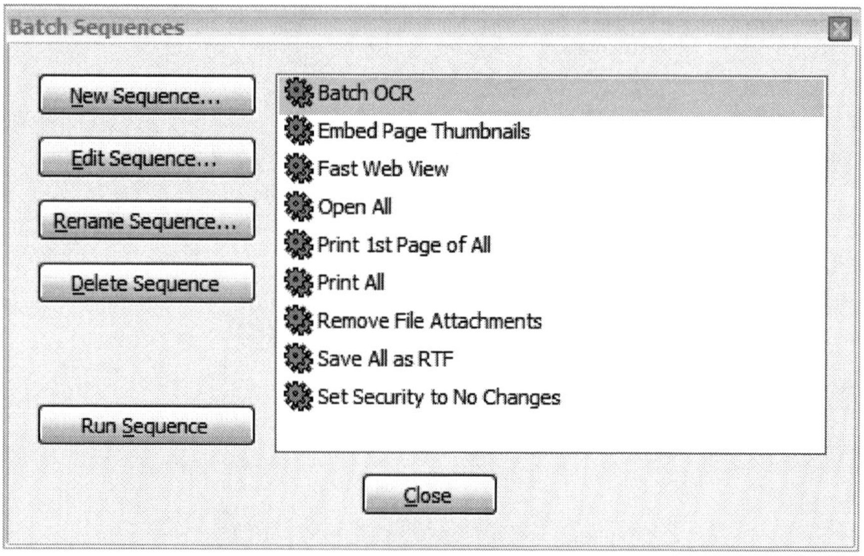

Figure 20.12

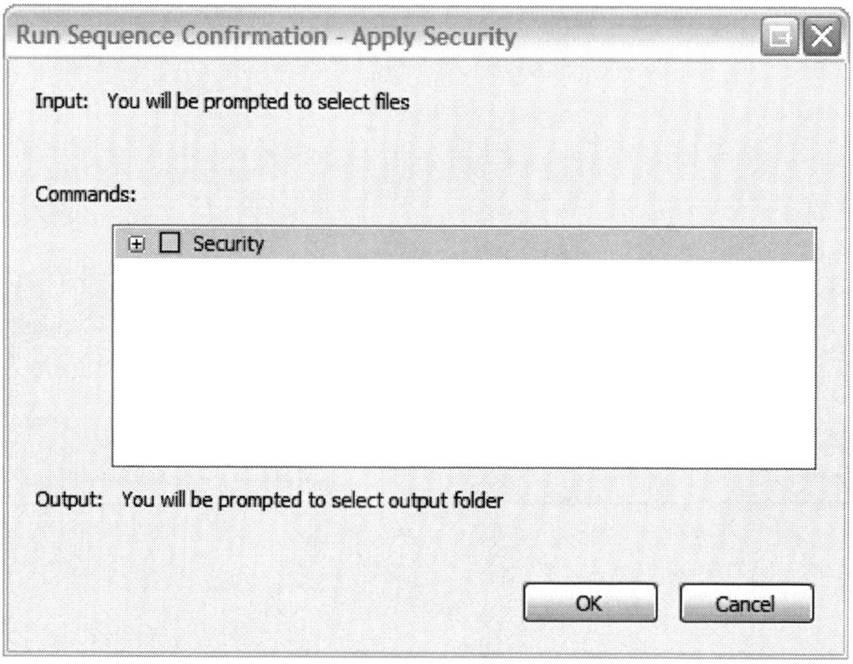

Figure 20.13

Notice that this window divides the information into three parts: Input; Commands; and Output. The **Apply Security** batch sequence calls for the user to specify the input (what files will be processed) and the output (where the files will be saved). The middle section (commands) informs you that the security command will be applied. Because the selected process (Apply Security) requires the user to specify the input, when you click **OK** (in the **Run Sequence Confirmation** window) the next thing you see will be a **Select Files to Process** window (Figure 20.14). Select a folder or files to run the sequence on, click **OK** and you are presented with a window to **Browse For Folder** where the output (processed) files will be saved (Figure 20.15). Click **OK**, the sequence will run, and the files will be batch processed.

§ 20.3 Batch Process Summary

This chapter described the process to create and run a single batch process. Hopefully you now have a sense of how powerful this feature can be. Think of thousands of pages in multiple PDF files that you would like to OCR. Simply run the OCR batch sequence, specify a new output folder and presto—a giant task can be run in the background or after hours. When you create your own batch sequences keep in mind that multiple "commands" can be included in the sequence; just add the desired commands then move them up or down in the order that you want them to run. Whether you use batch processing to apply security, run OCR, or some other task, it makes sense to save the out-

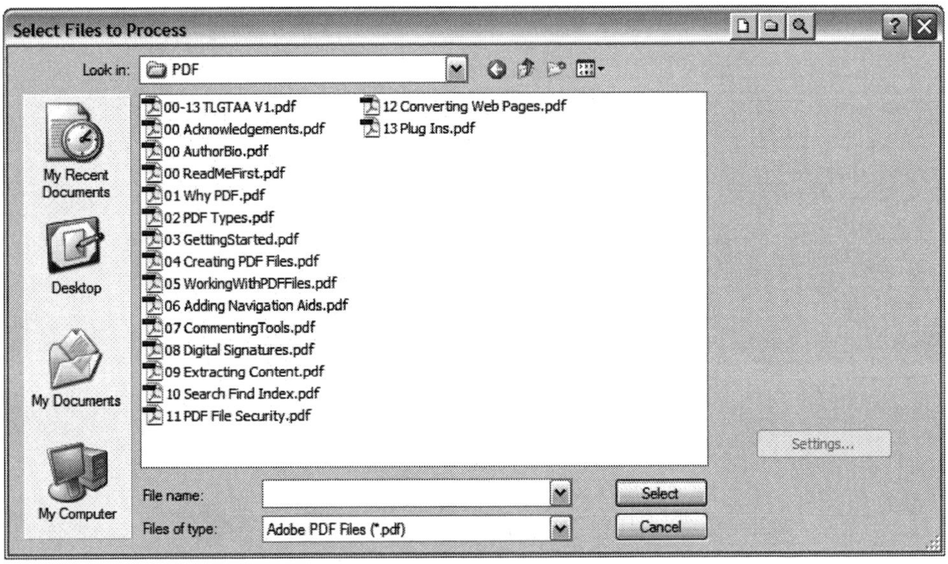

Figure 20.14

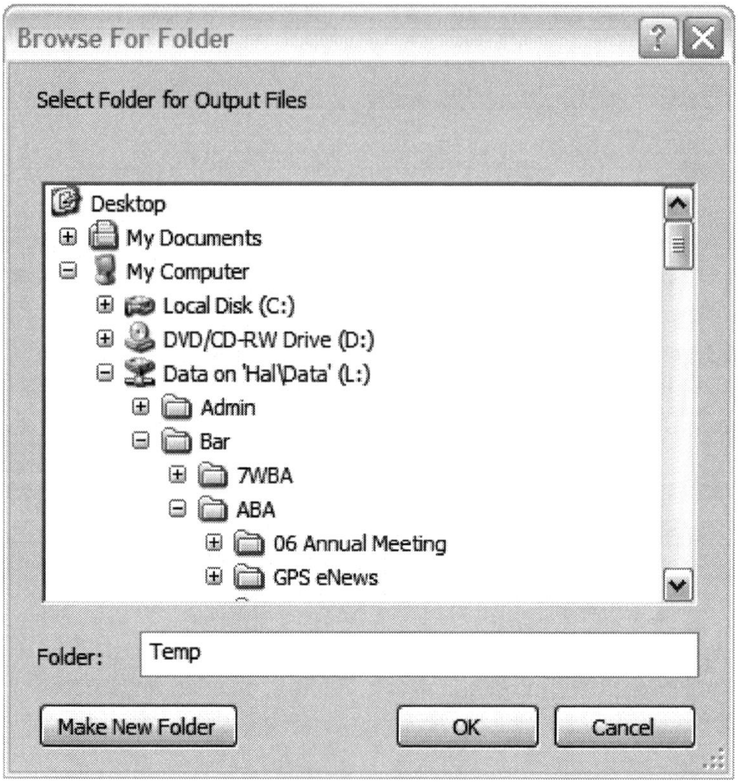

Figure 20.15

put to a new folder or at least give the output files new names. That way, if something goes wrong (say, you mistyped the password and can't seem to replicate it) you have your original files to go back to. If all works as planned, then you can retain or delete the original files.

Examine Document (Remove Metadata) | **21**

In addition to removing visible content from documents, legal professionals also need to verify that no hidden information exists, including metadata, before those documents are distributed. The Examine Document feature can scan through your document and alert you to hidden information that you may not be aware of, including metadata, comments, file attachments, and other elements. You can then remove some or all of those element with a single click.

To examine the open PDF file for hidden information:

Menu (Examine Document): **Document > Examine Document**

Keystroke (Examine Document): **Alt+D-I**

The **Examine Document** window opens and displays a list of the information associated with the document (Figure 21.1).

Make sure that the check boxes are selected only for the items that you want to remove from the document.

- ◆ *Metadata:* includes information about the document and its contents, such as the author's name, keywords, and copyright information, that can be used by search utilities. To view metadata: **File > Properties** or **Ctrl+D** and click on the **Description** tab and the **Additional Metadata** button.

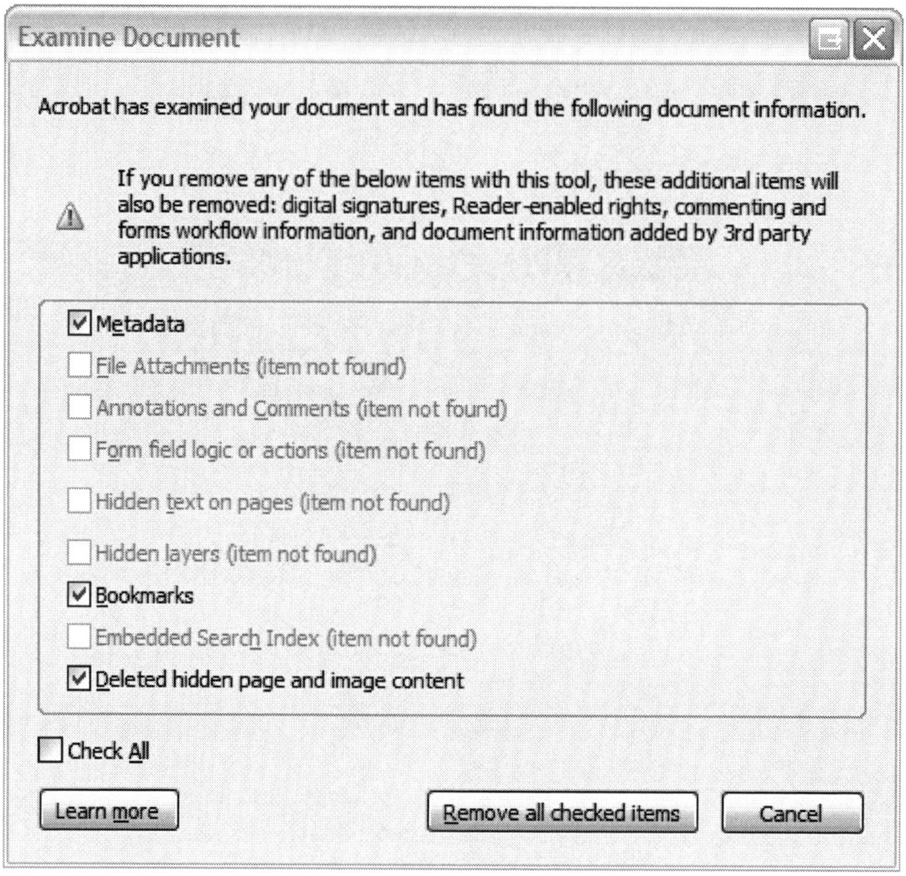

Examine Document

Acrobat has examined your document and has found the following document information.

⚠ If you remove any of the below items with this tool, these additional items will also be removed: digital signatures, Reader-enabled rights, commenting and forms workflow information, and document information added by 3rd party applications.

☑ Metadata

☐ File Attachments (item not found)

☐ Annotations and Comments (item not found)

☐ Form field logic or actions (item not found)

☐ Hidden text on pages (item not found)

☐ Hidden layers (item not found)

☑ Bookmarks

☐ Embedded Search Index (item not found)

☑ Deleted hidden page and image content

☐ Check All

Learn more   Remove all checked items   Cancel

Figure 21.1

◆ *File Attachments:* Files of any format can be attached to the PDF as an attachment. To view attachments, choose **View > Navigation Panel > Attachments** or click on the **Attachments** icon (a paperclip in the lower-left work area).

◆ *Annotations and Comments:* This includes all Comments that were added to the PDF using the **Comment and Markup** tools, including files attached as comments. To view comments, choose **View > Navigation Panel > Comments** or click on the **Comments** icon in the lower-left work area (Figure 21.2).

Figure 21.2

- *Form field logic or actions:* Includes form fields (including signature fields), and all actions and calculations associated with form fields. Caution: if you remove this item, all form fields are flattened and can no longer be filled out, edited, or signed.
- *Hidden text:* This item indicates text in the PDF that is either transparent, covered up by other content, or the same color as the background. To view hidden text, click **Preview**. Click the double arrow buttons to navigate pages that contain hidden text, and select **Options** to show hidden text, visible text, or both.
- *Hidden layers:* PDF files can contain multiple layers that can be shown or hidden. Removing hidden layers removes these layers from the file and flattens remaining layers into a single layer. To view layers, choose **View > Navigation Panel > Layers**.
- *Bookmarks:* Links that take users to specific pages in the PDF file. To view bookmarks, choose **View > Navigation Panel > Bookmarks** or click on the **Bookmark** icon.
- *Embedded Search Index:* An embedded search index speeds up searches in the file. To determine if the file contains a search index, choose **Advanced > Document Processing > Manage Embedded Index.** Removing indexes decreases file size but increases search time.
- *Deleted hidden page and image content:* PDF files sometimes retain content that has been removed and which is no longer visible, such as cropped or deleted pages, or deleted images.

If an item description, and its corresponding check box, is "grayed-out," Acrobat has determined that the file does not contain that type of information. Click **Remove all checked items** to delete selected items from the file, and click **OK**. If you don't want to overwrite the original file, save the file to a different name, location, or both. The selected content is permanently removed when you save the file. If you close the file without saving it, you'll have to repeat this process.

Printing PDF Files **22**

Alright, here we are, almost done with the book. After all the discussion of creating and working with PDF files, the paper-free office and electronic briefs, you're probably asking yourself, why a chapter on printing PDF files? Isn't the point to be rid of paper and work instead with electronic documents? Yes, but there will be times when you want or need to print a PDF file to paper. There may even be occasions when you want to print a portion of a PDF file to PDF (an explanation will follow in due course). When you tell an application to print a file you probably don't pay much attention to the printer dialog box. Other than selecting the desired printer there's not much else to be concerned with. When you print a document from Acrobat the usual dialog box appears, but this one merits closer examination.

§ 22.1 What to Print (Comments and Forms)

Open a PDF file, click the **Print** button on the **Tasks** toolbar, or do one of the following:

> Menu (Print): **File > Print**
> Keystroke (Print): **Ctrl+P**
> Keystroke (Print): **Alt+F-P**

The **Print** dialog box opens (Figure 22.1).

In the Printer (top) section of the **Print** dialog box, there is an easily overlooked drop-down menu under the caption **Comments and Forms** (Figure 22.2). The menu options are:

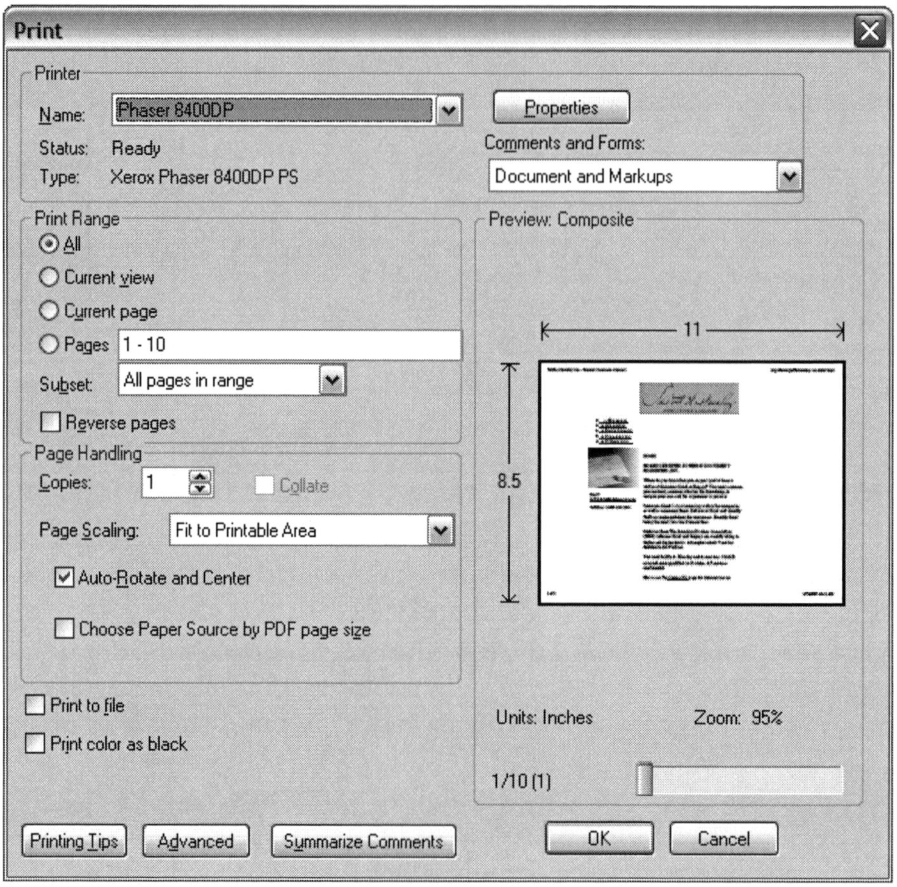

Figure 22.1

- ◆ *Document:* Prints the document contents and form fields.
- ◆ *Document and Markups:* Prints the document contents, form fields, and comments.
- ◆ *Document and Stamps:* Prints the document, form fields, and stamps, but no other markups, such as notes.
- ◆ *Form Fields only:* Prints interactive form fields but not document contents.

If you applied your signature stamp to the document, then you need to select **Document and Markups** or **Document and Stamps**. Otherwise, your signature will not appear on the printed page. Likewise, if you used the **Highlight** tool to mark text in the PDF file, and you want the highlights to appear on the printed page (you'll need a color printer) you need to need to select **Document and Markups**. Conversely, if you want to print a clean copy of the document without any markups, select **Document**.

The Preview area, below the **Comments and Forms** menu, provides a thumbnail view of what will print. Look for your signature if you want it to

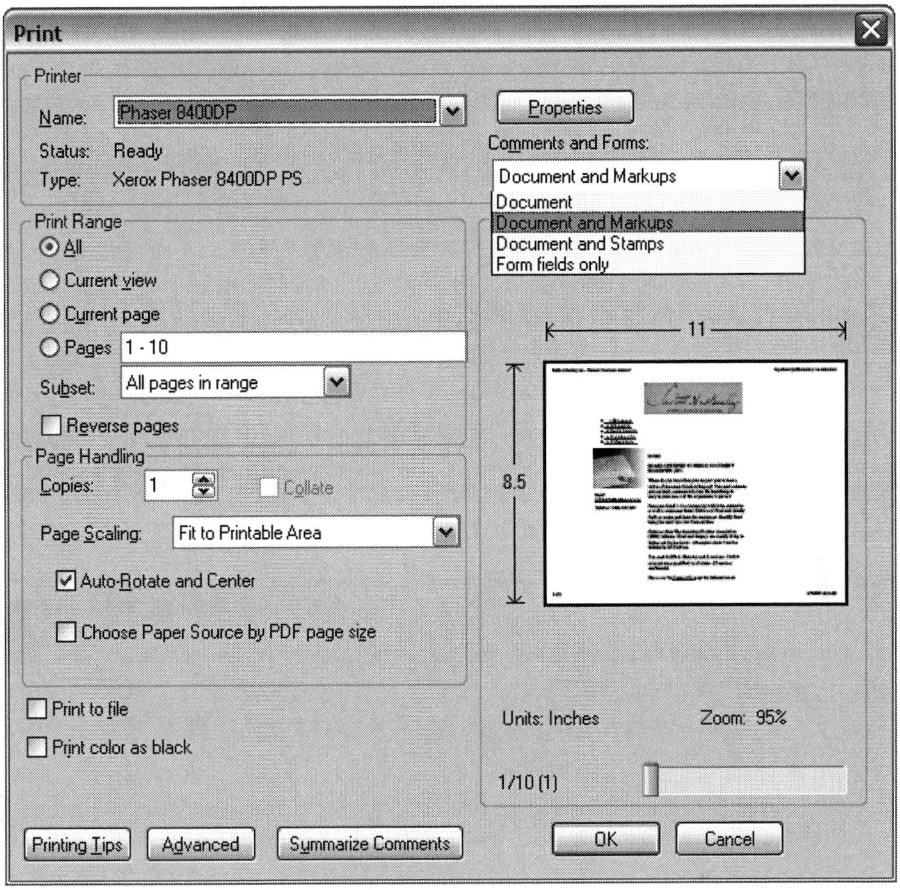

Figure 22.2

print. You can use the slider below the thumbnail to scroll through the pages of the file.

§ 22.2 What to Print (Print Range)

The **Print Range** section of the **Print** dialog box allows you to specify all pages, the current view, the current page, or specified pages. This may seem overly obvious but it was the print current view option that provided the impetus for this chapter (and the idea of printing a portion of a PDF file to PDF).

If you happen to be working with a PDF file that represents a large format physical document, such as a map or survey plat, the print current view is a cool option. Zoom in on a particular area, click the **Print** button (or **Ctrl+P**), select **Current View** in the **Print Range** section, and what you see on the screen (the current view) will print to the size of the paper in the selected physical printer.

§ 22.3 Page Handling

The **Page Handling** section of the **Print** dialog box allows you to specify the number of copies to print, whether or not to collate those copies, and specify page scaling. This last item, **Page Scaling**, deserves more attention. PDF files can be as large as 15,000,000 inches square (whoa!). While you're not likely to encounter a PDF file that size, it's not uncommon to have maps and plats scanned full size (e.g., 24 inches by 36 inches). Print scaling provides various ways to print oversized documents on standard desktop printers (Figure 22.3).

You can print each page in pieces, called tiles, and then trim and assemble those pieces. You can also increase the scale of a standard-sized document and print it on multiple pages. If all pages of the document are oversized, select **Tile all pages**. If some of the pages are standard-sized, choose **Tile large pages**.

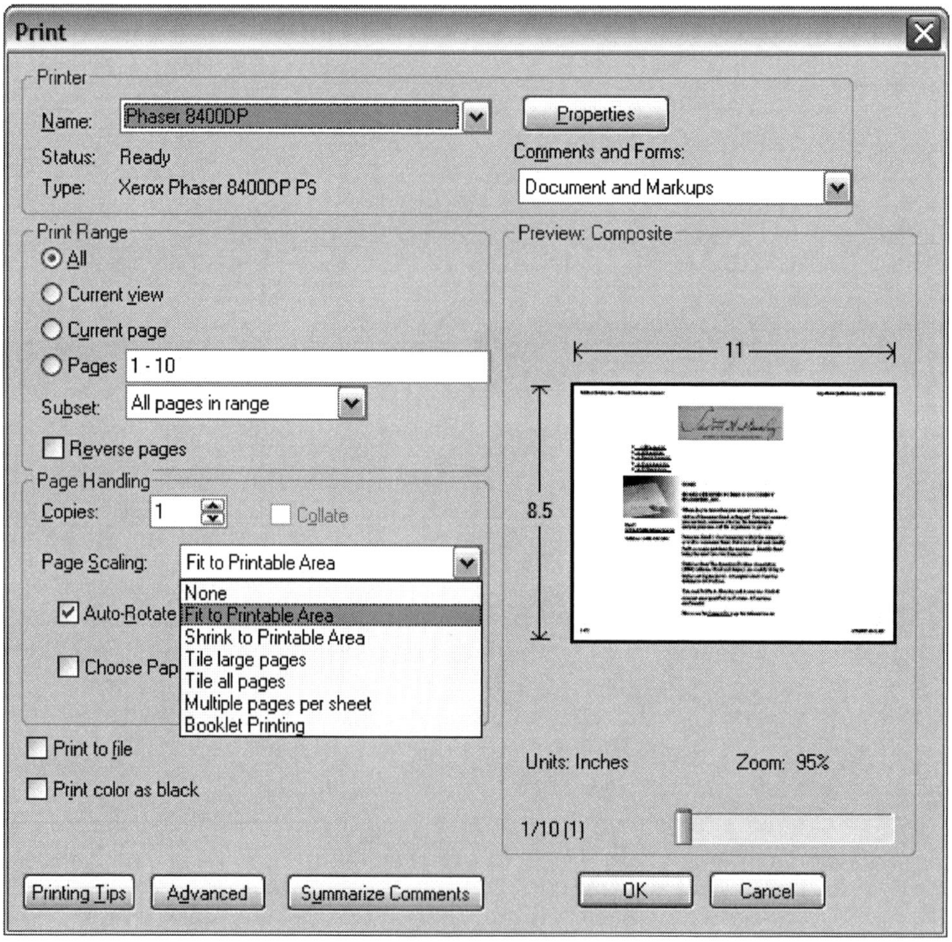

Figure 22.3

To print an oversized PDF file on paper that has smaller dimensions, for example printing a 24" x 36" plat on 8.5" x 11" or 11" x 17" paper, you can scale the document's width and height to fit. From the **Page Scaling** menu, choose **Fit to Printable Area** or **Shrink to Printable Area**. Page scaling works the other way too. Lets say you scanned a personal check (approximately 3 by 6 inches). If you select **Fit to Printable Area**, the check will be enlarged to fit the size of paper selected.

§ 22.4 Print PDF to PDF

Just as you can zoom in on a portion of a PDF file and print the current view to a physical printer, you can print the current view to PDF by selecting Adobe PDF as the printer. In Figure 22.4, a portion of a plat that was scanned

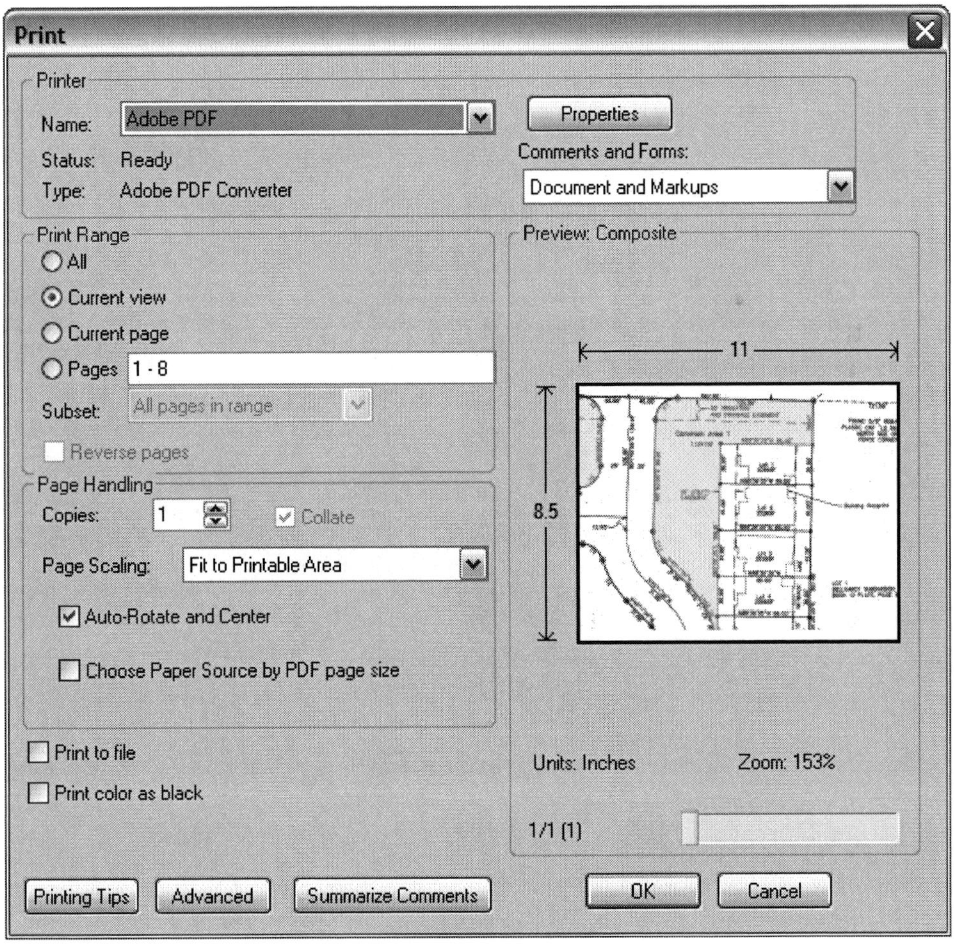

Figure 22.4

full size (24" x 36") to PDF has been selected, **Current view** has been selected in the **Print Range** section, and **Adobe PDF** selected in the **Printer** section. Clicking **OK** will generate a new PDF file of the "page size" specified in the **Adobe PDF Document Properties** window (Figure 22.5). The new PDF file can be used as an exhibit displayed with a projector, printed and attached to a paper document, or inserted into another PDF file. Experiment with this function and you'll find many uses.

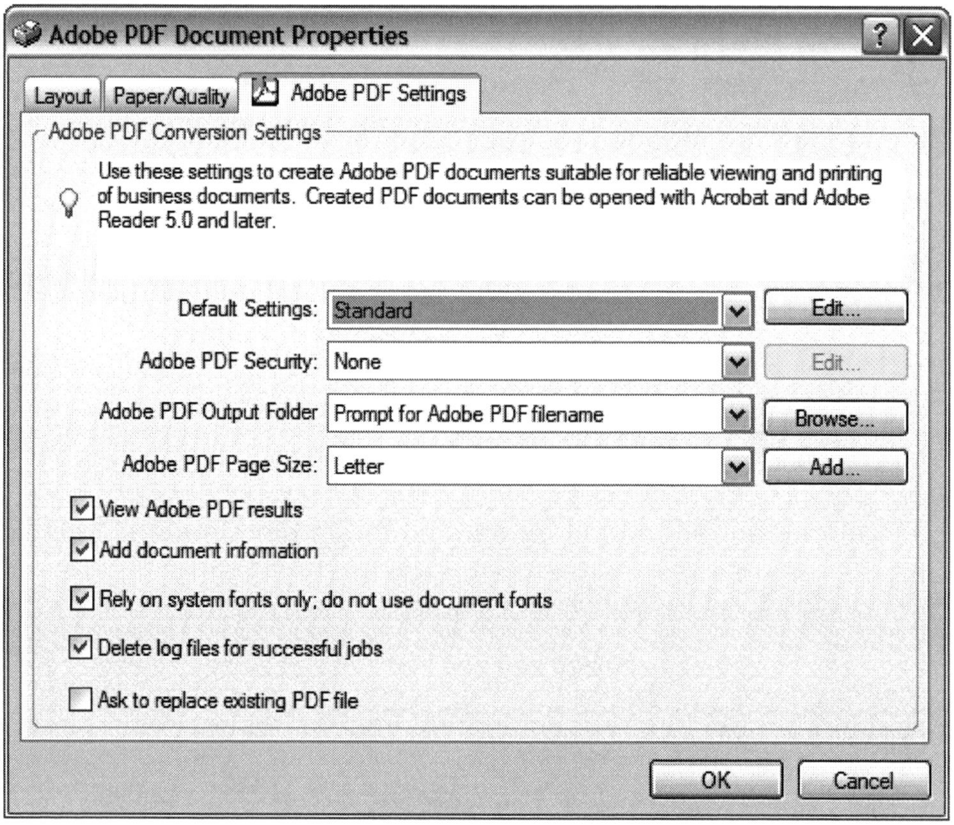

Figure 22.5

Reduce—Reuse—Recycle 23

Despite the advent of electronic—paper-free—technologies, paper use continues to grow. In 2000, over 4.6 million tons of copy paper were shipped in the United States; 1 million tons more than 1995. The growing demand for paper comes at a high cost to the environment. The direct economic consequences to your office of paper use are also significant: include the costs for purchasing, printing, storing, copying, retrieving, recycling, disposal, and postage, and the numbers quickly add up. The full cost associated with office paper can run more than twenty times the purchase price. Paper use also has significant environmental costs.

- In the United States, 500 million acres, an area almost three times the size of Texas, is used to grow wood for paper.
- One-third of all wood harvested in the United States is used for paper products.
- Paper production is the third most energy-intensive of all manufacturing industries in the United States, according to Department of Energy statistics, and uses 11.5% of all energy in the industrial sector. Paper production is the third most energy-intensive of all manufacturing.

Offices use nearly 1.5 pounds of paper per person per day, according to a survey of Los Angeles offices. The typical U.S. office worker uses about 10,000 sheets of copy paper each year. How much paper is 10,000 sheets?

- A ream (500 sheets) of unused paper is about 2 inches thick, which translates to about 250 sheets per inch, or 3,000 sheets per foot.
- In one large stack, 10,000 sheets of unused paper weighs about 100 pounds and is over 4 feet tall (for a variety of reasons, as you use paper it takes up more space).
- "Standard" office paper is 20 lb. weight; each sheet is 8.5 x 11 inches and covers about 0.65 square feet.
- There are about 200,000 sheets (400 reams) per ton, or about 100 sheet per pound.
- Paper prices vary, but a typical bulk cost is $1,000.00 per ton, which is $2.50 per ream, half a cent per sheet, or 50 cents per pound.

Reducing the amount of paper used in businesses presents enormous potential savings for the environment. Unfortunately, despite technology's promise of the paper-free office, paper use is on the rise—a telling statistic that helps account for the fact that about one-third of waste sent to municipal landfills is paper and packaging.

Reduce. Use less paper. Transition your office to electronic client files. Use electronic court filing systems. Create your letterhead in a word processing application so that you can print letters to PDF to send to clients and opposing counsel via electronic mail. Create hard copies only when absolutely necessary. In many cases you don't need a paper copy of a document. An electronic copy may be fine. The advantages of electronic copies are paper, postage, and storage space savings. They also allow electronic search capabilities you don't have with paper documents. Electronic filing and retrieval saves time when you need the document again. Try to review and edit draft documents on screen rather than on paper. If you need to print large documents consider adjusting margins, line spacing, and page settings that allow more information to fit on each page. Use electronic mail to share documents. Print or capture web pages to PDF rather them printing to paper.

Use two-sided printing and copying when possible. Paper has a large embodied energy content. It requires 15 watt-hours of energy to make a virgin sheet of copy paper. That's more energy than the paper would use in a copier, printer, or fax machine. The embodied energy has become a concern in offices that want to reduce the environmental impact of their activities. One simple but highly effective step to take is to change printer and copier settings to duplex. This saves a substantial amount of paper—and money. When you need new office equipment, purchase copiers and printers that automatically print on both sides.

Reduce paper use and you will reduce costs.

Reuse paper when possible. If you print drafts to paper to markup and edit, save the pages and use the clean side for your drafts. If you print draft or pre-bills to review each month, you have a ready supply of "draft" paper.

When opposing counsel sends you disclosure or discovery documents on paper, save it and reuse it to print drafts.

Recycle. Natural systems ultimately recycle everything. We can do the same with resources such as paper. Paper is a large component of the waste going into landfills, and offices are a primary source of that paper. Consider using recycled paper. The term "recycled" is often used to describe paper that includes scraps and wastes generated in the paper production process. Post-consumer fiber content is what really counts. Look for post-consumer content that is at least 30 percent or more. Thirty percent post-consumer recycled office papers can match the quality specifications of virgin for copy paper. There are a number of paper products with 100 percent post-consumer content. Figure 23.1 shows the recycling symbol.

Paper with post-consumer recycled content can meet your business needs while greatly improving environmental performance. By choosing recycled, you reduce the amount of wood, water, and energy that would otherwise be used to make paper. Buying recycled paper also diverts waste paper from landfills and provides economic incentives for better recycling.

Lots of expensive paper, paper with very real business and environmental costs, is thrown out with the trash. Although paper-recycling rates are at an all-time high, less than half of all office paper is recovered. Recycle to prevent this waste.

Figure 23.1

Keyboard Shortcuts and Resources

Keyboard Shortcuts

There are many, many keyboard shortcuts in Acrobat. See the Complete Adobe Acrobat 8 Help (**F1** key), contents topic, Keyboard Shortcuts. The list below includes common shortcuts, not too many to remember, that you will use on a regular basis.

Ctrl+B Create Bookmark at the present location.

Ctrl+E Properties Bar (displays the properties bar associated with the currently active object [e.g., Sticky Note] in the open PDF file).

Ctrl+F Find (find a word or character string within the current document).

Ctrl+Shift+D Delete pages (opens a dialog box where you specify the pages to be deleted—use with caution).

Ctrl+Shift+I Insert Pages (opens a dialog box where you specify one or more PDF files to insert into the currently open file).

Ctrl+Shift+N Go to a specific page number.

Ctrl+Shift+R Rotate pages (opens a dialog box where you specify the rotation direction and which pages to rotate).

Ctrl+Shift+S Save As (save the current PDF file with a new name).

Alt+D-X Extract pages (opens a dialog box where you specify the pages to copy from the current file to a new [unnamed] file).

Ctrl+D Opens the Document Properties window where you can supply summary information, apply security, and specify the initial view.

253

Ctrl+L Full Screen Mode, use the Escape key to return to normal view.

F4 Toggles the navigation panels on and off. Handy for quickly hiding or showing the Bookmark panel.

F8 Hides or displays the toolbars.

F9 Hides or displays the menu bar.

Web Sites

www.adobe.com/products/acrobat—The mother lode for all kinds of information about Acrobat and Portable Document Format.

www.pdfforlawyers.com—"How to use PDFs in the practice of law—Tips & Techniques," a web site maintained by Ernest Svenson (Ernie the Attorney), a business litigator in the greater New Orleans area.

www.planetpdf.com—"The home of the PDF community." Planet PDF caters to anyone and everyone with an interest in PDF, from professional Web or print publishers seeking appropriate tools, to rank beginners wondering exactly what "PDF" stands for. Assisting PDF users since 1998, Planet PDF is a comprehensive, popular and independent Web site exclusively focused on Adobe Acrobat/PDF users and uses. Note: Planet PDF is a division of Nitro PDF Software.

www.pdfzone.com—"The online authority for PDF and document management professionals." PDF Zone is produced by Ziff Davis Enterprise.

Index

About files, 188, 192
Acrobat, xv, 7–8
Actual Size view, 16, 17, 20, 64
Adding. *See also* Creating
    comments, 82, 85–86, 85–86
    pages, 48, 184
    sticky notes, 82
    text boxes, 85–86
Adobe. *See* Acrobat; Live Cycle Designer; Photoshop; Reader
Appearance. *See also* Page display
    of bookmarks, 65, 67
    of callout text boxes, 94–95
    of comments, 82, 83, 85, 94–95
    of comment summaries, 89
    of drawing markup tools, 94–95
    for Full Screen Mode, 176–77
    of lines, 94–95
    of links, 73, 186, 187
    of shapes, 94–95
    of signatures, 106–7
    of stamps, 94–95, 163, 165, 166
    of sticky notes, 82, 83, 94–95
    of text boxes, 85, 94–95
    of text markup, 94–95
Archive standards, 2
Area Measuring tool, 87–88
Arrows, 90–93, 171, 172
Artwork, 97
Attachments, 15, 240

Author, 58–59, 95
Auto-run features, 190

Batch processing, 229–38
Bates numbers
    in Acrobat generally, 207–11
    bookmarks and, 166
    copies and, 166
    extracting and, 117
    IntelliPDF BATES, 165–67
    optical character recognition (OCR)
        and, 122–23, 162
    for page numbers, 76–78
    plug-ins for, 162–67, 208
    prefixes for, 162, 164–65
    StampPDF, 163–65
    with word processing applications,
        162, 207–8
Blank pages, 44–45
BMP, 180
Bookmarks. *See also* Links
    appearance of, 65, 67
    arrangement of documents with,
        62–63
    Bates numbers and, 166
    comments and, 84–85
    creating, 63–64
    deleting, 66–67, 241
    destination of, 65–66
    editing, 65–66

for exhibit notebooks, 84–85
hierarchy for, 67, 68
for image-on-text files, 64–65
initial view options for, 55–57
navigation with, 15, 18, 61–69
page display and, 64
searching for, 126–27
security for, 68–69
text boxes and, 84–85
for Web pages, 155
wrapping long ones, 67
Briefs
contents of, 188, 191
copying to CDs, 187–90
creating, 180–82, 184
filing and service of, 2–3, 103, 179,
190–91
indexes for, 188–90
links in, 180, 185–87
organization of, 182–84
overview of, 179

Callout text boxes, 85–86, 93–96
Capture settings, 155–59
Case Management and Electronic Case
Files (CM/ECF) system, 2–3
Case-Sensitive, 126, 128
Catalog. See Indexing
Certificates, 104–5, 109–12, 134, 149
Clipboard, 43–44
Clouds, 90–93
Combine function, 35–42
Comments. See also Stamps; Sticky
notes; Text boxes; Text markup
adding, 82, 85–86
appearance of, 82, 83, 85, 94–95
author of, 95
bookmarks and, 84–85
deleting, 83, 93, 240
drawing markup tools, 89–93
editing, 83
for exhibit notebooks, 84–85
Find function for, 79–80
fonts for, 94
hiding, 95
for image-on-text files, 86–87
lines and shapes, 90–93
making, 95–96
measuring tools, 87–88
navigation with, 15

opacity of, 92, 94
overview of, 79–80, 101
pop-ups for, 94, 95–96
preferences for, 26
printing, 89, 243–45
properties of, 82, 83, 85, 93–96
searching for, 79–80, 101, 127
security for, 97, 99–100
show function for, 80
summaries for, 89–90, 101
toolbars for, 80–81
Contents, 59, 188, 191
Conversion, 2, 30, 33–34
Copies, 166
Copy function, 113–14, 117–18, 187–90.
See also Extracting
Court filings, 2–3, 103, 179, 190–91. See
also Briefs
Creating. See also Adding
from blank pages, 44–45
bookmarks, 63–64
briefs, 180–82, 184
from clipboard, 43–44
by combining, 35–42
comment summaries, 89
by drag and drop, 33, 180
exhibit notebooks, xiv
forms, 223–28
image-on-text files, 5–6, 122–23
indexes, 129–31, 188–90
links, 70–72, 75, 185–87
by packaging, 40–42
PDF files generally, 2, 29–45, 122–23,
180–82
with print function, 29, 30–31, 197,
198, 247–48
by scanning, 30, 31–33
signatures, 105–7
from source materials, 182, 184
stamps, 96–100
from Web pages, 42–43, 151–59
Cropping, 52–53, 98, 99
Cross-Out Text tool, 86–87
Custom-made stamps, 96–98

Deleting
after extracting, 51
bookmarks, 66–67, 241
comments, 83, 93, 240
indexes, 241

links, 74
pages, 51–52
with redaction, 221
sticky notes, 83
Destination, 65–66, 74–75
Digital formats, 1–4. *See also* Portable
    Document Format (PDF)
Digital information, xiii–xiv. *See also*
    Paper-free office
Digital storage requirements, 205
Discovery, 210
Display. *See* Page Display
Display mode. *See* Full Screen Mode
Distance Measuring tool, 87
Document management, 194–205
Document open security, 134, 135–37,
    141–44
Document properties, 55–59, 135–40,
    181. *See also* Properties
Documents, 26
Drag and drop, 33, 180
Drawing markup tools, 89–90, 90–93,
    93–96. *See also* Highlighter tool
Dual-folder system, 201–2
Dynamic Zoom, 23–25

Editing, 65–66, 83
Electronic briefs. *See* Briefs
Enter key, 171, 172
Erasers, 90–93
Examine Document feature, 239–41
Excel, 30–31
Exhibit notebooks, xiv, 84–85, 174–76
Export function, 119
Extracting. *See also* Copy function
    copy function for, 113–14, 117–18
    deleting after, 51
    export function for, 119
    graphic images, 116–19
    from image-on-text files, 113
    page display and, 114
    pages generally, 49–51
    from PDF files, 113–19
    save as function for, 114–16, 118
    word processing applications for,
        116

Facing pages, 57
File attachments, 240
File-naming conventions, 202–3

Filing systems (office), 198–204. *See
    also* Court filings
Find function, 79–80, 121–22, 127–28.
    See also Searching
Firm size, xv
First Page, 16, 17
Fit Page view, 16, 17, 21, 57, 64
Fit Visible, 57
Fit Width view, 16, 17, 21–22, 57, 64
Fonts, 94
Formats. *See* Digital formats
Form fields, 241
Forms, 223–28, 241, 243–45
Full Screen Mode, 25, 169–77

Go To, 17, 172
Governments, 2–3
Graphic images, 116–19

Headers and footers, 155–56, 208–9
Hidden layers, 241
Hidden text, 241
Hiding, 95, 169–70. *See also* Show func-
    tion
Hierarchy, 67, 68
Highlighter tool, 86–87, 93. *See also*
    Drawing markup tools

Identity, 27
Image-only files, 5, 90–93, 121, 167, 215
Image-on-text files
    bookmarks for, 64–65
    comments for, 86–87
    creating, 5–6, 122–23
    extracting from, 113
    optical character recognition (OCR)
        for, 6, 215
    overview of, 5–6
    redaction of, 215
    searching, 121–22, 124–27
    text markup for, 86–87
    from Web pages, 152
Indexing, 121–22, 129–31, 188–90, 241
Information management systems,
    194–205
Initial view options, 55–57
Inserting. *See* Adding
IntelliPDF BATES, 165–67
International Organization for Stan-
    dardization (ISO), 2
Internet Explorer, 30–31, 42–43

JPEG
    as common, 2
    conversion from, 33–34, 180
    extracting and, 117
    as image-only files, 6
    for stamps, 97
Judiciary, 2–3

Keyboard shortcuts, 253–54
Keystrokes, 10
Keywords, 58–59

Last Page, 16, 17
Layers, 55–57, 99, 241
Layout, 19, 57. *See also* Page display
Left-right arrows, 16
Lines, 90–93, 93–96
Links. *See also* Bookmarks
    appearance of, 73, 186, 187
    in briefs, 180, 185–87
    creating, 70–72, 75, 185–87
    deleting, 74
    destination of, 74–75
    moving, 73
    navigation with, 18, 61–62, 69–76
    properties of, 73
    security for, 75–76
    for source materials, 185–87
    toolbar for, 70, 186–87
Live Cycle Designer, 225–28
Logical folder system, 199–201

Magnification, 57. *See also* Zooming
Marking, 215–19
Marquee Zoom, 25
Measuring tools, 87–88
Memory requirements, 205
Menus, 8–10
Metadata, 133, 239–41
Mouse, 26–27
Moving, 73

Navigation
    by attachments, 15
    basics of, 16–17, 61–62
    with bookmarks, 15, 18, 61–69
    with comments, 15
    in Full Screen Mode, 171–74
    icons for, 14–15
    with links, 18, 61–62, 69–76
    with page numbers, 62, 76–78
    by pages, 15
    page size and, 16, 17
    by signatures, 15
Nesting. *See* Hierarchy
Next Page, 16
Next View, 17
Notes. *See* Sticky notes
Numbers. *See* Page numbers

Objects, 114
Opacity, 92, 94
Open security, 134, 135–37, 141–44
Optical character recognition (OCR).
    See also Scanning
    batch processing for, 237–38
    Bates numbers and, 122–23, 162
    for image-on-text files, 6, 215
    quality of, 3, 123–24
    searching and, 121–24
    for source materials, 182
Organization, 182–84
Orientation, 19
Ovals, 90–93

Packaging, 40–42
Page display. *See also* Appearance
    bookmarks and, 64
    extracting and, 114
    Full Screen Mode, 25, 169–77
    generally, 18
    initial view options for, 55–57
    layout and orientation, 19, 156–57
    magnification, 57
    preferences for, 27
    for printing, 246–47
    size, 20–23
    for Web pages, 156–59
    zooming, 22–25, 26–27, 176
Page Down, 16, 17, 21, 171
Page Handling function, 246–47
Page layout. *See* Page display
Page numbers, 62, 76–78
Page order, 54–55
Pages
    adding, 48, 184
    cropping, 52–53
    deleting, 51–52

extracting, 49–51
initial view options for, 55–57
navigation by, 15
rearranging order of, 54–55
replacing, 49
rotating, 53–54
working with, 47–48
Page size, 16, 17, 20–23
Page Up, 16, 17, 171
Page views. *See* Page display
Paper, 249–51
Paper-free office
   digital storage requirements in, 205
   document management basics in,
      196–98
   filing systems for, 198–204
   information management systems in
      generally, 194–96
   paper use in, 249–51
   possibility of, xiii–xiv, 4, 8, 193–94
Passwords. *See* Security
PDF drivers, 3
PDF files. *See also* Pages
   from blank pages, 44–45
   from briefs, 180–82
   from clipboard, 43–44
   combining, 35–42
   conversion to, 30, 33–34
   creating, 2, 29–45, 122–23, 151–59,
      180–82
   digital storage requirements for, 205
   document management systems for,
      194–205
   drag and drop for creating, 33, 180
   extracting from, 113–19
   initial view options, 55–57
   packaging, 40–42
   print function for creating, 29,
      30–31, 152–53, 180, 182, 197, 198,
      247–48
   printing, 243–48
   scanning for creating, 30, 31–33,
      180–81, 182
   security for, 99–100, 133–49
   from source materials, 182
   types of, 5–6
   from Web pages, 42–43, 151–59
   working with, 47–59
PDF packages, 40–42

PDF printers, 30
PDF tags, 155
Pencil erasers, 90–93
Pencils, 90–93
Percentage views, 57
Perimeter Measuring tool, 87–88
Permissions, 134–35, 138–40, 145–48
Photoshop, 171
Plug-ins, 161–67, 208, 213
Polygonal lines, 90–93
Polygons, 90–93
Pop-ups, 94, 95–96
Portable Document Format (PDF), 2,
     104. *See also* PDF files
PowerPoint, 30–31, 170–71
Preferences, 25–27, 169, 176–77. *See
   also* Properties
Previous Page, 16
Previous View, 17
Printers, 30, 250
Printing
   comments, 89, 243–45
   comment summaries, 89
   creating PDF files by, 29, 30–31,
      152–53, 180, 182, 247–48
   in document management systems,
      197, 198
   forms, 243–45
   Page Handling function, 246–47
   PDF files, 243–48
   from PDF packages, 41
   range for, 245
   signatures, 244
   stamps, 244
Professional responsibility, xiii, 3
Properties. *See also* Preferences
   of callout text boxes, 93–96
   of comments, 82, 83, 85, 93–96
   document properties, 55–59, 135–40,
      181
   of drawing markup tools, 93–96
   of lines, 93–96
   of links, 73
   for redaction, 219–20
   of shapes, 93–96
   of stamps, 93–96
   of sticky notes, 82, 83, 93–96
   of text boxes, 85, 93–96
   of text markup, 93–96

Public Access to Court Electronic
    Records (PACER) program, 3
Publish function, 30–31

Reader, xv, 7–8
Rearranging, 54–55
Record index numbers, 76–78
Rectangles, 90–93
Recycling, 251
Redaction
    applying, 220–22
    deleting with accidentally, 221
    marking for, 215–19
    overview of, 213–15
    plug-ins for, 167, 213
    properties for, 219–20
    searching for, 215–19
    security of, 213–14
Redax, 167, 213
Reduce, 250
Replacing, 49
Reuse, 250–51
Right-click, 185–86
Rotating, 53–54

Save As function, 114–16, 118
Save function, 187–90, 221, 228
Scanning. *See also* Optical character
    recognition (OCR)
    creating PDF files by, 30, 31–33,
        122–23, 180–81, 182
    in document management systems,
        196–98, 203–4
    searching and, 121–24
Searching. *See also* Find function
    for bookmarks, 126–27
    for comments, 79–80, 101, 127
    for document properties, 57–59
    image-only files, 5, 121
    image-on-text files, 121–22, 124–27
    optical character recognition (OCR)
        and, 121–24
    overview of, 121–22
    for redaction, 215–19
    refining searches, 126–27
    scanning and, 121–24
    for sticky notes, 79–80, 101
    for text boxes, 79–80, 101

Security
    batch processing for, 232–33, 236–37
    for bookmarks, 68–69
    certificates for, 134, 149
    for comments, 97, 99–100
    document open, 134, 135–37, 141–44
    with document properties, 135–40
    for links, 75–76
    overview of, 133–35
    for PDF files generally, 99–100, 133–49
    permissions, 134–35, 138–40, 145–48
    policies for, 137–50
    of redaction, 213–14
    for signatures, 97, 99–100, 103
    for stamps, 97, 99–100, 103
Select Image tool, 70, 72
Select Object tool, 114, 117–18
Select Text tool, 70, 72
Select tool, 114, 117–18
Service, 190–91. *See also* Court filings
Shapes, 90–93, 93–96
Shortcuts, 253–54
Show function, 80. *See also* Hiding
Signatures
    appearance of, 106–7
    certificates for, 104–5, 109–12
    creating, 105–7
    cropping, 98, 99
    layers for, 99
    navigation by, 15
    overview of, 103
    printing, 244
    security for, 97, 99–100, 103
    signing with, 107–8
    stamps for, 97–100, 103
    tagged Image File Format (TIFF) for,
        106
    using, 104–5, 107–8
    validating, 104–5, 109–12
Single page, 19, 57, 114
Single page continuous, 19, 57, 114
Source materials, 182, 184, 185–87
Space bar, 171, 172
StampPDF, 163–65
Stamps
    appearance of, 94–95, 163, 165, 166
    for Bates numbers, 163–67
    cropping, 98, 99

extracting and, 117
layers for, 99
overview of, 96–100
printing, 244
properties of, 93–96
security for, 97, 99–100, 103
for signatures, 97–100, 103
Sticky notes
adding, 82
appearance of, 82, 83, 94–95
deleting, 83, 93
editing, 83
overview of, 81–83
properties of, 82, 83, 93–96
searching for, 79–80, 101
Subject, 58–59
Summaries, 89–90, 101

Tagged Image File Format (TIFF)
conversion from, 2, 33–34, 180
extracting and, 117
as image-only files, 6
for signatures, 106
for stamps, 97
Text boxes
adding, 85–86
appearance of, 85, 94–95
bookmarks and, 84–85
callout text boxes, 85–86
deleting, 93
for exhibit notebooks, 84–85
overview of, 84–86
properties of, 85, 93–96
searching for, 79–80, 101
Text markup, 86–87, 93–96
Title, 58–59
Toolbars, 10–14, 70, 80–81, 169–70, 186–87

Two-up, 19
Two-up continuous, 19
Typewriter tool, 223

Underline Text tool, 86–87
Up-down arrows, 16
U.S. Food and Drug Administration, 2

Validating, 104–5, 109–12
View. *See* Page display

Web pages
bookmarks for, 155
capture settings for, 155–59
creating PDF files from, 42–43, 151–59
headers and footers for, 155–56
image-on-text files from, 152
page display for, 156–59
PDF tags for, 155
Web sites, 254
Whole Words Only, 126, 128
Windows Explorer, 204
Word. *See* Word processing applications
Wordperfect. *See* Word processing applications
Word processing applications
Bates numbers with, 162, 207–8
creating PDF files from, 29, 30–31
for extracting, 116
forms from, 223
metadata from, 133
need for, 1, 4
PDF drivers in, 3

Zooming, 22–25, 26–27, 176. *See also* Magnification

Selected Books from . . .
THE ABA LAW PRACTICE MANAGEMENT SECTION

The Essential Little Book of Great Lawyering
By James A. Durham

In a convenient, pocket-sized handbook, veteran marketer Jim Durham shares his secret on how to be a great lawyer. His core thesis is simple: being a great lawyer IS the best business development plan. You'll benefit from his wisdom and guidance as he communicates how to set the stage for greatness, the essence of great lawyering, the common characteristics of great lawyers, and more. He explains that being a great lawyer means that you truly understand your client's business. It's a classic pocketbook to share with your colleagues and members of your firm.

The Lawyer's Guide to Marketing on the Internet, Third Edition
By Gregory H. Siskind, Deborah McMurray, and Richard P. Klau

In today's competitive environment, it is critical to have a comprehensive online marketing strategy that uses all the tools possible to differentiate your firm and gain new clients. The Lawyer's Guide to Marketing on the Internet, in a completely updated and revised third edition, showcases practical online strategies and the latest innovations so that you can immediately participate in decisions about your firm's Web marketing effort. With advice that can be implemented by established and young practices alike, this comprehensive guide will be a crucial component to streamlining your marketing efforts.

The Lawyer's Field Guide to Effective Business Development
By William J. Flannery, Jr.

"In this wonderful book, Bill Flannery, who changed the legal marketplace forever, does what he's been doing so effectively throughout his extraordinary career—he teaches lawyers how to sell. How can you build your firm's business without it?"
    —Richard S. Levick, Esq., President and CEO, Levick Strategic Communications

Long-term, profitable client relationships form the foundation for the enduring success of any law firm. Winning and retaining long-term, attractive clients doesn't happen by accident. In his new book, The Lawyer's Field Guide to Effective Business Development, renowned legal marketer Bill Flannery shares his practical approach to acquiring and refining the face-to-face skills necessary for winning and keeping valuable clients.

In a handy, pocket-sized format, this unique guidebook is designed so you can take it with you as you travel in search of new business. The chapters are organized chronologically to take you step by step from your initial search for clients through the process of building and maintaining long-term profitable client relationships.

The Electronic Evidence and Discovery Handbook: Forms, Checklists, and Guidelines
By Sharon D. Nelson, Bruce A. Olson, and John W. Simek

The use of electronic evidence has increased dramatically over the past few years, but many lawyers still struggle with the complexities of electronic discovery. This substantial book provides lawyers with the templates they need to frame their discovery requests and provides helpful advice on what they can subpoena. In addition to the ready-made forms, the authors also supply explanations to bring you up to speed on the electronic discovery field. The accompanying CD-ROM features over 70 forms, including, Motions for Protective Orders, Preservation and Spoliation Documents, Motions to Compel, Electronic Evidence Protocol Agreements, Requests for Production, Internet Services Agreements, and more. Also included is a full electronic evidence case digest with over 300 cases detailed!

The Lawyer's Guide to Extranets: Breaking Down Walls, Building Client Connections
By Douglas Simpson and Mark Tamminga

An extranet can be a powerful tool that allows law firms to exchange information and build relationships with clients. This new book shows you why extranets are the next step in client interaction and communications, and how you can effectively implement an extranet in any type of firm. This book will take you step-by-step through the issues of implementing an extranet, and how to plan and build one. You'll get real-world extranet case studies, and learn from the successes and failures of those who have gone before. Help your firm get ahead of the emerging technologies curve and discover the benefits of adopting this new information tool.

The Law Firm Associate's Guide to Personal Marketing and Selling Skills
By Catherine Alman MacDonagh and Beth Marie Cuzzone

This is the first volume in ABA's new groundbreaking Law Firm Associates Development Series, created to teach important skills that associates and other lawyers need to succeed at their firms, but that they may have not learned in law school. This volume focuses on personal marketing and sales skills. It covers creating a personal marketing plan, finding people within your target market, preparing for client meetings, "asking" for business, realizing marketing opportunities, keeping your clients, staying in touch with your network inside and outside the firm, and more. An accompanying trainer's manual illustrating how to best structure the sessions and use the book is available to firms to facilitate group training sessions.

Many law firms expect their new associates to hit the ground running when they are hired on. Although firms often take the time to bring these associates up to speed on client matters, they can be reluctant to invest the time needed to train them how to improve personal skills such as marketing. This book will serve as a brief, easy-to-digest primer for associates on how to develop and use marketing and selling techniques.

ABA LAW PRACTICE MANAGEMENT SECTION
MARKETING • MANAGEMENT • TECHNOLOGY • FINANCE

The Lawyer's Guide to Marketing Your Practice, Second Edition
Edited by James A. Durham and Deborah McMurray
This book is packed with practical ideas, innovative strategies, useful checklists, and sample marketing and action plans to help you implement a successful, multi-faceted, and profit-enhancing marketing plan for your firm. Organized into four sections, this illuminating resource covers: Developing Your Approach; Enhancing Your Image; Implementing Marketing Strategies and Maintaining Your Program. Appendix materials include an instructive primer on market research to inform you on research methodologies that support the marketing of legal services. The accompanying CD-ROM contains a wealth of checklists, plans, and other sample reports, questionnaires, and templates—all designed to make implementing your marketing strategy as easy as possible!

The Lawyer's Guide to Increasing Revenue: Unlocking the Profit Potential in Your Firm
By Arthur G. Greene
Are you ready to look beyond cost-cutting and toward new revenue opportunities? Learn how you can achieve growth using the resources you already have at your firm. Discover the factors that affect your law firm's revenue production, how to evaluate them, and how to take specific action steps designed to increase your returns. You'll learn how to best improve performance and profitability in each of the key areas of your law firm, such as billable hours and rates, client relations and intake, collections and accounts receivable, technology, marketing, and others. Included with the book is a CD-ROM featuring sample policies, worksheets, plans, and documents designed to aid implementation of the ideas presented in the book. Let this resource guide you toward a profitable and sustainable future!

The Lawyer's Guide to Strategic Planning: Defining, Setting, and Achieving Your Firm's Goals
By Thomas C. Grella and Michael L. Hudkins
This practice-building resource is your guide to planning dynamic strategic plans and implementing them at your firm. You'll learn about the actual planning process and how to establish goals in key planning areas such as law firm governance, competition, opening a new office, financial management, technology, marketing and competitive intelligence, client development and retention, and more. The accompanying CD-ROM contains a wealth of policies, statements, and other sample documents. If you're serious about improving the way your firm works, increasing productivity, making better decisions, and setting your firm on the right course, this book is the resource you need.

The Successful Lawyer: Powerful Strategies for Transforming Your Practice
By Gerald A. Riskin
Available as a Book, Audio-CD Set, or Combination Package.
Global management consultant and trusted advisor to many of the world's largest law firms, Gerry Riskin goes beyond simple concept or theory and delivers a book packed with practical advice that you can implement right away. By using the principles found in this book, you can live out your dreams, embrace success, and awaken your firm to its full potential. Large law firm or small, managing partners and associates in every area of practice—all can benefit from the information contained in this book. With this book, you can attract what you need and desire into your life, get more satisfaction from your practice and your clients, and do so in a systematic, achievable way.

How to Start and Build a Law Practice, Platinum Fifth Edition
By Jay G Foonberg
This classic ABA bestseller has been used by tens of thousands of lawyers as the comprehensive guide to planning, launching, and growing a successful practice. It's packed with over 600 pages of guidance on identifying the right location, finding clients, setting fees, managing your office, maintaining an ethical and responsible practice, maximizing available resources, upholding your standards, and much more. You'll find the information you need to successfully launch your practice, run it at maximum efficiency, and avoid potential pitfalls along the way. If you're committed to starting—and growing—your own practice, this one book will give you the expert advice you need to make it succeed for years to come.

Flying Solo: A Survival Guide for Solo and Small Firm Lawyers, Fourth Edition
Edited by K. William Gibson
This fourth edition of this comprehensive guide includes practical information gathered from a wide range of contributors, including successful solo practitioners, law firm consultants, state and local bar practice management advisors, and law school professors. This classic ABA book first walks you through a step-by-step analysis of the decision to start a solo practice, including choosing a practice focus. It then provides tools to help you with financial issues including banking and billing; operations issues such as staffing and office location and design decisions; technology for the small law office; and marketing and client relations. Whether you're thinking of going solo, new to the solo life, or a seasoned practitioner, *Flying Solo* provides time-tested answers to real-life questions.

30-Day Risk-Free Order Form
Call Today! 1-800-285-2221
Monday–Friday, 7:30 AM – 5:30 PM, Central Time

Qty	Title	LPM Price	Regular Price	Total
_____	The Essential Little Book of Great Lawyering (5110579)	$ 9.95	$ 11.95	$_____
_____	The Lawyer's Guide to Marketing on the Internet, Third Edition (5110585)	74.95	84.95	$_____
_____	The Lawyer's Field Guide to Effective Business Development (5110578)	49.95	59.95	$_____
_____	The Electronic Evidence and Discovery Handbook: Forms, Checklists, and Guidelines (5110569)	99.95	129.95	$_____
_____	The Lawyer's Guide to Extranets: Breaking Down Walls, Building Client Connections (5110494)	59.95	69.95	$_____
_____	The Law Firm Associate's Guide to Personal Marketing and Selling Skills (5110582)	39.95	49.95	$_____
_____	Trainer's Manual for the Law Firm Associate's Guide to Personal Marketing and Selling Skills (5110581)	49.95	59.95	$_____
_____	The Lawyer's Guide to Marketing Your Practice, Second Edition (5110500)	79.95	89.95	$_____
_____	The Lawyer's Guide to Increasing Revenue (5110521)	59.95	79.95	$_____
_____	The Lawyer's Guide to Strategic Planning (5110520)	59.95	79.95	$_____
_____	The Successful Lawyer: Powerful Strategies for Transforming Your Practice (5110531)	64.95	84.95	$_____
_____	How to Start and Build a Law Practice, Platinum Fifth Edition (5110508)	57.95	69.95	$_____
_____	Flying Solo: A Survival Guide for Solo and Small Firm Lawyers, Fourth Edition (5110527)	79.95	99.95	$_____

*Postage and Handling	
$10.00 to $24.99	$5.95
$25.00 to $49.99	$9.95
$50.00 to $99.99	$12.95
$100.00 to $349.99	$17.95
$350 to $499.99	$24.95

**Tax
DC residents add 5.75%
IL residents add 9.00%

*Postage and Handling	$_____
**Tax	$_____
TOTAL	$_____

PAYMENT

❏ Check enclosed (to the ABA)

❏ Visa   ❏ MasterCard   ❏ American Express

_____
Account Number   Exp. Date   Signature

Name _____ Firm _____

Address _____

City _____ State _____ Zip _____

Phone Number _____ E-Mail Address _____

Guarantee
If—for any reason—you are not satisfied with your purchase, you may return it within 30 days of receipt for a complete refund of the price of the book(s). No questions asked!

Mail: ABA Publication Orders, P.O. Box 10892, Chicago, Illinois 60610-0892
♦ Phone: 1-800-285-2221 ♦ FAX: 312-988-5568

E-Mail: abasvcctr@abanet.org ♦ Internet: http://www.lawpractice.org/catalog

Are You in Your Element?

Tap into the Resources of the ABA Law Practice Management Section

ABA Law Practice Management Section Membership Benefits

The ABA Law Practice Management Section (LPM) is a professional membership organization of the American Bar Association that helps lawyers and other legal professionals with the business of practicing law. LPM focuses on providing information and resources in the core areas of marketing, management, technology, and finance through its award-winning magazine, teleconference series, Webzine, educational programs (CLE), Web site, and publishing division. For more than thirty years, LPM has established itself as a leader within the ABA and the profession-at-large by producing the world's largest legal technology conference (ABA TECHSHOW®) each year. In addition, LPM's publishing program is one of the largest in the ABA, with more than eighty-five titles in print.

In addition to significant book discounts, LPM Section membership offers these benefits:

ABA TECHSHOW
Membership includes a $100 discount to ABA TECHSHOW, the world's largest legal technology conference & expo!

Teleconference Series
Convenient, monthly CLE teleconferences on hot topics in marketing, management, technology and finance. Access educational opportunities from the comfort of your office chair – today's practical way to earn CLE credits!

Law Practice Magazine
Eight issues of our award-winning *Law Practice* magazine, full of insightful articles and practical tips on Marketing/Client Development, Practice Management, Legal Technology, and Finance.

Law Practice Today
LPM's unique Web-based magazine covers all the hot topics in law practice management today — identify current issues, face today's challenges, find solutions quickly. Visit www.lawpracticetoday.org.

Law Technology Today
LPM's newest Webzine focuses on legal technology issues in law practice management — covering a broad spectrum of the technology, tools, strategies and their implementation to help lawyers build a successful practice. Visit www.lawtechnologytoday.org.

LawPractice.news
Brings Section news, educational opportunities, book releases, and special offers to members via e-mail each month.

To learn more about the ABA Law Practice Management Section, visit www.lawpractice.org or call 1-800-285-2221.

MARKETING • MANAGEMENT • TECHNOLOGY • FINANCE

LawPractice Management Section

MARKETING • MANAGEMENT • TECHNOLOGY • FINANCE